50% OFF Online Nurse Executive Prep Course!

Dear Customer,

We consider it an honor and a privilege that you chose our Nurse Executive Study Guide. As a way of showing our appreciation and to help us better serve you, we have partnered with Mometrix Test Preparation to offer you **50% off their online Nurse Executive Prep Course**. Many Nurse Executive courses are needlessly expensive and don't deliver enough value. With their course, you get access to the best Nurse Executive prep material, and **you only pay half price**.

Mometrix has structured their online course to perfectly complement your printed study guide. The Nurse Executive Prep Course contains **in-depth lessons** that cover all the most important topics, **750 practice questions** to ensure you feel prepared, and more than **380 digital flashcards**, so you can study while you're on the go.

Online Nurse Executive Prep Course

Topics Included:
- Human Resource Management
  - Federal Employment Laws
  - Communication
- Quality and Safety
  - Change Management Frameworks
  - Systems Theories and Management Structures
- Business Management
  - Reimbursement Methods
  - Financial Management and Budgeting
- Health Care Delivery
  - Ethics
  - Scope and Standards of Practice

Course Features:
- Nurse Executive Study Guide
  - Get content that complements our best-selling study guide.
- Full-Length Practice Tests
  - With 750 practice questions, you can test yourself again and again.
- Mobile Friendly
  - If you need to study on the go, the course is easily accessible from your mobile device.
- Nurse Executive Flashcards
  - Our course includes a flashcard mode with over 380 content cards to help you study.

To receive this discount, visit them at mometrix.com/university/nurseexec or simply scan this QR code with your smartphone. At the checkout page, enter the discount code: **NURSEEXEC50TPB**

If you have any questions or concerns, please contact them at support@mometrix.com.

Sincerely,

Online Resources & Audiobook

Included with your purchase are multiple online resources. This includes the practice tests in an interactive format and this book in audiobook format. There is also a convenient study timer to help you manage your time.

Instructions for accessing these resources can be found on the last page of this book.

Nurse Executive Study Guide 2025-2026
4 Full-Length Practice Tests and NE-BC Review Book for ANCC Certification [2nd Edition]

Lydia Morrison

Copyright © 2025 by TPB Publishing

All rights reserved. No part of this publication may be reproduced, distributed, or transmitted in any form or by any means, including photocopying, recording, or other electronic or mechanical methods, without the prior written permission of the publisher, except in the case of brief quotations embodied in critical reviews and certain other noncommercial uses permitted by copyright law.

Written and edited by TPB Publishing.

TPB Publishing is not associated with or endorsed by any official testing organization. TPB Publishing is a publisher of unofficial educational products. All test and organization names are trademarks of their respective owners. Content in this book is included for utilitarian purposes only and does not constitute an endorsement by TPB Publishing of any particular point of view.

ISBN 13: 9781637755983

Table of Contents

Welcome 1
   FREE Videos/DVD OFFER 1

Quick Overview 2

Test-Taking Strategies 3

Introduction 7

Study Prep Plan for the Nurse Executive Test 9

Human Resource Management 13
   Knowledge 13
   Skills 19
   Practice Quiz 38
   Answer Explanations 39

Quality and Safety 40
   Knowledge 40
   Skills 81
   Practice Quiz 87
   Answer Explanations 88

Business Management 89
   Knowledge 89
   Skills 92
   Practice Quiz 100
   Answer Explanations 101

Health Care Delivery 102
   Knowledge 102

Skills 118
Practice Quiz 131
Answer Explanations 132

Practice Test #1 133
Answer Explanations #1 158
Practice Test #2 179
Answer Explanations #2 204
Nurse Executive Practice Test #3 & #4 225
Online Resources & Audiobook 227

Welcome

Dear Reader,

Welcome to your new Test Prep Books study guide! We are pleased that you chose us to help you prepare for your exam. There are many study options to choose from, and we appreciate you choosing us. Studying can be a daunting task, but we have designed a smart, effective study guide to help prepare you for what lies ahead.

Whether you're a parent helping your child learn and grow, a high school student working hard to get into your dream college, or a nursing student studying for a complex exam, we want to help give you the tools you need to succeed. We hope this study guide gives you the skills and the confidence to thrive, and we can't thank you enough for allowing us to be part of your journey.

In an effort to continue to improve our products, we welcome feedback from our customers. We look forward to hearing from you. Suggestions, success stories, and criticisms can all be communicated by emailing us at info@studyguideteam.com.

Sincerely,
Test Prep Books Team

FREE Videos/DVD OFFER

Doing well on your exam requires both knowing the test content and understanding how to use that knowledge to do well on the test. We offer completely FREE test taking tip videos. **These videos cover world-class tips that you can use to succeed on your test.**

To get your **FREE videos**, you can use the QR code below or email freevideos@studyguideteam.com with "Free Videos" in the subject line and the following information in the body of the email:

   a. The title of your product
   b. Your product rating on a scale of 1-5, with 5 being the highest
   c. Your feedback about the product

If you have any questions or concerns, please don't hesitate to contact us at info@studyguideteam.com.

Quick Overview

As you draw closer to taking your exam, effective preparation becomes more and more important. Thankfully, you have this study guide to help you get ready. Use this guide to help keep your studying on track and refer to it often.

This study guide contains several key sections that will help you be successful on your exam. The guide contains tips for what you should do the night before and the day of the test. Also included are test-taking tips. Knowing the right information is not always enough. Many well-prepared test takers struggle with exams. These tips will help equip you to accurately read, assess, and answer test questions.

A large part of the guide is devoted to showing you what content to expect on the exam and to helping you better understand that content. In this guide are practice test questions so that you can see how well you have grasped the content. Then, answer explanations are provided so that you can understand why you missed certain questions.

Don't try to cram the night before you take your exam. This is not a wise strategy for a few reasons. First, your retention of the information will be low. Your time would be better used by reviewing information you already know rather than trying to learn a lot of new information. Second, you will likely become stressed as you try to gain a large amount of knowledge in a short amount of time. Third, you will be depriving yourself of sleep. So be sure to go to bed at a reasonable time the night before. Being well-rested helps you focus and remain calm.

Be sure to eat a substantial breakfast the morning of the exam. If you are taking the exam in the afternoon, be sure to have a good lunch as well. Being hungry is distracting and can make it difficult to focus. You have hopefully spent lots of time preparing for the exam. Don't let an empty stomach get in the way of success!

When travelling to the testing center, leave earlier than needed. That way, you have a buffer in case you experience any delays. This will help you remain calm and will keep you from missing your appointment time at the testing center.

Be sure to pace yourself during the exam. Don't try to rush through the exam. There is no need to risk performing poorly on the exam just so you can leave the testing center early. Allow yourself to use all of the allotted time if needed.

Remain positive while taking the exam even if you feel like you are performing poorly. Thinking about the content you should have mastered will not help you perform better on the exam.

Once the exam is complete, take some time to relax. Even if you feel that you need to take the exam again, you will be well served by some down time before you begin studying again. It's often easier to convince yourself to study if you know that it will come with a reward!

Test-Taking Strategies

1. Predicting the Answer

When you feel confident in your preparation for a multiple-choice test, try predicting the answer before reading the answer choices. This is especially useful on questions that test objective factual knowledge. By predicting the answer before reading the available choices, you eliminate the possibility that you will be distracted or led astray by an incorrect answer choice. You will feel more confident in your selection if you read the question, predict the answer, and then find your prediction among the answer choices. After using this strategy, be sure to still read all of the answer choices carefully and completely. If you feel unprepared, you should not attempt to predict the answers. This would be a waste of time and an opportunity for your mind to wander in the wrong direction.

2. Reading the Whole Question

Too often, test takers scan a multiple-choice question, recognize a few familiar words, and immediately jump to the answer choices. Test authors are aware of this common impatience, and they will sometimes prey upon it. For instance, a test author might subtly turn the question into a negative, or he or she might redirect the focus of the question right at the end. The only way to avoid falling into these traps is to read the entirety of the question carefully before reading the answer choices.

3. Looking for Wrong Answers

Long and complicated multiple-choice questions can be intimidating. One way to simplify a difficult multiple-choice question is to eliminate all of the answer choices that are clearly wrong. In most sets of answers, there will be at least one selection that can be dismissed right away. If the test is administered on paper, the test taker could draw a line through it to indicate that it may be ignored; otherwise, the test taker will have to perform this operation mentally or on scratch paper. In either case, once the obviously incorrect answers have been eliminated, the remaining choices may be considered. Sometimes identifying the clearly wrong answers will give the test taker some information about the correct answer. For instance, if one of the remaining answer choices is a direct opposite of one of the eliminated answer choices, it may well be the correct answer. The opposite of obviously wrong is obviously right! Of course, this is not always the case. Some answers are obviously incorrect simply because they are irrelevant to the question being asked. Still, identifying and eliminating some incorrect answer choices is a good way to simplify a multiple-choice question.

4. Don't Overanalyze

Anxious test takers often overanalyze questions. When you are nervous, your brain will often run wild, causing you to make associations and discover clues that don't actually exist. If you feel that this may be a problem for you, do whatever you can to slow down during the test. Try taking a deep breath or counting to ten. As you read and consider the question, restrict yourself to the particular words used by the author. Avoid thought tangents about what the author *really* meant, or what he or she was *trying* to say. The only things that matter on a multiple-choice test are the words that are actually in the question. You must avoid reading too much into a multiple-choice question, or supposing that the writer meant something other than what he or she wrote.

5. No Need for Panic

It is wise to learn as many strategies as possible before taking a multiple-choice test, but it is likely that you will come across a few questions for which you simply don't know the answer. In this situation, avoid panicking. Because most multiple-choice tests include dozens of questions, the relative value of a single wrong answer is small. As much as possible, you should compartmentalize each question on a multiple-choice test. In other words, you should not allow your feelings about one question to affect your success on the others. When you find a question that you either don't understand or don't know how to answer, just take a deep breath and do your best. Read the entire question slowly and carefully. Try rephrasing the question a couple of different ways. Then, read all of the answer choices carefully. After eliminating obviously wrong answers, make a selection and move on to the next question.

6. Confusing Answer Choices

When working on a difficult multiple-choice question, there may be a tendency to focus on the answer choices that are the easiest to understand. Many people, whether consciously or not, gravitate to the answer choices that require the least concentration, knowledge, and memory. This is a mistake. When you come across an answer choice that is confusing, you should give it extra attention. A question might be confusing because you do not know the subject matter to which it refers. If this is the case, don't

eliminate the answer before you have affirmatively settled on another. When you come across an answer choice of this type, set it aside as you look at the remaining choices. If you can confidently assert that one of the other choices is correct, you can leave the confusing answer aside. Otherwise, you will need to take a moment to try to better understand the confusing answer choice. Rephrasing is one way to tease out the sense of a confusing answer choice.

7. Your First Instinct

Many people struggle with multiple-choice tests because they overthink the questions. If you have studied sufficiently for the test, you should be prepared to trust your first instinct once you have carefully and completely read the question and all of the answer choices. There is a great deal of research suggesting that the mind can come to the correct conclusion very quickly once it has obtained all of the relevant information. At times, it may seem to you as if your intuition is working faster even than your reasoning mind. This may in fact be true. The knowledge you obtain while studying may be retrieved from your subconscious before you have a chance to work out the associations that support it. Verify your instinct by working out the reasons that it should be trusted.

8. Key Words

Many test takers struggle with multiple-choice questions because they have poor reading comprehension skills. Quickly reading and understanding a multiple-choice question requires a mixture of skill and experience. To help with this, try jotting down a few key words and phrases on a piece of scrap paper. Doing this concentrates the process of reading and forces the mind to weigh the relative importance of the question's parts. In selecting words and phrases to write down, the test taker thinks about the question more deeply and carefully. This is especially true for multiple-choice questions that are preceded by a long prompt.

9. Subtle Negatives

One of the oldest tricks in the multiple-choice test writer's book is to subtly reverse the meaning of a question with a word like *not* or *except*. If you are not paying attention to each word in the question, you can easily be led astray by this trick. For instance, a common question format is, "Which of the following is...?" Obviously, if the question instead is, "Which of the following is not...?," then the answer will be quite different. Even worse, the test makers are aware of the potential for this mistake and will include one answer choice that would be correct if the question were not negated or reversed. A test taker who misses the reversal will find what he or she believes to be a correct answer and will be so confident that he or she will fail to reread the question and discover the original error. The only way to avoid this is to practice a wide variety of multiple-choice questions and to pay close attention to each and every word.

10. Reading Every Answer Choice

It may seem obvious, but you should always read every one of the answer choices! Too many test takers fall into the habit of scanning the question and assuming that they understand the question because they recognize a few key words. From there, they pick the first answer choice that answers the question they believe they have read. Test takers who read all of the answer choices might discover that one of the latter answer choices is actually *more* correct. Moreover, reading all of the answer choices can remind you of facts related to the question that can help you arrive at the correct answer. Sometimes, a misstatement or incorrect detail in one of the latter answer choices will trigger your memory of the subject and will enable you to find the right answer. Failing to read all of the answer choices is like not reading all of the items on a restaurant menu: you might miss out on the perfect choice.

11. Spot the Hedges

One of the keys to success on multiple-choice tests is paying close attention to every word. This is never truer than with words like *almost*, *most*, *some*, and *sometimes*. These words are called "hedges" because they indicate that a statement is not totally true or not true in every place and time. An absolute statement will contain no hedges, but in many subjects, the answers are not always straightforward or absolute. There are always exceptions to the rules in these subjects. For this reason,

you should favor those multiple-choice questions that contain hedging language. The presence of qualifying words indicates that the author is taking special care with his or her words, which is certainly important when composing the right answer. After all, there are many ways to be wrong, but there is only one way to be right! For this reason, it is wise to avoid answers that are absolute when taking a multiple-choice test. An absolute answer is one that says things are either all one way or all another. They often include words like *every*, *always*, *best*, and *never*. If you are taking a multiple-choice test in a subject that doesn't lend itself to absolute answers, be on your guard if you see any of these words.

12. Long Answers

In many subject areas, the answers are not simple. As already mentioned, the right answer often requires hedges. Another common feature of the answers to a complex or subjective question are qualifying clauses, which are groups of words that subtly modify the meaning of the sentence. If the question or answer choice describes a rule to which there are exceptions or the subject matter is complicated, ambiguous, or confusing, the correct answer will require many words in order to be expressed clearly and accurately. In essence, you should not be deterred by answer choices that seem excessively long. Oftentimes, the author of the text will not be able to write the correct answer without offering some qualifications and modifications. Your job is to read the answer choices thoroughly and completely and to select the one that most accurately and precisely answers the question.

13. Restating to Understand

Sometimes, a question on a multiple-choice test is difficult not because of what it asks but because of how it is written. If this is the case, restate the question or answer choice in different words. This process serves a couple of important purposes. First, it forces you to concentrate on the core of the question. In order to rephrase the question accurately, you have to understand it well. Rephrasing the question will concentrate your mind on the key words and ideas. Second, it will present the information to your mind in a fresh way. This process may trigger your memory and render some useful scrap of information picked up while studying.

14. True Statements

Sometimes an answer choice will be true in itself, but it does not answer the question. This is one of the main reasons why it is essential to read the question carefully and completely before proceeding to the answer choices. Too often, test takers skip ahead to the answer choices and look for true statements. Having found one of these, they are content to select it without reference to the question above. The savvy test taker will always read the entire question before turning to the answer choices. Then, having settled on a correct answer choice, he or she will refer to the original question and ensure that the selected answer is relevant. The mistake of choosing a correct-but-irrelevant answer choice is especially common on questions related to specific pieces of objective knowledge.

15. No Patterns

One of the more dangerous ideas that circulates about multiple-choice tests is that the correct answers tend to fall into patterns. These erroneous ideas range from a belief that B and C are the most common right answers, to the idea that an unprepared test-taker should answer "A-B-A-C-A-D-A-B-A." It cannot be emphasized enough that pattern-seeking of this type is exactly the WRONG way to approach a multiple-choice test. To begin with, it is highly unlikely that the test maker will plot the correct answers according to some predetermined pattern. The questions are scrambled and delivered in a random order. Furthermore, even if the test maker was following a pattern in the assignation of correct answers, there is no reason why the test taker would know which pattern he or she was using. Any attempt to discern a pattern in the answer choices is a waste of time and a distraction from the real work of taking the test. A test taker would be much better served by extra preparation before the test than by reliance on a pattern in the answers.

Introduction

Function of the Test

The American Nurses Credentialing Center (ANCC) helps nurses demonstrate their competencies and knowledge through certification in many different areas of care. The Nurse Executive Board Certification Exam is an assessment that demonstrates the proficiency of the nurse executive. This exam is accredited by both the Accreditation Board for Specialty Nursing Certification (ABSNC) and the National Commission for Certifying Agencies (NCAA). After meeting eligibility requirements and passing the certification exam, this credential will be awarded to the test taker and is valid for five years.

Prior to scheduling examination, test takers must apply online with documentation demonstrating eligibility. In order to be eligible, the test taker must hold a current, active RN license in the U.S. (or a recognized equivalent from another country), report at least 2,000 hours of experience managing daily operations for a unit within the last three years, and complete 30 hours of continued education focused on leadership within the last three years. For more information visit https://www.nursingworld.org/our-certifications/nurse-executive/.

The assessment will test the taker's competency and knowledge of entry-level topics that nurse executives are expected to have. Among these skills include strategies for overseeing a group of nurses or non-nursing staff, managing daily operations, staffing fundamentals, and assessing individual and group improvement. The following guide is intended to help you study and assess your own knowledge of these topics in preparation for the exam. The practice tests are representative of the types of questions you may see when taking the exam.

Test Administration

The Nurse Executive Board Certification Exam is offered in the United States via computer at a Prometric testing center. Once the test taker submits an application and all necessary documentation, they should schedule their exam. The exam must be scheduled within 120 days of submitting an application. If the test taker needs to reschedule or cancel their exam, they may do so for no additional cost at least 48 hours prior to the exam and within the 120-day window.

If a test taker requires special accommodations while sitting for the exam, the required documentation may be submitted to the ANCC Certification Special Accommodations department. It is important to note that this request must be done prior to scheduling a test appointment, and the test taker should wait for confirmation of special accommodations before scheduling their exam.

Test Format

The exam lasts 180 minutes (3 hours) and contains 150 questions, including 125 scored questions and 25 unscored pretest questions. Pretest questions are used to determine the efficacy of these questions before they are included in the exam as scored questions. While the test taker's score is only calculated on the 125 scored questions, the unscored questions are indistinguishable from the scored, so it is important to answer all available questions.

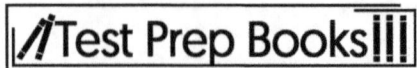

The content areas of the Nurse Executive Board Certification exam include Human Resource Management, Quality and Safety, Business Management, and Health Care Delivery. The following table depicts a breakdown of the number of questions included from each category.

Section	Questions
Human Resource Management	40
Quality and Safety	21
Business Management	20
Health Care Delivery	44
Total	125

Scoring

Test takers will receive a score of pass or fail at the end of their exam. Official passing certificates are issued by mail after the exam date. Test takers who do not pass the exam will receive a detailed score report that differentiates their performance across subject areas to aid in studying to re-take the examination at a later date.

Study Prep Plan for the Nurse Executive Test

1 **Schedule** - Use one of our study schedules below or come up with one of your own.

2 **Relax** - Test anxiety can hurt even the best students. There are many ways to reduce stress. Find the one that works best for you.

3 **Execute** - Once you have a good plan in place, be sure to stick to it.

One Week Study Schedule		
	Day 1	Human Resource Management
	Day 2	Quality and Safety
	Day 3	Skills
	Day 4	Health Care Delivery
	Day 5	Skills
	Day 6	Practice Test #1
	Day 7	Take Your Exam!

Two Week Study Schedule				
	Day 1	Human Resource Management	Day 8	Business Management
	Day 2	Promote Outreach, Diversity, and Inclusion	Day 9	Health Care Delivery
	Day 3	Quality and Safety	Day 10	Skills
	Day 4	Confidentiality/Information Security	Day 11	Practice Test #1
	Day 5	Legal Reporting Obligations	Day 12	Practice Test #2
	Day 6	Evaluating the Appropriateness...	Day 13	Practice Test #3
	Day 7	Skills	Day 14	Take Your Exam!

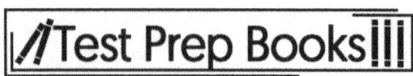

Study Prep Plan for the Nurse Executive Test

One Month Study Schedule

Day 1	Human Resource Management	Day 11	Evaluating the Appropriateness of...	Day 21	Technology Evaluation and Integration
Day 2	Employee Performance...	Day 12	When to Use Restraints	Day 22	Practice Test #1
Day 3	Promote Outreach, Diversity, and Inclusion	Day 13	Standard Precautions/Transmission-Based...	Day 23	Answer Explanations #1
Day 4	Americans with Disabilities Act (ADA)	Day 14	Skills	Day 24	Practice Test #2
Day 5	Quality and Safety	Day 15	Research Related to Performance...	Day 25	Answer Explanations #2
Day 6	Confidentiality/Information Security	Day 16	Business Management	Day 26	Practice Test #3
Day 7	Ethical Practice	Day 17	Leadership Styles	Day 27	Answer Explanations #3
Day 8	Legal Reporting Obligations	Day 18	Health Care Delivery	Day 28	Practice Test #4
Day 9	Referral Process	Day 19	Unconsciousness or Unresponsiveness	Day 29	Answer Explanations #4
Day 10	Transfer Devices	Day 20	Skills	Day 30	Take Your Exam!

Build your own prep plan by visiting:

testprepbooks.com/prep

As you study for your test, we'd like to take the opportunity to remind you that you are capable of great things! With the right tools and dedication, you truly can do anything you set your mind to. The fact that you are holding this book right now shows how committed you are. In case no one has told you lately, you've got this! Our intention behind including this coloring page is to give you the chance to take some time to engage your creative side when you need a little brain-break from studying. As a company, we want to encourage people like you to achieve their dreams by providing good quality study materials for the tests and certifications that improve careers and change lives. As individuals, many of us have taken such tests in our careers, and we know how challenging this process can be. While we can't come alongside you and cheer you on personally, we can offer you the space to recall your purpose, reconnect with your passion, and refresh your brain through an artistic practice. We wish you every success, and happy studying!

Human Resource Management

Knowledge

Federal Employment Laws

The **Family Medical Leave Act** (FMLA) was passed to allow eligible employees to take up to twelve weeks of job-protected, unpaid leave during a twelve-month period for specific family and medical reasons. Employees are covered under this act if their employer has at least fifty employees—full- or part-time—working within seventy-five miles of a given workplace. Additionally, the employee must have worked for their employer for at least twelve months and for a total of 1,250 hours over the past year.

FMLA covers leave for the following reasons:

- The birth of a child, adoption, or foster-care placement

- The serious health condition of a spouse, child, or parent

- The serious health condition of the employee, one requiring inpatient care or continuing treatment by a healthcare provider

- Qualifying exigency leave, or leave to address the most common issues that arise when an employee's spouse, child, or parent is on active duty or call to active-duty status—e.g., making financial and legal arrangements or arranging for alternative childcare

- Military caregiver leave or leave to care for a covered service member, such as the employee's spouse, child, parent, or their next of kin, with a serious injury or illness. Employees are to be granted up to twenty-six weeks of job-protected, unpaid leave during a twelve-month period to care for a covered service member.

Instead of taking all of their leave at once, employees can choose to take FMLA leave intermittently or in blocks of time for specific, qualifying reasons as approved by their employer. One reason for doing so would be for an employee to attend medical appointments for their ongoing treatment and testing for a serious health condition.

Spouses who work for the same employer must share the amount of FMLA time they take for the birth of a child, adoption, or foster care placement or for the serious health condition of a child or parent. The total amount of leave taken by both spouses must add up to twelve weeks for the reasons stated above or twenty-six weeks for the care of a covered service member.

Employers also have the right to require employees to take unpaid FMLA leave concurrent with any relevant paid leave, such as sick time or vacation time, to which the employees are entitled under their current policies. In addition, a week containing a holiday still counts as a full week of FMLA, whether or not the holiday is considered to be paid time.

Employers are required to maintain an employee's group health care coverage while they are out on FMLA leave when the employee was covered under such a plan prior to leave. Once an employee's

FMLA leave has ended, they are to be reinstated to their original job or to an equivalent job with equivalent conditions of employment, pay, and benefits.

Employers who fail to comply with the FMLA act may face both civil and criminal penalties. Also, if the Department of Labor finds that an employer did not post FMLA rights and responsibilities notices in the workplace, then a penalty of $211 can be assessed for willful failure to post.

The **Americans with Disabilities Act** (ADA) is a federal law that prevents discrimination based on disability. This law requires employers to provide reasonable accommodations to employees with a disability. For example, an employer may accommodate a disabled employee by building a wheelchair accessible ramp to enter and exit the building. Additionally, the ADA stipulates that public entities be accessible for disabled persons. The ADA does include both mental and physical medical conditions, and temporary conditions may qualify as a disability. ADA protections apply to every aspect of job application procedures, employment, and promotions.

Other important regulations include the **Fair Labor Standard Act** (FLSA) which establishes rules such as minimum wage and overtime pay, standards for child labor, and definitions for exempt and non-exempt employees. The Family and Medical Leave Act (FMLA) outlines standards for when employees are permitted to take unpaid, job-protected family and medical leave. The Occupational Safety and Health Act of 1970 created the **Occupational Safety and Health Administration** (OSHA), which ensures that employers provide a safe and healthy workplace. Examples of OSHA regulations include eliminating or reducing hazards when possible, providing free safety equipment, informing employees about chemical hazards, providing comprehensive and comprehensible safety training, keeping records of work-related injuries and illnesses, and displaying the official OSHA poster describing employees' rights and employers' responsibilities.

Employees may choose to be represented by a **labor union**. However, there are other forms of employee representation as well. The **National Labor Relations Act** of 1935 (NLRA; also known as the Wagner Act) is administered by the National Labor Relations Board (NLRB) and protects the rights of private sector workers to join labor unions. Additionally, it constrains employee representation in nonunionized companies. Nevertheless, **nonunion employee representation** plans can be found in many organizations where employees want a voice in the workplace. Like unions, these groups allow employees to advocate for fair treatment and improved employment conditions while also creating a channel for communication where employees can give input into the decision-making process.

However, the decisions ultimately rest with management. Unlike unions, nonunion employee representation plans keep all decisions and bargaining within the organization. One example of this type of body is a **works council**, which generally represents employees on a more local level than a trade union. A works council operates within an organization to improve communication between employers and employees and to increase employees' **bargaining power**. In the United States., a works council must be elected by employees without interference by the employer in order to be recognized as lawful. In other cases, employees may also choose to be represented by legal counsel or a governmental body to assist in negotiations or resolving disputes.

Principles and Styles of Communication

Communication Strategies

There are numerous helpful **communication** strategies that companies can implement. For instance, a **brown bag lunch program** is an informal meeting including employees and management that is used to

Human Resource Management

discuss company problems. The company-provided meal can help create a relaxed setting for exchanging ideas. Additionally, department meetings allow everyone involved to share solutions to company challenges.

Town hall meetings are formal gatherings for the entire company that are commonly referred to as "all-hands meetings." They tend to focus on sharing information "from the top down" concerning the overall organization. Thus, town hall meetings are not usually designed to allow feedback from employees about smaller detail issues. An **open-door policy** is used to establish a relationship where employees feel comfortable speaking directly with management about problems and suggestions. In essence, an open-door policy enables a supervisor to be a "human suggestion box." There are several potential roadblocks to a successful open-door policy. In certain situations, it can be difficult to create an environment where employees feel comfortable discussing problems in person. In addition, depending on the problem reported, it may not be possible to maintain confidentiality. However, in the right situation, an open-door policy can help companies identify problems quickly without having to wait for a formal meeting.

Management by Walking Around (MBWA), as the name suggests, involves having managers and supervisors physically get out of their offices and interact with employees in person. MBWA allows management to check on employee progress, inquire about potential issues, and gain other feedback without relying on employees to "make the first move" through an open-door policy or online suggestion form. This strategy prevents management from becoming isolated behind a desk and disinterested in employees' problems.

Communication Types

There are multiple means that a company can use to communicate with its employees. Each method has its own potential advantages and drawbacks. Email makes it easy to get information to a lot of people very quickly. However, this communication method can result in employees suffering from "information overload" from too many emails, making it more likely that important information is overlooked. Also, there is a danger that confidential information may be accidentally communicated to the wrong people.

The **intranet** (internal website and computer network) has the benefit of eliminated risk of important information being accessed by someone outside the organization. Intranets can be very effective at communicating important ongoing information about the company, such as policies and procedures. In addition, companies often store necessary workplace documentation, such as HR-related forms, on an intranet. This allows employees to access that information when necessary. However, if outside parties need information on the intranet, they cannot access it. In addition, intranet communication is often "top-down" and does not allow for feedback from employees. It is also important to note that some intranet systems are not user-friendly, causing employees to be discouraged from using them.

Newsletters can provide a variety of information and have the potential to do so in an engaging, welcoming manner. However, newsletters can be labor-intensive. Since they are relatively infrequent (compared to the ease of sending an email), newsletters are not always useful for communicating urgent or immediate information. In addition, newsletters do not allow for formal two-way communication from employees (although this can be remedied by involving employees in the creation of the newsletter).

Finally, word-of-mouth communication can quickly spread information throughout a group of people. However, as in the children's game "Telephone," information can become muddled, misinterpreted, and downright unrecognizable as it is passed from person to person. A manager or supervisor has no control over misinterpretations and misunderstandings that can result from word-of-mouth communication.

Cultural Humility

Cultural humility is a method of evaluating one's own values and biases to bring awareness and sensitivity to how these may be projected onto opinions and decisions. Nurse executives must be adept at emphasizing cultural humility and cultural competence in order to support openness and respect.

Cultural competence is related to cultural humility; it is the ability to effectively understand, communicate, and collaborate in the midst of cultural differences. Nurse executives must develop and uphold policies aimed at creating diverse teams, ensuring that comprehensive care is consistently delivered to meet the needs of the community. There are four tenets at the forefront of cultural humility and competence: diversity, equity, inclusion, and belonging.

Diversity

Diversity is the presence of differences in a particular setting. It can include race, ethnicity, gender identity, religion, age, language, or socioeconomic status. Nurse executives are responsible for understanding how diverse backgrounds and experience can affect patients' beliefs about health, communication approaches, and preferences of care. Committing to cultural competence enables nurse leaders to recognize these unique characteristics, and cultural humility allows for openness when meeting these demands. Promoting cultural diversity strengthens collaboration in the multi-disciplinary team, improves care, and builds a united front to better serve colleagues and patients.

Equity

Fair treatment, inclusivity, and accessibility are the foundations of equity. When power imbalances are transparent and tackled head on, nurse executives can better address systemic barriers and process failures that lead to gaps in care caused by inequity. When the issues are known, resource allocation, hiring practices, and patient care strategies can be tailored to be supportive and fair.

Inclusion

Inclusive environments are more likely to make all team members feel respected and valued. Nurse executives can influence their organization's culture by pursuing initiatives that allow the voices of patients and staff to be heard. One strategy to accomplish this is leadership rounding. Improved communication that welcomes feedback and suggestions ensures that leaders have honest and accurate information, which can help them improve morale and secure a safer, more collaborative culture.

Belonging

Belonging is not just about being heard but feeling engaged and connected to an organization. Nurse leaders must strive to build trust among staff members by upholding values and engaging with authenticity. This can be accomplished by listening to staff, limiting judgement, and acknowledging individuals' differences. Affirming the cultural values and identities of the staff can be accomplished through building a meaningful and shared purpose driven by the organization's mission. This mission should include principles such as psychological safety, staff recognition, career development, and a servant leadership stance.

Human Resource Management

Styles of Leadership

The most effective and efficient way for those in executive positions in healthcare to utilize the resources at their disposal is for them to carefully consider how they interact with those they lead. Regardless of how perfect a provider's understanding of a disease may be, they will still need to rely on other individuals (e.g., emergency medical technicians [EMTs], nurses, and laboratory personnel) to treat patients with that disease effectively and efficiently. They must understand how to communicate with others, utilize their staff members, and balance each person's unique assets and potential liabilities. Each of these diverse tasks, and how best to navigate them as a leader, form the basis for discussions around leadership styles—specifically, which styles of leadership work best in healthcare settings.

Discussions on the best traits for those seeking to be leaders have existed for as long as humans have lived in organized society. One dominant theory for much of recorded history is called the **"Great Man Theory of Leadership"**. According to the theory, great leaders are born, not made. Implicit in such a theory is the idea that leadership cannot be taught—either one has the ability to lead, and will, or one does not, and will not. The Great Man Theory of Leadership is largely dismissed today. Increasing psychological and scientific evidence has sufficiently attested to the idea that characteristics associated with effective and efficient leadership are not only given to a select few; instead, they are patterns of behavior that can be understood, taught, and replicated.

Almost all other theories on leadership styles promote the idea that being a great leader is a learnable and practicable skill. In the mid-20th century, psychologist Kurt Lewin was credited with popularizing three basic styles of leadership: Autocratic, Democratic, and Laissez-Faire. Lewin had formulated these three distinct styles of leadership while watching schoolchildren complete a project together, although intending his theory to be applied directly to the business world. According to his theory, an **autocratic leadership** style (also sometimes referred to as an authoritarian leadership style) occurs when only the leader is involved in the decision-making process, and input from other team members is not expected or invited. On the other end of the scale, a **democratic leadership** style involves the active gathering of input from team members by the leader, with the goal of incorporating feedback into the final decision-making process. A leader can still be democratic even if they make the decision alone; what makes a leader democratic is how they go about their decision-making process. Finally, a **laissez-faire leadership** style occurs when a leader is largely not involved in the decision-making process. Even if a laissez-faire leader does ultimately decide on a course of action at the end of a process, they are still considered laissez-faire, as they were hands-off in the majority of the work process.

In the time since Lewin's theories on leadership first became popular, there has been much further research done on the various techniques and strategies individuals employ in leadership positions. One distinction that has been highlighted is the difference between transformational leadership and transactional leadership. Central to both styles is the concept that a leader is most effective when those they lead are most satisfied in their work, because satisfied workers will have more natural motivation to work hard. With the **transactional leadership** style, the belief is that team members are most satisfied when their objectives and rewards are clear. In other words, the transactional aspect of the relationship, in which the team members put in effort with the expectation of an appropriate reward, is what defines the leadership style. In a **transformational leadership** style, there is the same focus on motivating employees to perform, but the type of motivation is different. Instead of trying to transactionally motivate their employees, a transformational leader is one who motivates their employees by establishing an environment in which the employees feel the most personal growth and connection to their work. Whereas a transactional leader may look to entice an employee into better performance by offering a bonus for a certain quality of performance, a transformational leader will look to improve employee performance by ensuring there is a workplace culture of caring for and nurturing employees.

In order to better understand the kind of mindset and behaviors that underlie transformational leadership style, consider the style's four main components, typically called the "four I's." First, *intellectual stimulation* refers to the quality among transformational leaders to inspire and support innovative ways of thinking in the workplace. Instead of working under the assumption that past policy should dictate present and future action, transformational leaders encourage new ways of thinking and problem solving. Second, *individual consideration* refers to transformational leaders' ability to serve as mentors to their employees. Rather than simply behaving as a boss to their subordinates, a transformational leader seeks to engage with their employees and encourage them to improve both themselves and the organization. Third, *inspirational motivation* is embodied by leaders who can motivate their employees to commit to the organization's vision. Such leaders can convince their employees to internalize the goals and objectives of the organization, resulting in better alignment with their own goals and objectives. Finally, idealized influence refers to leaders who serve as **role models** to their employees. In this way, a transformational leader might inspire their employees simply by leading by example, displaying the behaviors they wish to see more of in their employees. Unlike the other leadership styles, the more ephemeral nature of transformational change and leadership makes it more difficult to discuss the exact actions and behaviors one may want to exhibit. Therefore, the "four I's" provide a multifaceted, if not comprehensive, view of how a transformational leader may act.

Human-centered leadership is a newer leadership style that puts the employees first, focusing on understanding and meeting employee's needs. Examples of using human-centered leadership include offering professional growth opportunities as well as personal support for employees. The human-centered leadership style requires leaders to be empathetic and understanding of their employee's wants and needs.

The **coaching** style of leadership, like the human-centered style, focuses on the individual development of employees. Leaders who practice this style work on building relationships with employees and actively invest in the betterment of their team. One key aspect of the coaching style of leadership is the importance of providing feedback and praise for employees. Leaders who practice this style will generally have strong relationships and trust with the people they manage.

Another leadership style that has gained popularity in recent years is called **situational leadership**. As the name suggests, situational leadership maintains that the most important quality for a leader to have is the ability to adapt to a specific situation. Implicit in such a theory is the idea that no single disposition or mentality for a leader will result in the best outcome every time. For example, a democratic leadership style, although potentially advantageous when considering treatment options for a patient, may not be acceptable in an emergency in which discussion needs to be quick and to the point. Situational leadership style, like transformational leadership style, can be practiced in many ways; however, it is the philosophy supporting the actions that matters.

The main reason situational leadership has gained prominence in recent years, especially in discussions around healthcare leadership, is a growing acknowledgment that for certain workplaces, there is no single style of leadership that will always garner the best outcomes. This is particularly true in a healthcare setting where different patients and scenarios will require leaders to act and plan in different ways. For example, a patient who arrives to the emergency room in some stage of cardiac arrest will

Human Resource Management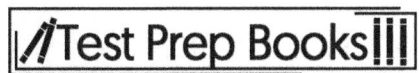

clearly require a more direct and autocratic leadership style than a patient who arrives at the hospital stable but with chronic pain of unknown origin. There are also certain types of healthcare environments, such as the operating room, that can better support a democratic leadership style due to the team-based nature of the unit. A situational leadership perspective best prepares healthcare professionals and leaders for any circumstance that may arise by acknowledging that the best way to lead will vary depending on the patient, the team members, and the resources at hand.

For a healthcare leader to best engage with and practice a situational leadership style, it is necessary for them to have a complete and thorough understanding of their team members' strengths and weaknesses. Having an in-depth knowledge of other leadership styles will improve a leader's ability to lead situationally, since they will be better equipped to properly handle a wide variety of circumstances. As a result, such leaders will be capable of preparing and organizing not only themselves, but also the distinct members of their team. Such adaptability can be helpful in both managing the day-to-day activities of a healthcare facility as well as preparing for the often difficult process of securing proper public health accreditation. When the leaders of a healthcare organization are adaptable and cognizant of the varying abilities of their team members, they are best prepared to handle whatever challenges may come their way, whether they involve caring for a patient or caring for the financial health of the entire organization.

Skills

Employee Performance Management

While managers can sometimes fall into the mindset of thinking of employees as resources, it is important to remember that every nurse and staff member is human and has their own thoughts, ideas, and feelings. A large part of employee management, then, comes down to communication.

Communication

There are five key principles for effective communication. The first is that telling is not the same as communicating. Communication involves the participation of both parties. Simply telling someone to do something is not effective communication. The other person must acknowledge the information and either ask questions, request clarification and further information, or communicate that they understand. This two-person exchange is communication.

The second key principle is that communication must be clear. It is not the responsibility of the secondary party to determine what the primary party meant by their communication. The primary party must make their communication clear without the need for interpretation.

The communicator should use simple, precise language. Care should be taken to avoid flowery, unusual, or ambiguous language when possible. The message cannot be adequately communicated if it is obscured by muddy language.

Communication requires the participation of both parties, which means that feedback is encouraged. If the receiving party did not fully understand the information, the primary communicator must be willing to hear and respond to queries, even when they are not positive.

The last principle is that direct communication is best. Communicate directly with the party who needs the information, whether that is in writing or via face-to-face conversation. Avoid having people pass verbal messages to others as those messages can get distorted or miscommunicated.

Even when these principles are followed, there can still be barriers to effective communication. The most obvious of these barriers are physical barriers. Distance, such as being on opposite sides of a room, and noise can make effective communication difficult. Similarly, trying to communicate in less-than-ideal surroundings, such as outside in bad weather, can cause misunderstandings.

There can also be psychological and social barriers, such as strained communication between employees who do not get along well or with employees who are intimidated by their managers. Fear, stress, distrust, and anger all inhibit communication. When tempers flare or when either party is feeling stressed, overwhelmed, or upset, it is best to wait to discuss the situation if at all possible. If communication must occur, both parties need to set their feelings aside in order to focus on the conversation and make the communication as effective as possible. In these situations, communicating in writing, such as via email, may be a better option than face-to-face.

Communication is also sometimes limited by semantics. What one party clearly interprets, another might find confusing. Using unfamiliar words or symbols, writing shorthand notes, or writing with poor penmanship can negatively affect communication. For example, if a manager writes notes for the next incoming nursing shift, but the manager's handwriting is illegible, the incoming staff may find it unreadable and incomprehensible. Thus, the communication was ineffective.

Assessment

When management and staff have good communication, it becomes easier for managers to convey important information, such as employee evaluations and performance assessments. **Nursing competency** involves several aspects, including general knowledge, job skills, attitudes, and behaviors. The nurse must have sufficient knowledge to do the job effectively. They must also have the necessary skills to apply that knowledge to patient care, and they must be able to do the job with an appropriate attitude and behavior. A nurse who is knowledgeable and skilled may not do well if the patients feel uncomfortable with them or do not trust them. Similarly, a nurse can have the best personal rapport with their patients, but without the proper knowledge or skills, they could do more harm than good. It is the responsibility of the manager, therefore, to ensure that each staff member has a suitable mix of knowledge, skills, and attitudes to do their jobs effectively.

There are several ways that managers can assess the staff. The nurses can perform **self-assessments**, in which the nurse considers specific questions about their own performance and abilities. These assessments may ask the nurse to list their best attributes or strongest skills, along with areas where they feel they could improve. They might be asked to describe situations in which they feel like they excelled as well as situations that they found difficult to manage. Self-assessments can also include information about career goals, feedback about their current job description, and execution of the required duties. Formatting of the assessments can include both open-ended questions and checklists for nurses to rank the information (e.g., on an agree-disagree scale).

Nurse executives and managers can also assess staff through observation, by accompanying them on their rounds, for example, and having the nurse explain what they are doing and why. The manager can pose questions to the nurse to get a fuller picture of the nurse's knowledge and thought process when dealing with patient care. Additionally, managers can perform audits of the nursing staff's notes, review patient files, and conduct peer reviews to get a full picture of a nurse's performance. If the manager finds areas that may be weak, having the nurse review information or complete practice simulations can help assess whether the weakness is due to knowledge, skills, lack of attention to detail, or a poor attitude about the job.

Periodically, a full appraisal of each nurse and staff member should be completed. An **employee appraisal** generally consists of ratings as well as written notes and observations. For example, the nurse may be given a score of one to five on a particular aspect of the job, and then the appraiser may include notes supporting or explaining that score. Employee appraisals often include information about the employee's schedule, attendance record, interactions with management and peers, and patient feedback. Ideally, the appraisal should also include direct information from the nurse, including any concerns they may have, their career goals, and their feedback about their work and their position within the organization. These appraisals are usually completed by the nurse's immediate supervisor or manager, reviewed by upper management, and placed into the nurse's permanent employment record.

Regardless of the type of evaluation, managers should ensure that the information and analysis align with the organization's mission and values. It would be unfair to evaluate a nurse based on criteria that they were unaware were part of their job requirements. Similarly, nurses should be given frequent feedback, both positive and critical, so that they can make adjustments on an ongoing basis. It would not be fair or effective management to withhold information or observations just so they can be included in an evaluation or appraisal at a later time. Nurses and staff want to be good at their jobs and want to know both what they are doing well as well as how they can improve.

Additionally, evaluation feedback should be clear and well-documented to avoid any type of "he said, she said" situation. If a nurse is given critical feedback and instructed on techniques for making improvements in that area, that feedback should be documented and acknowledged by both parties. By doing this, misunderstanding can be avoided if the nurse fails to make the necessary improvements or if the nurse makes changes that the manager says were unnecessary and/or incorrect.

Finally, evaluations and feedback should focus on employee retention and growth. Overly critical analysis without any acknowledgment of successes only serves to make the employee less satisfied with their job. It creates feelings of inadequacy and adds unnecessary stress to the employee. Instead, feedback should be growth-focused. While it is important to let staff know when an area needs improvement, this must be done in a way that allows the employee to learn and grow rather than making them feel as though they are incompetent or unvalued.

Similarly, when an employee is doing well and receives a good evaluation, the assessment should include specific details and explanations about what they are doing well and how that can translate to career growth and future potential. This way, the employee knows what they should continue doing and can take pride and ownership of a job well done.

Employee Engagement Strategies

On-Boarding
On-boarding, also known as organizational socialization, is the process by which new hires obtain the knowledge, skills, and behaviors they need in order to become valued, productive contributors to the company. The success of on-boarding programs is crucial because new employees decide if they will stay with an organization during their first six months of work. Therefore, it is important for companies to ensure that new employees feel supported and adjust to the social and performance aspects of their new roles quickly.

On-boarding can begin by having an employee's new managers and teammates reach out to them via email to welcome them even prior to their formal start date with the company. On the first day at work, the manager can introduce the new hire to the team member who will serve as their "buddy," to whom

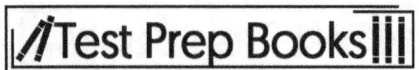

they can feel free to go to with any questions or concerns. Taking the new hire out of the office for a welcome lunch on the first day with a couple of staff members is always a nice gesture, as well as ensuring they have lunch partners for the first couple of weeks on the job.

Other aspects of successful on-boarding programs involve the new hire's manager scheduling meet-and-greet appointments to learn more about the roles that each teammate in the department plays and how the new hire will interact with them. These types of meetings can also be scheduled with individuals throughout the company who have key relationships with the department, such as members of IT, Marketing, Human Resources, etc. Additionally, providing the new hire with an on-boarding schedule that involves a variety of team members who will train on various processes and applications can be helpful. It is also important for the manager to provide clear expectations by meeting with the new hire to discuss their performance and development plans for the first three months. Finally, to help a new hire build contacts throughout the company, it is imperative to get them involved in a cross-functional project.

There is no set time limit for on-boarding programs, but at some companies, these programs can last throughout an employee's first year.

Retention

After taking the necessary time to recruit the right employees, it is important for companies to work to retain them. Employee turnover has high costs associated with it—lost time and lost productivity. There are many different ways that companies attempt to retain staff, and not one method works for all employees. For example, some employers feel that offering a competitive benefits package that includes health care, a retirement program, and life insurance is the best way to retain employees. However, sometimes low or no cost options that improve employees' work/life balance, such as flextime, telecommuting, and allowing employees to wear jeans to work every day (unless they are attending customer-facing meetings) are the best way to go. In addition, staff can be grateful for, and tend to stay longer at, workplaces that provide perks that are meaningful to them. Examples of these include on-site childcare, tuition reimbursement, dry cleaning pickup, and free doughnuts on Fridays.

Employers can stay in touch with how their employees are feeling about the work environment by conducting what is known as **stay interviews**. During these interviews, topics including why employees came to work for the employer, why the employees have stayed at the employer, what would make the employees consider leaving, and what the employees would want to see changed are discussed. This allows management to make necessary improvements before they find themselves conducting exit interviews.

Finally, in a workplace that is serious about retention, open communication between management and employees about the company's mission and future goals is key. It is also important for management to show concern for employees' continued development and to promote from within when possible.

Exit Interviews

Individuals who are leaving a company are given an exit interview to uncover their reasons for parting ways with the organization. **Exit interviews** are typically conducted by a neutral party, such as an HR professional, rather than by the departing employee's direct supervisor. HR will typically summarize and analyze the data from exit interviews at regular intervals to share information with management regarding possible improvement opportunities.

Human Resource Management

Alumni Program
Employee engagement can continue even after employees have left the organization. One way is through an **alumni program** that allows HR to communicate with and keep up with former employees. There are several reasons to maintain an alumni program. First, former employees can be a valuable source of referrals and rehires because they are already familiar with the structure, culture, and skills involved with the company. Former employees may also later become clients, customers, or consultants for the company.

One way to ensure the effectiveness of such a program is to have a positive and professional process when employees leave the company. This ensures that former employees leave with a great impression of their former company, allowing them to act as ambassadors and relationship builders for the company even as they continue their careers elsewhere. Learning about an employee's future goals and securing their contact information before they leave sets the stage for future ongoing communication, which is also imperative. Personalized outreach messages—for example, information about entry-level positions for former interns versus consultancy opportunities for former specialists—ensure that communications are relevant and effective. Ways to evaluate the effectiveness of the company's alumni program include analyzing the number of rehires and how long they stay with the company upon rehire; analyzing the number and value of business connections made through former employees; and tracking the number of hiring referrals from former employees.

Employee Engagement Data
Although HR can gain valuable insights into employee engagement by hearing from individual employees, conducting organization-wide studies allows HR to build a larger dataset. This provides an overall picture of how employees in the aggregate are engaging with the company, identify patterns, and highlight areas in need of improvement.

Generally, organizations collect data through **employee engagement surveys**. Some companies choose to work with third-party vendors that provide surveys and data analysis services. Some advantages of contracting out data analysis are the ease of implementation (no need for a company to design its own questions and response software) and the availability of benchmarking (third-party vendors work with many companies and have access to other datasets to provide comparisons of where other companies stand with engagement). Some companies choose to create surveys themselves, perhaps to save costs or have more control over the survey format.

Either way, even when working with a vendor that provides a survey template, management should review and select the types of questions. In fact, most surveys are structured as statements, and respondents are then asked to rank their level of agreement or disagreement (this discrete ranking response is called a **Likert scale**). Statements fall into common categories such as leadership (how leaders communicate with and motivate employees), alignment (how well employees' knowledge, skills, and abilities match their tasks), development (whether employees have opportunities for professional growth), facilitation (whether employees have access to the tools and resources they need to perform their jobs), and company culture (the personality of a company). The scores that employees assign to each statement can then be translated into quantitative data on engagement. Surveys also typically include a few open-ended response questions that allow employees to share comments or concerns that may not be covered by other parts of the survey.

After gathering data, the next step is for HR to analyze it. To make the data meaningful, there needs to be a point of comparison. For example, having similar or identical survey items every year allows HR to

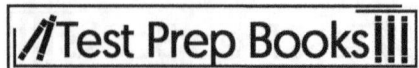 Human Resource Management

track if certain aspects of engagement are changing or remaining stable. However, HR also must judge whether any change is statistically meaningful. After pulling meaningful results from the data, the next step is to see what story they tell. This involves relating the survey results to other organizational metrics. For example, HR might notice that this year, there was a 10% increase in respondents who agreed with the statement, "I have many opportunities to challenge myself." HR finds that the highest positive responses came from the newest employees. Since HR implemented a new cross-training program for new hires last year, they might conclude that the program led to increased employee engagement in the realm of development.

In communicating the results of the survey, HR must look at the bigger picture of what the organization is trying to achieve and how employee engagement supports that goal. In the above example, HR might demonstrate how the cross-training program leads to more highly qualified employees who stay with the company longer, resulting in decreased hiring costs and increased customer retention. Employee engagement metrics should be considered in the context of overall business metrics.

Organizational Climate and Culture

How employees think and feel about a company is critical to an employer. If members of an organization have negative associations with their workplace, it can be difficult to motivate them. The overall "mood" of an organization is known as its **climate**, and organizational climate cannot be directly controlled. However, climate is closely affected by work environment, company standards, interactions, and a general sense of "how things are done around here." Together, these factors add up to what is called organizational culture. So, if an employer wants to improve the company's climate, they need to make changes to the company culture.

Encouraging Communication and Involvement

Encouraging communication and involvement is often a step in the right direction toward changing company culture. And much like climate and culture, communication and involvement are closely related, but not necessarily identical. For example, if John's boss gives him increased responsibility over an aspect of his work, then John has become more involved. However, if John does not have input from his boss on the decision process or a formal way to share his ideas with management, then the boss has not encouraged communication. Conversely, if John's boss starts sending regular memos detailing company activities and the strategies behind them, this is an increase in communication. However, if John and other employees do not have a way to contribute to this knowledge, then the boss has not encouraged involvement. To make meaningful changes to company culture, both communication and involvement should be addressed.

Involvement Strategies

There are numerous involvement strategies that companies can use. For example, the act of delegating authority allows an employee to make more decisions. By granting a staff member more responsibility, an employer can encourage them to take a greater sense of ownership over a company's successes. An employee survey can be used to ask employees how they feel about the company. Surveys can be formal (written or online) or informal (casual conversation), and can address topics such as concerns, suggestions for improvement, and priorities. It should be noted that, even in an anonymous survey, employees may feel hesitant to share their true feelings if the workplace culture is viewed as unfriendly.

In addition to surveys, a **suggestion program**, via an idea box or an online submission form, allows employees to recommend ways to address company problems. Unlike a survey, a suggestion program is an ongoing part of company involvement. Employees can also work together in a formal capacity as part

Human Resource Management

of a committee to address company concerns. Committees may be temporary or ongoing, and employees' service on a committee may also be for a specific term or a permanent appointment.

Moreover, an **employee-management committee** is a specific kind of committee where employees work alongside management to address company concerns. Sometimes known as employee participation groups, these committees also can be temporary or ongoing, depending on the needs of the organization.

Finally, employees can also serve on a **task force**, which is similar to a committee but focused on a specific problem and is usually temporary in nature. Employees on a task force work to determine the cause of a problem and develop a solution.

Federal Laws to Promote Outreach, Diversity, and Inclusion

Affirmative action aids employers in identifying imbalances in the workforce and assists them with placing a focus on hiring, training, and promoting groups of workers who are underrepresented. The following employers are required to have **affirmative action plans** (AAPs) in place (otherwise, having an AAP is voluntary):

- Employers with fifty or more employees and $50,000 in federal contracts
- Employers who are a member of the federal banking system
- Employers who issue, sell, or redeem U.S. Savings Bonds

The following sections contain detailed information about the major elements that make up an AAP.

Introductory Statement

An **introductory statement** is essentially a company overview that includes information concerning headcount, along with any significant employment changes that have taken place in the past calendar year. In addition, the company's policy on affirmative action and equal opportunity employment is also mentioned.

Organizational Profile

An **organizational profile** depicts the organization's staffing patterns, to determine if any barriers exist to equal opportunity employment. The organizational structure can be presented in a variety of formats (e.g., graphical chart, spreadsheet, etc.) to show the following information:

- Unit names
- Employees' job titles, gender, and minority status
- Total number of males and females
- Total number of males and females who are also minorities

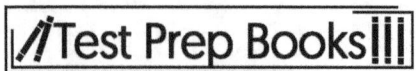

Job Group Analysis

A **job group analysis** is a list of all titles that comprise each job group. Jobs are grouped according to those with similar content, responsibilities, salaries, and opportunities for advancement. This analysis represents jobs by functional alignment versus departmental alignment.

Job Group Analysis											
Title	Salary	Total	Male Female	White	Black	Hispanic	Asian	Native Hawaiian	Indian	Two or More	Minority
Vice President Operations	28	1	1	1	0	0	0	0	0	0	0
			0	0	0	0	0	0	0	0	
Vice President Sales	28	1	1	0	0	1	0	0	0	0	1
			0	0	0	0	0	0	0	0	
Chief Financial Officer	29	1	0	0	0	0	0	0	0	0	1
			1	0	1	0	0	0	0	0	
Chief Operating Officer	30	1	1	1	0	0	0	0	0	0	0
			0	0	0	0	0	0	0	0	
Chairman	32	1	1	1	0	0	0	0	0	0	0
			0	0	0	0	0	0	0	0	
Summary of 1A – Executive		5	4	3	0	1	0	0	0	0	2
			1	0	1	0	0	0	0	0	

Availability Analysis

Organizations examine the internal (employees who are trainable, promotable, and transferable) and external (candidates in the reasonable geographical recruitment area) availability of women and minorities to determine their theoretical availability. External availability statistics can be obtained through state and local governments, which provide statistical data and may even publish it on their websites.

Utilization Analysis

The availability of women and minorities is compared with their current representation in each job group at the company. Companies typically define **underutilization** as the "80 percent rule." This rule is used to determine adverse impact in the employee selection process by comparing the rates at which different groups of people are hired for a job. Eighty percent was arbitrarily selected as an indication of underutilization. Then, for job groups where underutilization is found, reasonable placement goals are set (expressed as placement rates). It is also important to note that a company can have underutilization without experiencing adverse impact.

Other Required Elements

- Identify the individual who is ultimately accountable for the affirmative action plan
- List each identified problem area
- Detail the action-oriented affirmative action programs that will aid in reaching set goals
- Discuss how the affirmative action program will be monitored and reported to management
- Provide executive approval and signature on the affirmative action plan

- Create separate affirmative action plans for qualified, covered veterans and individuals with disabilities

- Ensure proper notices are posted on company bulletin boards about affirmative action and equal opportunity employment

Promote Outreach, Diversity, and Inclusion

A commitment to diversity and inclusion improves a company's relationship with its employees, customers and clients, and the community. Both a business case and a legal case can be made for engaging in diversity and inclusion initiatives. Additionally, the **Equal Employment Opportunity Commission (EEOC)** prohibits discriminatory hiring practices. Companies may also be subject to affirmative action laws in their states, and those that have contracts with the federal government must comply with several federal laws. Section 503 of the Rehabilitation Act of 1973, which applies to contractors with contracts over $10,000, requires those employers to take affirmative action for qualified individuals with disabilities. The Vietnam Era Veterans' Readjustment Assistance Act of 1974 (VEVRAA), later amended by the Jobs for Veterans Act, requires companies to have an affirmative action plan for veterans with service-connected disabilities and applies to contractors with 50 or more employees and contracts of $100,000 or over. Executive Order 11246 requires contractors with 50 or more employees and contracts of $10,000 or more to maintain an affirmative action program regarding women and minorities

One common way for companies to improve community outreach and develop a new generation of diverse employees is through an **internship program**. Having interns can be a win-win for the company and the community. People who are new to their field have a chance to develop their skills and learn more about the business. Meanwhile, the company can evaluate new talent and build a pool of prospective employees. Many companies hire full-time employees from previous interns, and these employees already have a great deal of loyalty to and knowledge about the organization. However, federal law should still be considered when designing an internship program. The FLSA establishes clear guidelines regarding wages and overtime pay for employees. Furthermore, for-profit companies planning unpaid internship programs must ensure that their interns are not in fact employees, utilizing a seven-point test created by the Department of Labor. Generally, the test evaluates whether unpaid interns are primarily gaining educational benefit, understand they will not be compensated, and are not displacing paid employees.

Organizations may also have **employee resource groups** (ERGs), which are formed by groups of employees who belong to similar demographic groups (e.g., an ERG for female employees or one for veterans). ERGs help employees to feel represented within the organization, build relationships, share experiences with others who understand their background, and give employers valuable insights into the unique needs and perspectives of a specific employee group.

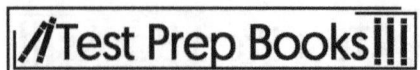

Workplace Programs Related to Health, Safety, Security, and Privacy

Workplace policies should strictly follow federal laws in order to legally secure a workplace that satisfies minimum health, safety, security, and privacy standards. Failure to meet federal standards can result in fines or the loss of a license. Federal laws and regulations function as minimum standards that all workplace policies must meet. Employers are allowed to pursue policies that go beyond what is legally required if they believe such policies will benefit the organization. Many employers strive to understand the delicate balance between meeting federal guidelines and maintaining high profit margins. Therefore, organizations often find innovative ways to meet federal standards while using efficient business strategies.

Four examples of federal agencies and laws regarding workplace issues are the Occupational Safety and Health Administration (OSHA), the Drug-Free Work Place Act, the Health Insurance Portability and Accountability Act, and the Sarbanes-Oxley Act.

The **Occupational Safety and Health Act,** passed in 1970, established the Occupational Safety and Health Administration (OSHA) of the federal government in 1971. This agency creates and enforces workplace safety standards. Employers who are engaged in commerce and have one or more employees must observe the regulations established by OSHA. However, partial exemptions are allowed to employers with fewer than 10 employees. These employers do not need to keep OSHA injury and illness records unless requested, however, work-related fatalities, hospitalizations, and amputations must still be reported. Not only does OSHA set minimum standards, the agency also ensures job training for workers in a language they can understand. Additionally, OSHA protects employees who work in substandard conditions and informs them of their rights. A critical provision of OSHA is the protection of employees who file a complaint to open an investigation of their working conditions; these employees are protected by OSHA from employer retaliation. OSHA regulations empower employees to advocate for safety and security in their workplace.

OSHA regulations focus on employer and employee rights and responsibilities. Employers are required to meet all OSHA safety standards, attempt to reduce hazards to workers, and supply free protective equipment to workers. Additionally, they must provide safety training and prominently display OSHA posters that detail employee rights. Employers must keep accurate records of any injuries or illnesses that occur in the workplace and notify OSHA promptly of any injuries. Furthermore, employers may not retaliate if an employee uses their right to report an OSHA violation.

OSHA regulations provide specific rights to employees. Examples of these include the right to obtain information concerning work hazards, request a workplace inspection without fear of employer retaliation, and meet privately with a licensed OSHA inspector. Additionally, OSHA regulations allow employees to refuse work that may be abnormally dangerous or life-threatening.

The **Drug-Free Workplace Act of 1988** requires organizations to establish a drug-free workplace, provide a copy of this policy to their employees, and institute a drug awareness program. This law applies to federal contractors with contracts of $100,000 or more and all organizations that are federal grantees. Penalties exist for employers who do not comply with the act, including contract suspension or contract termination. Although an employer may discuss alcohol and tobacco use in its policies, the Drug-Free Workplace Act does not address the use of these substances.

The **Health Insurance Portability and Accountability Act** of 1996 (**HIPAA**) addresses issues of healthcare access and portability as well as aspects of healthcare administration. HIPAA provisions allow workers that change jobs or become unemployed to transfer and continue their healthcare coverage.

Additionally, HIPAA regulations establish standards for healthcare administration in order to reduce waste, fraud, and abuse. HIPAA laws strengthen privacy standards and provide benchmarks for medical records in areas such as electronic billing.

HIPAA is applicable to health insurance plans issued by companies, HMOs, Medicare, and Medicaid. Moreover, these regulations apply to healthcare providers who conduct transactions electronically and healthcare clearinghouses that process certain information. HIPAA's Privacy Rule gives rights to the insured regarding the disclosure of medical information, such as the ability to view health records and request an edit of inaccurate information. Additionally, individuals may file a complaint if rights are denied or health information is not protected. Patient information with heightened protection is placed in the insurer's database and may include conversations about patients between medical professionals and billing information. Lastly, HIPAA creates strict rules regarding how healthcare information is disseminated and specifies who is given access.

The **Sarbanes-Oxley Act of 2002**, or **SOX**, is federal legislation that is designed to establish higher levels of accountability and standards for U.S. public institution boards and senior management. The act was passed in reaction to major global corporate and accounting scandals such as WorldCom and Enron, companies that were caught engaging in dubious financial practices. Sarbanes-Oxley specifically targets senior executives responsible for accounting misconduct and record manipulation. The law protects shareholders from any activity that conceals or misleads investors about the firm's finances. The firm has a mandate to report financial information transparently and accurately either to shareholders or the Securities and Exchange Commission (SEC). Moreover, SOX imposes more stringent penalties for white-collar crime and requires detailed reporting to the SEC if a company's finances significantly alter.

Employee Handbooks

Employee handbooks are important tools to communicate information to staff concerning the company's culture, work hours, safety, harassment, attendance, benefits, pay, electronic communication policies, and discipline policies. It is important for companies to keep employee handbooks current, simple to read, and to make accommodations for any multilingual requests. Additionally, a disclaimer should be included that the employee handbook is not intended to be a contractual agreement between the company and the employee. By making the employee handbook accessible on the company's intranet site, this eliminates outdated paper copies from floating around the office, and employees can access important policies at any time. It is good practice to have employees sign a form stating that they have received and read the latest version of the employee handbook.

SOP, Time and Attendance, and Expenses

There are many reasons to promote formalized policies and procedures in the workplace. They can guide and clarify standards of employee behavior, ensure fairness and consistency in employee treatment, promote compliance with federal law, and reduce risk of lawsuits. Although HR generally gives employees an overview of these policies and procedures during onboarding, employees may need reminders throughout their period of employment. When policies change, it is the responsibility of the HR department and management to communicate those changes.

The first step is to clarify the policies and procedures in HR before promoting them throughout the organization. Policies must be written in clear, plain language that includes a purpose statement (why the policy is needed), specific details (what the policy entails), implementation section (who is

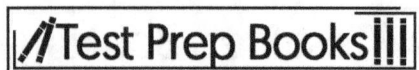

responsible for carrying out which aspects of the policy), effective date (when the policy will go into effect), and glossary (what specific terms mean within the context of the policy).

HR can then begin promoting the new policy throughout the organization. Depending on the organization's size and structure, several approaches are available, and HR may choose to use several of them. Particularly for large and decentralized organizations, HR should hold face-to-face meetings with managers and supervisors to communicate the specifics of the policy, state the business case for the policy, describe relevant changes from previous policy, emphasize the legal implications (if any) of violating the policy, and answer any questions. Because managers have more daily interaction with employees, their buy-in is key. HR may then have other meetings with employees or send a policy notice by email. Either way, employees should be required to sign off on the new policy and acknowledge their understanding. HR should keep a file of employee acknowledgement forms.

Time and attendance policies guide rules such as when employees arrive at and leave the office, how they record their time, overtime procedures, and requests for time off. A **standard operating procedure**, or **SOP**, is a written description of the steps involved in completing a specific task. It may conform to industry standards, legal regulations, or company-specific rules. **Expense policies** describe how employees can charge business expenses for items such as travel, accommodations, food, and other covered costs incurred in carrying out their job function.

Settling Discrimination Charges

Unfortunately, discrimination exists in some organizations, and sometimes official charges are brought forth. In these cases (and even in cases where the organization is confident that no wrongdoing has taken place), an organization has a decision to make. It can follow the process through the Equal Employment Opportunity Commission (EEOC) and be investigated by a Fair Employment Practices Agency (FEPA) at the local or state level. Alternatively, the organization may choose to settle the charges rather than face an investigation. Employee charges of discrimination must be filed with the EEOC within 180 days of the alleged incident. If probable cause is found, then the EEOC will attempt conciliation, and the employer is required to settle.

The complaint charge is either settled or the process may move to litigation with either the EEOC or a private court. If the EEOC is not able to determine probable cause, the employee can request a right-to-sue letter after the end of the 180-day period and must file suit in court within ninety days. Finally, if the EEOC does not find probable cause, the employer and employee are both notified. The employee can request a right-to-sue letter, and the EEOC's involvement with the case ends. The employee can then sue the employer in court.

There are a number of factors that can influence a company's decision to settle discrimination charges. One is the financial cost of an investigation. Lawyers and court fees can be a financial strain on a company's finances, not to mention additional obligations if the court rules against the company. There are also the challenges of the investigation itself to consider. If charges are brought to the EEOC or FEPA, a company may be required to devote considerable time and resources to cooperating with the investigation. Thus, an organization may decide that a one-time financial penalty is preferable to an extended period of disruption.

A company must also weigh the risk of damage to its reputation when considering the best path of settlement. A long, drawn-out trial and investigation, potentially widely covered on social and traditional media, can do irreparable harm to the company's image. Even in cases where the company is found to be blame-free in the case, the general public may still associate the organization with the charges of

Human Resource Management

discrimination. Therefore, a company may find it is better to accept the financial expense to avoid the potential long-term damage to its reputation. Finally, there are systemic problems to think about. If the company is aware of deeper issues of discrimination among its employees, it may choose to settle charges to avoid having the investigation uncover an ongoing pattern that may be hard to address.

Front Pay

If a company is found guilty of workplace discrimination, it is usually required to allow the individual in question to return to their position within the organization. However, in some instances, the court may rule that the company should require front pay. **Front pay** is money awarded to an individual in a workplace discrimination case and is generally equal to lost earnings. Front pay is usually required when the position is not available, the employer has not made any effort to address an ongoing issue of discrimination throughout the company, or the employee would be forced to endure a hostile work environment if they were to return to the original position.

Mediation Process

Mediation often serves as a precursor to the more official step of arbitration. In general terms, arbitration is sometimes thought of as a form of mediation, but legally there are important differences. Most notably, a mediator doesn't serve as a final "judge" of the dispute, but rather attempts to work with both parties to help them reach a resolution without having to take additional legal steps.

The mediation process usually begins with both parties agreeing to use a mutually acceptable mediator. The mediator sets the ground rules for the process and defines details such as what the dispute is about, who is involved, when and where the negotiations will take place, and the negotiation procedure. When the actual meeting takes place, the mediator reiterates the ground rules for the process. Both sides present their case and the mediator attempts to help both parties reach a compromise or find other solutions. If both sides agree to a compromise, a written document will be signed to ensure that both sides will follow through on the agreed-upon actions. If both sides do not agree, they may choose to pursue arbitration or litigation (court action).

Constructive Confrontation

Constructive confrontation is a type of mediation used in some particularly complicated or contentious disputes, such as when neither party can agree to a compromise. Constructive confrontation can sometimes break these stalemates by temporarily skipping the main issue in dispute, and instead, focusing first on secondary issues. Sometimes, by first resolving these smaller details, a mediator can affect parties' willingness to compromise on bigger issues.

Arbitration

Arbitration is a way to settle disputes without taking the issue to court. In a general sense, arbitration is a form of mediation. However, arbitration typically refers to a more formal process that takes place after an initial mediation attempt has failed. In arbitration, a neutral third party (known as an arbitrator) makes a decision based on the facts presented. There are different kinds of arbitration, decisions, and arbitrators.

In **compulsory arbitration**, the disputing parties are required by law to go through the arbitration process. This could be the result of a court order, but it could also arise from a contract that dictates that arbitration take place in certain situations.

In **voluntary arbitration**, the disputing parties choose to undergo the arbitration process, usually because they cannot come to an agreement, but do not want to go through a potentially expensive and time-consuming lawsuit.

In a **binding decision**, the disputing parties are required by law to follow the decision reached as a result of the arbitration process. This means that the losing party must follow the actions laid out by the decision, such as payments or reinstatement to a disputed position. In addition, a binding decision marks the end of the legal process. Neither party may pursue further legal action after the decision has been reached.

As the name suggests, **non-binding decisions** do not carry legal weight. Either party may choose to follow or not follow the terms of the decision. In addition, a dissatisfied party may choose to pursue additional legal action after the decision of the arbiter is reached.

A **permanent arbitrator** is someone who routinely judges arbitration cases for a company or other organization. An arbitrator may be trained and certified by a professional organization or a mutually trusted individual to provide an unbiased opinion on the dispute.

An **ad-hoc arbitrator** may also be a certified professional or a mutually trusted third party. But unlike permanent arbitrators, ad-hoc arbitrators do not have a regular arbitration relationship with either party. Instead, they are chosen as a one-time solution to address only the unique dispute in question.

An **arbitrator panel** functions just like an ad-hoc arbitrator, but it is comprised of multiple arbitrators (usually three). They are sometimes called arbitral tribunals or tripartite arbitration panels.

Americans with Disabilities Act (ADA)

The Americans with Disabilities Act (ADA) was passed in 1990 to protect individuals with disabilities against discrimination in relation to aspects such as employment, pay, and benefits. The EEOC defines such disabled individuals as having a physical or mental impairment that limits one or more major life activities.

The ADA applies to companies and organizations with fifteen or more employees. The act dictates that unless a company or organization undergoes "undue hardship," they are required to make reasonable accommodations for any disabled employees. Examples of such modifications include improving existing facilities to make them more accessible or adjusting the circumstances under which a job is performed. It is important to know that disabled employees must still be able to perform the essential functions of their job positions, with or without accommodations, when hired.

Identifying reasonable accommodations is an interactive four-step process. First, barriers to the performance of the essential job functions must be identified for a disabled employee. Then, possible accommodations that may be helpful in overcoming the barriers are discussed. The feasibility of each of the accommodations is assessed, including if the accommodations are the employer's responsibility or will impose an undue hardship to the employer. Finally, the appropriate accommodations are chosen for the disabled employee. An employer is allowed to ask for proof of a disability if it is not obvious, along with information about the accommodation before deciding to make it. An employer cannot ask if an individual has a disability during a job interview. However, if a candidate comes to an interview in a wheelchair, the employer can ask the individual what type(s) of accommodations would be needed.

Examples of reasonable accommodations include the following:

- Modifying work sites
- Accessible facilities
- Flexi-time
- Flexi-place
- Providing readers and interpreters
- Modifying work schedules
- Assistive devices
- Reassignment (only available as a last resort)

Pregnancy Discrimination Act

The **Pregnancy Discrimination Act**, passed in 1978, was an amendment to Title VII of 1964. The act applies to all employers with fifteen or more employees and states that while pregnant women are working, they are to be treated in the same way as other employees who are performing their jobs. Therefore, pregnancy must be treated in the same manner as any other type of temporary disability.

Under this legislation, an employer:

- Cannot refuse to hire a pregnant woman
- Cannot force a woman to take leave or terminate her employment because she is pregnant
- Must give a woman a comparable position to the one that she held prior to her maternity leave (if the company already does so with employees taking short-term disability) upon her return to work
- Must provide a pregnant woman with reasonable accommodation(s) if she is unable to do her job and approaches her manager to that effect
- Cannot discriminate against a woman who has undergone an abortion

When a pregnant woman is interviewing for a job position, she is not required by law to disclose the fact that she is pregnant. If it is obvious that a female interview candidate is pregnant, a prospective employer can only state the job requirements for the position (ignoring the pregnancy) and ask the candidate when she is available to start work.

Uniform Guidelines on Employee Selection Procedures

The **Uniform Guidelines on Employee Selection Procedures**, passed in 1978, were designed to prohibit selection procedures that have an adverse impact on protected groups. Adverse impact occurs when the rate for a protected group is less than 80% of the rate for the group with the highest selection rate. This is also known as the 80 percent rule, or the four-fifths rule. Below are two examples:

Example 1:

Four hundred white candidates applied and two hundred were hired – 50%. One hundred Hispanic candidates applied and forty-five were hired – 45%. 80% of 50 is 40. There is no adverse impact here. If the number was lower than forty, there would be.

Example 2:

Sixty male candidates interviewed and thirty were hired – 50%. Forty female candidates applied and ten were hired – 25%. 80% of 50 is 40. Yes, there is adverse impact here, since there were only 25% females hired. Females must be hired at a selection rate of 40%.

Under these guidelines, procedures that have an adverse impact on women and minorities must be proven to be valid in predicting and/or measuring performance, so as not to be viewed as discriminatory. The **"bottom line" concept** was an outcome of these guidelines, meaning that an employer is not required to evaluate each component of the selection process individually if the end result is shown to be predictive of future job performance.

If adverse impact is found (which is not always intentional), the employer has alternatives:

- Abandon the procedure
- Modify the procedure to eliminate adverse impact
- Demonstrate job relatedness
- Conduct validation studies
- Keep detailed records
- Investigate alternatives with less adverse impact
- Show the business necessity associated with the need to keep the procedure (which is difficult to do)

Immigration Reform and Control Act (IRCA)

The **Immigration Reform and Control Act (IRCA)** was passed in 1986 and amended in 1990. This act was created to prevent discrimination against individuals based on national origin or citizenship on elements such as employment, pay, or benefits, so long as they are legally able to work in the United States. Employers are also required to verify new employees by having them complete an **employment eligibility verification form (I-9)** and receiving proof of lawful status within their first three working days. The back of the I-9 form lists each of the documents that can be used to show legality to work in the United States, verifying an individual's right to work and identity. Employers must retain I-9 forms for three years, or for one year after an employee's termination, whichever comes later. In addition, this act established civil and criminal penalties for hiring illegal immigrants.

Furthermore, the IRCA instituted categories for visas, such as immigrant visas or green cards. While permanent or indefinite visas and are obtained through family relationships or employment, nonimmigrant visas are temporary. Another example is the H1-B visa, for which there is a yearly cap. This type of visa is set aside for certain kinds of working professionals who travel to the United States for a specified period of time.

Sexual Harassment in the Workplace

There are two types of sexual harassment that occur in the workplace: quid pro quo and hostile work environment. The translation of quid pro quo is "this for that." **Quid pro quo sexual harassment** takes place when a superior conditions employment (e.g., promotional opportunity, raise, etc.) on sexual favors.

The type of sexual harassment known as **hostile work environment** takes place when sexual or discriminatory conduct creates a work environment that a "reasonable person" would find threatening

Human Resource Management

or abusive (e.g., unwelcome advances, offensive gender-related language, and sexual innuendos). It is important to remember that male employees can also be victims of sexual harassment.

There are four well-known court cases that stemmed from sexual harassment in the workplace:

- *Meritor Savings Bank vs. Vinson*: The court held that sexual harassment violates Title VII. This case dealt with an employee who was plagued with unwanted sexual innuendos. The court said that the plaintiff did not need to prove concrete psychological harm, just an abusive or intimidating environment.
- *Harris vs. Forklift Systems, Inc.*: This case established the "reasonable person" standard for hostile environment sexual harassment.
- *Oncale vs. Sundowner Offshore Service, Inc.*: The court ruled that same-gender sexual harassment is actionable. This case dealt with all males working on an offshore oilrig, where a heterosexual male was threatened with rape.
- *Faragher vs. City of Boca Raton*: The court stated that employers can be held liable for supervisory harassment that results in an adverse employment action. This case dealt with female lifeguards who were sexually harassed. The city was held liable because the lifeguards' supervisors were not informed of the policy (it was not communicated effectively).

The following items are key elements to put in place in order to prevent sexual harassment from occurring in the workplace:

- Provide staff with a written, zero tolerance policy on sexual harassment that contains clear definitions and examples
- Provide a complaint procedure for staff to utilize
- Hold training sessions for employees and document attendees
- Investigate all sexual harassment complaints
- Follow through with corrective action (up through and including termination), if necessary
- Communicate the policy on sexual harassment to everyone in the company using multiple methods

Team Performance Management

No employee works alone. The unit or department is staffed by a team, and everyone, from the nurse executive and managers to the nurses and the staff, is part of that team. Managing a team means understanding the **team dynamics**—everyone's work styles, values, and goals—and how everyone works together to care for the patients.

It is important to understand that a group is not a team. A group of people can work in the same place, but they are not a team unless they can work together toward a common goal. Members of a team are engaged with one another and actively collaborate together to solve problems. They show respect for one another and keep the goal—providing the best care for the patients—always at the forefront.

It is the responsibility of the managers to create a cohesive team and cultivate a successful team dynamic within the unit or department. The first aspect of this is creating a common goal and developing a plan for reaching and maintaining that goal. Goals can be set for daily tasks or longer-term projects within the unit, department, or organization. Regardless of their scope, goals should be established using the **SMART** acronym: Specific, Measurable, Achievable, Relevant, and Time-Bound.

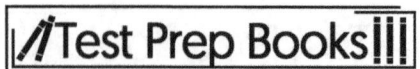

SMART Goals

A specific goal includes detailed information about who is expected to do each task or who will be impacted by each task. The goal should be precise, clear, and free of jargon, confusing, or ambiguous language. A basic, specific goal might be that nurses should visit all of their patients on the unit within the first hour of their shift.

The team's goal should also be measurable, meaning that it can easily be determined whether or to what extent the goal was reached. If a nurse has ten patients and visits only eight of them during the first hour of their shift, the nurse has reached 80% of the goal.

Goals should also be attainable. Setting goals that a team is wholly unable to achieve creates tension, anxiety, and feelings of hopelessness and inadequacy not only within the team but also for each individual member of the team. Unattainable goals can eventually lead to job dissatisfaction and result in losing employees. Instead, set goals that the team can achieve, even if they must put in more work or effort to get there. It would not be reasonable to ask a nurse with ten high-needs patients to complete visits to all of them within too short a time frame. The nurse will just become anxious and frustrated, and patient care could suffer.

Goals for the team should be relevant. Goals should make sense to the team, encourage better patient care, and allow the department to run more smoothly and efficiently.

The last aspect of SMART is that goals should be time-bound. There should be an end date by which the goal should be met. The team should have time to work toward achieving the goal, with enough urgency to make them strive to improve but not so urgent as to create stress and anxiety.

Team Dynamics

Once the team is established and working toward a common goal, the managers need to carefully assess the team dynamics, or how the members of the team interact with one another and collaborate together to achieve their common goal. It takes time and care to build a team that works together, communicates well, and collaborates effectively to provide superior healthcare to its patients. Common pitfalls must be avoided. One such pitfall is the "us" versus "them" mentality that can develop when things don't go as planned. For example, if a nurse neglects to complete a task that then falls on the next shift to finish, it can create negative feelings. It is important that everyone understands their role and is accountable for their responsibilities.

Managers can help alleviate these feelings by encouraging clear communication. Scheduling shifts that overlap slightly allows for staff on differing shifts to communicate with one another. A short meeting where the outgoing team can brief the incoming team on previous events and current patient status updates creates a sense of unity and collaboration between the different shifts. Furthermore, it reminds everyone that they are on the same team and working together to provide the best care for their patients.

Conflict Resolution

Despite everyone's best efforts, there will inevitably be conflicts that must be resolved. Ideally, team members will be able to communicate with one another and resolve minor issues between themselves, but that is not always the case. Nurse executives and managers must be prepared to assist in finding a mutually agreeable solution to conflicts.

The first step to **conflict resolution** is fully understanding the situation. Managers must be willing to listen to their employees. They must take the time to meet with the employee one-on-one, without other distractions, and actively listen to the employee's concerns. The manager should refrain from any judgment and instead seek to fully understand the situation, employee's feelings, and position within the conflict. Once the manager has heard from the initial party, the same time and consideration should be given to the other person, to hear their side of the situation.

Once the manager fully understands the conflict, they can determine the best path forward. Ideally, both parties should be involved in reaching resolution, with equal and due respect given to everyone. Sometimes the manager needs to act as a mediator, allowing the two parties to talk to one another, understand each other, and resolve their differences. Other times, the manager may need to resolve a dispute by deciding on which particular action to take. In all cases, though, the employees need to feel heard, understood, and valued throughout the resolution. They need to know that the resolution is in the best interest of the team and the patients.

Leveraging Diversity

Humankind is a unique mix of demographic differences in ethnicity, race, socioeconomic situation, gender, sexual orientation, and religion. **Diversity** can also come in the form of attitudes, ideas, beliefs, and experiences. In other words, people come from many different walks of life, and the healthcare team must be ready to manage patients from every background and situation. To this end, a diversified team can better relate to its patients, and patients feel more comfortable when they feel as though their team understands them and can relate to them. In addition to patient comfort and satisfaction, a diverse team leads to more innovative thinking and unique ideas for problem-solving. Generating creative and exciting ways to solve problems and meet team goals can invigorate the whole team, building on their sense of unity, respect, and appreciation for one another.

There are specific elements that managers can implement to foster a diverse work team and inclusive environment. First, management must create a safe space where everyone is valued, questions are welcomed, and the whole team is committed to understanding one another. In addition, managers should be aware of their own implicit biases and work to overcome those. The workplace policies and procedures should be reviewed to ensure that they are not adversely affecting any particular demographic, and employees should feel free and comfortable to bring any concerns to their managers.

Managers should also require a diverse pool of recruits when looking for new hires. Human resource departments and employee search firms should understand the needs and requirements of the team, both from a skilled professional standpoint as well as from a diversity and inclusion perspective. Managers should also ensure that everyone has equal access to professional development opportunities, while utilizing the unique knowledge, skills, and ideas of each team member to strengthen the team as a whole.

Practice Quiz

1. Two of Olivia's staff are having a dispute about which responsibilities are whose. What can she do to resolve the situation?
    a. Request that HR revise and clarify the job descriptions
    b. Establish a protocol within the department for handling job disputes
    c. Schedule a meeting with herself and the two employees to clarify the responsibilities of each person
    d. Tell the two employees to sit down and resolve the issue themselves

2. Which of the following are some of the differences that create diversity within the workplace?
    a. Gender
    b. Ethnicity
    c. Religion
    d. All of the above

3. How can a diverse nursing team better care for patients?
    a. Patients feel more comfortable when they feel as though their nurses can relate to them.
    b. A diverse team creates less potential for conflict.
    c. Different people have different styles of bedside manner.
    d. Patients like people with different personalities.

4. In reviewing her staffing needs for an upcoming hiring event, Megan has noticed that most of her staff are of the same racial and cultural background. She would like to work on creating a more diverse team. What is the first step she can take?
    a. Ask HR to provide a more diverse pool of applicants.
    b. Meet with other managers about exchanging some of her staff with theirs.
    c. Fire some of her staff and replace them with more diverse new hires.
    d. Cut back on the hours for some of her staff and give more hours to new, more diverse employees.

5. What is one thing that managers and nurse executives can do to foster a more diverse workplace?
    a. Increase professional development opportunities and requirements.
    b. Create a safe space where everyone is committed to inclusiveness and understanding one another.
    c. Set a schedule to change up team groupings every week.
    d. Strictly adhere to department policies and procedures.

See answers on the next page.

Answer Explanations

1. C: The most immediate and effective solution is to schedule a meeting with all three parties to resolve the confusion. Once that is done, then a request can be put in to HR or upper management for a revision to the job descriptions, Choice A, if necessary. Choice B can be helpful in the long term, but it would not immediately fix the current problem. Telling two people who are already at odds that they have to fix the problem themselves, Choice D, often just creates more conflict and can lead to resentment.

2. D: There are many different factors that can create diversity within a team. Gender, ethnicity, and religion are all examples of diversity that can exist amongst team members.

3. A: Patients feel more comfortable when they feel as though their nurses understand them and can relate to them, which leads to better care and a better experience for the patient. While all teams have the potential to experience conflict, Choice B, diversity does not necessarily make this more or less likely. It is also true that different personalities will care for patients differently, Choices C and D; however, that is not a characteristic of diversity.

4. A: Managers can require a diverse pool of recruits when looking for new hires. Megan can speak to Human Resources about her department's needs and ask that they actively seek out more diverse applicants. Shifting staff between departments, Choice B, is a drastic measure and may not be feasible given the level of knowledge and skill required for each unit or department. Firing or laying off someone based on demographics such as race, ethnicity, gender, or religion, Choice C, is a violation of federal law. Similarly, reducing someone's hours based on these characteristics, Choice D, is unlawful.

5. B: Creating a safe work environment where everyone is committed to understanding one another helps to foster a diverse team and an inclusive environment. While continuing education, Choice A, is important, it is not usually a factor in creating diversity. Changing up team groupings, Choice C, can actually create a more divisive environment. Adhering to the department's policies and procedures, Choice D, is generally a good practice, unless it goes against diversity and inclusion efforts. Instead, existing policies and procedures should be reviewed to ensure that they are not adversely affecting any particular demographic.

Quality and Safety

Knowledge

Change Management Frameworks

In order to remain competitive, adopt industry best practices, and adapt to changing markets, an organization will undergo change at many points. Change might be implemented to benefit company shareholders and increase the profitability of the company. Change can also occur to reduce costs and increase efficiency. However, especially from an HR perspective, it's important to keep in mind how change affects employees. The truth is that most people don't like change. Workforce changes, such as outsourcing or downsizing, are certain to be met with employee resistance. Even more minor changes like revised vacation policies may go through an unpopular adjustment period. Change management helps to smooth over these difficulties.

Change Management

Change is inevitable for any organization, especially in fields affected by global markets and technological innovation. **Change management** seeks to aid organizations through significant transitions in resource allocation, operations, business processes, or any other large-scale changes. Careful change management helps the organization to function effectively even while undergoing a major evolution.

Implementing Change

How should an organization implement change? The classic 1961 text *The Planning of Change* tackles this question. The book outlines three strategies for managing change: the empirical-rational strategy, the normative-reductive strategy, and the power-coercive strategy.

The **empirical-rational strategy** assumes that people are rational and will naturally follow any course that's in their self-interest. Therefore, they are more likely to accept change when they think it will directly benefit them. To implement change in line with this strategy, an organization must either 1) demonstrate the benefit of the change or 2) demonstrate the harm of the status quo (or both). One way of accomplishing this is to incentivize change. For example, a growing company is gaining new employees, but it doesn't want to expand its available parking. The company decides to limit the number of parking spots and encourage public transportation use. Employees are reluctant to give up the freedom to drive, so the company holds an educational seminar about how to save money by using public transportation and offers monthly reimbursement for employees who use public transportation.

The next approach proposed in *The Planning of Change* is the **normative-reductive strategy**. This strategy assumes that people will closely follow social norms and expectations. In order to implement change, it's necessary to first change one's idea of what is socially acceptable. This is the strategy that harnesses the power of advertising. For example, think of anti-tobacco advertising campaigns over the past few decades. Throughout most of the twentieth century, smoking was socially acceptable just about anywhere. However, especially in the 1990s and 2000s, aggressive anti-smoking advertisements attacked the tobacco industry and started anti-smoking education programs for students. The social norm turned against smoking in most public places, and now there are more anti-smoking laws than ever before.

Finally, the **power-coercive strategy** assumes that people are followers who will listen to authority and do as they are told. This approach to change is basically, "My way or the highway!" Where the empirical-rational strategy seeks to demonstrate how change will benefit employees, the power-coercive strategy argues that not following change will be harmful to employees, who might be punished or even fired for failure to comply. For example, a factory undergoes an intense safety inspection and decides to completely renovate its safety standards. Employees now have new dress code requirements. If they don't follow the dress code, they aren't allowed to work that day; after the third dress code violation, they will be fired.

Deciding which strategy to employ depends on the overall character of the organization as well as the importance and sensitivity of the change. For example, an otherwise friendly and collegial office might respond negatively to usage of the power-coercive strategy. The power-coercive strategy would be useful for changes with clear legal or financial liabilities, such as when an organization must follow new government regulations.

Culture of Safety

Just Culture

Just Culture refers to a supportive workplace environment that recognizes the reality of human error yet prioritizes safety tools and tactics to prevent errors. When a safety event does occur—whether it is an actual adverse event or merely a close call—it is viewed as preventable and non-punitive. Unless gross negligence is involved, the individuals involved in the event are not blamed. Instead, the process that allowed the error must be addressed.

To achieve such a culture, there must be a mindset of continuous improvement and striving to uphold patient safety. The concept of Just Culture stems from the premise that if staff are encouraged and feel safe to bring patient safety concerns forward, then a proactive approach can be taken to limit the errors and mistakes that play a role in the safety event.

Nurse executives and leadership must affirm this message through their words and actions in order for a true culture to be adopted. This may be accomplished through rounding, continuing education, and encouraging the reporting of safety events. In addition, nurse execs must ensure that their direct reports understand and adhere to the promise of a non-punitive system. Any retaliatory actions must be justified and should only occur in cases in which gross negligence, illegal activity, or purposeful work outside of scope has been discovered after investigation.

Workplace Violence

Workplace violence is a widespread problem in healthcare. It has been assumed for many years that workplace violence is common in healthcare, and staff have historically been reluctant to report events. Many nursing and executive leaders have moved towards adopting zero tolerance policies. This applies to both physical and non-physical violence, and it encompasses violence from patients as well as lateral violence amongst co-workers.

Nurse executives can organize workplace violence, or disruptive behavior, committees to review reported cases. Recommendations of appropriate actions can be voted upon, with results ranging from a warning letter to denial of care or employment.

Nurse leaders must uphold expectations in a fair manner and set a precedent of behavior. Workplace violence training for all staff across the organization is encouraged, with topics covering de-escalation

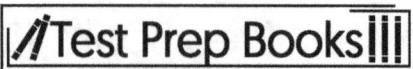

Quality and Safety

strategies, reporting methods, and defining both physical and non-physical violence. Addressing workplace violence can improve employee engagement and psychological safety while lowering attrition rates and rates of injury.

Every worker in healthcare has the right to be treated fairly, respectfully, and with their safety and best interests in mind. Affirming a zero tolerance of violence at any level in the healthcare system advocates for the safety of staff and patients.

High Reliability Principles

High Reliability Organizations (HRO) and industries prioritize safety. When prioritizing safety in healthcare, the focus is on preventing harm—whether to patients or to staff.

There are five basic HRO principles that the nurse exec must know and follow. These include:

1. Preoccupation with Failure: Failure is inevitable, but when it is anticipated, the organization can be better prepared. Nurse executives should know the risks inherent to the areas they lead and have strategies in place to reduce harm when failures occur.

2. Deference to Expertise: The wisest and most knowledgeable people in the room are not the executive leadership team, but the subject matter experts doing the actual work every day. When their expertise is recognized, these experts will bring issues to the upper level and be drivers for change.

3. Commitment to Resilience: When things go wrong, an organization with leadership support is resilient and can quickly pivot to adjust to unplanned outcomes. The nurse executive should be prepared for changes in staffing, shortages, and deviations from the regular flow of patient care, and back-up plans should be established and communicated widely.

4. Sensitivity to Operations: Reliable nurse executives keep a finger on the pulse of what is happening within the organization. This enables them to identify and bring awareness to issues that could be safety concerns or cause delays.

5. Reluctance to Simplify: Nurse executives acknowledge that the healthcare system is a challenging environment with many moving pieces, and they investigate the root of the problem rather than relying on a simple solution. When one piece is not in the right place or functioning as it should, safety events can occur. Building layers of safeguards assists in making systems safer, and identifying and solving root problems is most important.

Risk Management and Legal Compliance

Nurse administrators also have the responsibility of managing potential risks and maintaining legal compliance within their healthcare organization. Conducting regular **risk assessments** to determine potential areas that need improvement and implementing risk management programs are important functions of the nurse administrator. Maintaining liability insurance is also an important factor, which is often provided by major health systems. Nurse administrators need to have extensive knowledge of healthcare administration laws and regulations, such as employment laws and patient rights laws. When legal requirements are met, it prevents and reduces legal risks. It also generates an ethical and lawful environment that allows for safe, effective, and quality patient care.

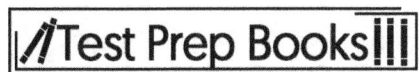

Advance Directives

Advance directives, such as a **living will** or **durable power of attorney**, are forms that state a patient's choices for treatment, including refusal of treatments, life support, and stopping treatments when the patient chooses. **Do not resuscitate (DNR) status**, and its varying types, is also included in advance directives. One area where these topics are often discussed is prior to a patient undergoing surgery. Therefore, the preoperative interview should include discussion of advance directives and DNR status. If the patient has advance directives, a copy should be placed in the medical record, and they should be reviewed by the nurse and physician. If the patient has a code status of anything other than full resuscitation, a conversation among the surgeon, anesthesiologist, and patient is necessary to discuss the patient's wishes in detail.

Older schools of thinking suggest all patients, regardless of preoperative DNR status, are considered full code while in the operating room; however, this is not true. A patient with DNR status of no intubation and no **cardiopulmonary resuscitation** (**CPR**) may proceed with the surgical procedure if the surgeon and anesthesiologist have a conversation with the patient and a plan is agreed upon among them. Consent must be obtained by the patient if there is a change in status or a suspension of the DNR order during surgery. However, if the patient wishes to keep DNR status of no intubation and no CPR during surgery, the surgeon and/or anesthesiologist may deem the patient a nonsurgical candidate. If a patient is entering surgery with a DNR order of anything other than full code, this must be communicated to the entire surgical team and documented in the medical record. **Healthcare power of attorney** is the legal term for the person appointed by the patient to make their healthcare decisions should they become incapacitated.

Reviewing Client Understanding of Advance Directives

The role of the nursing staff in coordinated care is to work in tandem with the entire health care team to ensure the needs and choices of each patient are effectively communicated across the participating departments. This involves reviewing advance directives with the patient and ensuring they understand what these directives entail. These are guideline documents utilized for instituting or continuing medical care and are a U.S. healthcare facility requirement as per The **Patient Self-Determination Act** of 1990. Many of the subjects they cover are delicate in nature, such as death-related legal and/or ethical matters, euthanasia, DNR (do not resuscitate) orders, organ donation, the bill of rights of a dying person, the living will of the patient, and giving over the power of attorney to a trusted person (durable power of attorney). As a result, the utmost care and empathy should be followed.

Making a note of any questions the patient asks regarding the concept of advance directives is a good way to assess their understanding of the process. For example, if a patient asks whether they are allowed to alter their directive, this raises a red flag to the nurse that they don't fully understand the process. If the patient doesn't offer any feedback voluntarily, asking them what they know about the process is a good way to determine their level of knowledge.

Client Care Assignments

Every day when the nurse reports to duty, a team of patients will be assigned to them. A caseload of patients will vary in size based on the acuity of the patients' illnesses and the policies of the unit.

Acuity refers to the severity of the patient's illness. Some patients are high acuity, meaning a greater amount of time and resources are required in their daily routine due to the severity of their illness. Others are low acuity and do not require as much complexity in the level of care. High acuity patients

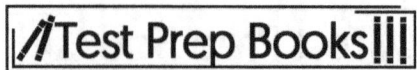

might be more difficult for many nurses because their care can often take away from the care of others. A team full of high-acuity patients, then, can be a great burden for a nurse to bear.

When patient assignments become too burdensome for nurses, evidence can be found in **nursing-sensitive indicators**, such as increases in patient falls and hospital-acquired pressure ulcers. When the nurse is busy with a team of high acuity patients, it is difficult to perform each required task thoughtfully and carefully. It is then in the best interest of those making team assignments for nurses to carefully weigh the patient load and ensure equitable and fair decisions are made.

Dividing up teams of patients is often the task of the charge nurse. To fairly assign patient teams to nurses, the charge nurse must bear in mind each patient's acuity. Conflict arises when nurses feel that there is inequity in the assignment of patients and they are unduly burdened with an unfair patient load compared to other teams or units.

Nurse satisfaction directly correlates with patient care. If nurses do not feel their patient assignments are fair and the burden is too great, their performance suffers as well as their job satisfaction. Nursing performance can be linked to the following nurse-sensitive indicators: how well patient pain is managed; the presence and treatment of pressure ulcers, patient falls, and medication errors; patient satisfaction; and nosocomial or hospital-acquired infections.

Client Rights

Each patient has certain rights that must be respected. When patients are admitted to a facility, they are put in a position of vulnerability. This special position of power held by the health care provider should never be abused to violate the rights of the patient. Caring for a patient is an honor, and certain rules of conduct should be followed.

The patient has the right to have health information kept private and only shared with those who are given permission to view it. The Health Insurance Portability and Accountability Act (HIPAA) was passed by Congress in 1996 to protect health information. HIPAA is responsible for patient privacy in each of the various means that personal health information can be shared: verbally, digitally, over the phone or fax, or through written messages.

Along with protecting the patient's health information, the nurse must be respectful of the patient's privacy in general. Knocking on the patient's door before entering the room, keeping the door shut to the busy corridor outside the room, and not asking unnecessary personal questions are all ways the nurse can extend common courtesy to the patient. The nurse-patient relationship is already quite personal in nature, so one must be careful not to exploit that relationship.

Each patient has the right to fair treatment. Care should not be provided in a way that shows favoritism, whether due to racial bias or unfair prejudice based on the nurse's personal opinions and beliefs. Giving one patient preferential treatment over another is a violation of the patient's rights, and the nurse will be subject to disciplinary action if they are discovered to be treating patients poorly.

No patient should ever be abused or neglected. This should go without saying, but it is a patient right that is perhaps the most important. Abuse can be physical, emotional, sexual, mental, or financial. Neglect is when the patient's needs are being ignored, usually resulting in patient harm.

The patient has the **right to self-determination**, which means that they have the right to make decisions regarding their own health care. Patients are members of the healthcare team along with the doctors and nurses. What the nurse may think is the right course of action for a patient may not align with what

Quality and Safety

the patient thinks is right, and that is to be respected. The healthcare team forms the plan of care and educates the patient as to what a plan entails, but it is the patient who makes the final decision to accept or reject a plan. If the patient is not capable of making their own decisions, the power of attorney—usually a close family member such as a wife, husband, or adult child—has the power to make healthcare decisions for the patient.

Along with self-determination, the patients also have the freedom to express themselves and their opinions. Simply being admitted to a facility does not take away their freedom of speech. Patients may have opinions about all aspects of their care, and they have every right to express these feelings. The nurse needs to be respectful, listen, and try to help when there is a problem that can be solved. Issues voiced by patients can always be escalated by the nurse, using the appropriate chain of command.

If a nurse suspects abuse or neglect, they are mandated to report it to the appropriate entity. The charge nurse and/or nurse manager should be notified, so the appropriate action can be taken to right the situation. There are also hotlines that can be called, such as the National Center on Elder Abuse (1-800-677-1116).

There are different types of abuse. **Physical abuse** involves injuries to the body from force, such as punching or kicking. If the nurse notes various bruises or cuts in various stages of healing without explanation, it may be a sign of physical abuse.

Sexual abuse is when sexual contact is made without the consent of one party, including rape, coercion into doing sexual acts, and fondling of genitalia. The nurse should look for unexplained bruising of or bleeding around the perineal area, new difficulty sitting or walking, or increased agitation as potential signs of sexual abuse.

Emotional abuse and **mental abuse** are not quite as obvious as physical abuse, as the damage inflicted is internal or hidden. Emotional and mental abuse is usually caused by verbal assault. The abuser may belittle and criticize the victim to the point that the victim feels worthless, insecure, and afraid. If the nurse senses an uncomfortable relationship between an informal caregiver or family member and the patient, this should be monitored, investigated, and reported if abuse is suspected.

Financial abuse is a type of abuse in which the abuser limits the victim's access to money and financial information, sometimes stealing directly from the victim without the victim's knowledge. Being the caregiver of an older person grants a person special access to personal documents and financial resources; this privilege can be abused. If the nurse suspects that checks and other financial means meant for the patient are being rerouted and misused by a caregiver, this abuse should be reported right away.

It is the patient's right to deny treatment. Patients can deny treatment if fully informed of their medical condition and the likely outcomes resulting from the refusal. This is known as the right to informed consent. They may decide to refuse treatment for several reasons, including religious or cultural beliefs, fear of the procedure or its side effects, or belief that the treatment is unnecessary. This right can be legally challenged if overwhelming reasons are determined to necessitate overriding the wishes of the patient, such as the endangerment of another person's life, a situation where a parent's decision threatens the life of a child, or the best interest of the public takes precedence over the patient's right. The nursing team needs to be able to contribute to a modified plan of care that includes these possibilities.

Collaboration with Interdisciplinary Team

Interdisciplinary rounding can provide an opportunity for team collaboration. Much like a clear hand-off process, interdisciplinary rounds reduce patient care errors, decrease mortality rates, and improve patient outcomes. Interdisciplinary rounds are an excellent place to discuss social service needs, nutritional care services, and transportation needs with all teams coordinating care for the patient in a single setting.

The patient's service needs may vary in depth for the inpatient stay and at the time of discharge; however, there should be an evaluation of these needs and a coordination of care for those services in which there is a need. Nurses document the action plan as it relates to services and requirements for the patient and collaborate with members of the interdisciplinary team to see that next steps are executed in a timely fashion. In many instances, rounding may not be possible due to the rapid pace and turnover of the medical environment, and thus, clear documentation will be needed to allow for synchronous care coordination.

Nurses, physicians, surgeons, nurse aids, physical and occupational therapists, mental health professionals, and medical assistants are just some of the members who may be collaborating on the care of one patient. Perception of power between these professionals can sometimes create a stressful environment that can also affect patient outcomes. Collaboration among team members is imperative so that patient safety does not become an issue. **Collaboration** involves joint decision-making activities between both disciplines, rather than nurses only following physician orders. Although each role may have a particular focus throughout the assessment and plan of care activities, they must jointly come together to formulate the best possible plan of care throughout the treatment period. Studies show that an attentive communication style between nurses and physicians has the most positive impact on patients.

Ongoing education of physicians and nurses may be a necessity to support a collaborative environment. In addition to continuing education and in-services, job shadowing can assist in promoting understanding and teamwork by exposing both the nurse and physician to one another's role.

Concepts of Management and Supervision

Delegation

Nursing staff take on many responsibilities that can be delegated to other clinical and non-clinical colleagues. However, learning how to safely delegate tasks, while still making patients feel cared for, is a skill that can take time to develop. It requires knowing not only what the needs of the patient are, but also the strengths and weaknesses of assistive personnel and how to best communicate professional needs with them. It also requires personal development in becoming comfortable with outsourcing responsibilities, as the nurse who delegates still remains accountable for the patient.

There are different types of assistive personnel that may be supervised by nurses. **Clinical assistive staff** can provide basic medical assistance, such as taking patients' vital signs, assisting with caretaking duties, monitoring any abnormalities or changes in the patient, maintaining a sterile and safe environment, and any other request made directly by nursing staff. **Non-clinical assistive personnel**, such as front desk staff, can assist with patient communication (such as wait times), managing paperwork and ensuring it is complete, and performing any other administrative task that may support the nursing staff's cases.

When nursing staff choose to delegate tasks, they may feel worried about risking their own accountability or work ethic. However, communicating with assistive personnel, understanding their strengths and weaknesses, and remaining transparent about the needs that are present in the department can ensure that delegated tasks are a good fit for the person who is taking the responsibility. In this regard, nursing staff take on a leadership and managerial role that requires developing their problem-solving, time management, and interpersonal skills. Some effective tools for delegation include standardized checklists that cover the procedure that is being delegated, meetings with assistive personnel to assess their comfort levels in performing certain tasks, and matching professional needs with individual qualifications. When **delegation** is effective, it can help the entire department work in a more efficient manner. Additionally, both nursing staff and assistive personnel are more likely to feel like part of a cohesive team and less likely to feel overworked or undervalued.

Supervision

After the nurse has successfully and effectively delegated a task, the nurse then takes on the role of supervisor of the person to whom they delegated the task. Delegation requires supervision to ensure the task is done appropriately and protect the nurse's own licensure.

The key to supervision is the follow-up. After the task is delegated, the nurse must then make a note to investigate whether the task was completed correctly and in a timely manner. Asking the person who was supposed to perform the task to report back is appropriate. All conversations and interactions must be performed professionally and with respect for both the inferior and superior party.

Many nurses were once **certified nursing assistants (CNAs)** and understand the role and responsibility of the person they now delegate to. If the two nurses were former co-workers and one has risen to the role of nurse from CNA, tensions may arise. Tensions that arise between nursing staff and those they delegate to may be resolved through careful interactions. Each party must be respectful and recognize they are working together with the best interest of the patient at the forefront of their minds.

At times, it may be necessary for the nurse to coach and support the staff member, giving tips for better performance where appropriate. Again, this interaction must be done with professionalism and respect. It is important as an employee in any field to be receptive to constructive criticism, as well as being able to offer it when appropriate and allowing plenty of discussion on the point.

The nurse must ensure that the task delegated, such as taking vital signs or cleaning up an incontinent patient, has been appropriately documented. Documentation is necessary for legal reasons, to show that proper care was given to the patient. If the person to whom the task was delegated did not document the task, it is necessary for the nurse to confront them directly and confirm that it was done.

Recognizing and Reporting Staff Conflict

Staff conflict occurs when team members have different views or thoughts on an issue. Conflict on the job can be disturbing and anxiety-provoking. However, it is an inevitable part of working as a team.

Recognizing and reporting conflict involves the following steps:

- *Defining the conflict*: Conflicts occur when two or more people have differing attitudes or viewpoints. Conflict can be helpful when it is resolved in a healthy manner, equally fulfilling to both parties, and results in closure.

- *Evaluating the various factors that can provoke conflict*: Arguments, a lack of trust, workflow disruptions, impaired interpersonal relationships, criticism of others, and frustration are examples of issues that can incite conflict.

- *Recognizing the variations of personality types*: It is imperative to embrace the various ways team members think and feel and how these diverse factors will affect the outcome of the conflict.

- *Distinguishing types of communication*: Team members can display a wide range of communicative techniques during any type of interaction. However, conflict can cause people to behave in varying ways, such as becoming guarded or aggressive. It is important for team members to be aware of this possibility.

Here are a few ways to resolve team conflict:

- *Collaboration and Open Communication*: Working together and maintaining an open exchange between team members helps to cultivate relationships among group members. By encouraging the conflicting parties to actively participate in the resolution, a more in-depth understanding of the dispute can be achieved.

- *Compromise and Negotiation*: Maintaining a level playing field encourages both parties to remain confident but not belligerent, promoting equality between team members. Discussing the issue rationally allows team members to focus on common goals and interests, rather than individual parties and their diverse opinions. As a result, the conflicting parties can separate themselves from the conflict and issue at hand.

- *Mediation*: Sometimes one-on-one communication with each team member is required in order to discern each person's concerns, beliefs, and opinions. Once this occurs, the team can investigate resolving the conflict via methods that are satisfactory to all involved.

There are six stages of team conflict resolution:

1. Clarifying the disagreement and making sure both sides agree on the topic of the issue.
2. Establishing a common goal agreed upon by those involved in the conflict.
3. Discussing the various techniques the team can use to gain a common understanding.
4. Defining the issues that are in the way of reaching the common goal.
5. Coming to an agreement regarding the best way(s) to resolve the conflict.
6. Agreeing upon a solution and deciding the responsibilities of each member.

Furthermore, it is important to remember that every conflict and team dispute is unique. Keep the following in mind when deciding how to approach a situation:

- *Acknowledge personal reactions of team members*: Every team member may have a totally different response to conflict and how it is being handled by the team. These include being evasive, dominating, accommodating, collaborative, or cooperative.

- *Choose useful conflict resolution techniques*: When a conflict arises, it is important to be aware of the fact that team members will have varying principles and priorities on how to settle it. Therefore, selecting the best technique for resolving conflict will depend on each situation and those involved.

- *Recognize the benefits and drawbacks of team conflict-resolution strategies*: These include dealing with the issue, thinking it through, discussing it in person, using a mediator, apologizing when needed, and communicating clearly and effectively.

Quality and Safety

- *Be aware of situations that typically require employee disciplinary action*: Since conflict can disrupt the workflow of the whole team and covers a wide range of behaviors, sometimes disciplinary action is required.

Confidentiality/Information Security

Patient privacy and **confidentiality** are constant concerns for all healthcare providers. Given the sensitivity of medical procedures, the healthcare team must maintain strict patient confidentiality. Under the Health Insurance Portability and Accountability Act (HIPAA), a patient's information is required to be protected and kept confidential regardless of the form, including electronic, written, and spoken communication. **Protected health information (PHI)** should be shared only on an as-needed and minimum necessary basis. When discussing patients or cases in settings where other personnel may overhear the conversation, the medical team should be careful not to include any PHI that may violate the patient's confidentiality. Additionally, when information is displayed electronically to families and visitors in waiting rooms, patient names should be avoided. HIPAA violations can have negative consequences for the providers and/or the facility.

The nurse plays an important role in keeping a patient's health information private. Sharing personal details—such as a patient's name, condition, and medical history—in an inappropriate way violates the person's right to privacy. For example, a nurse telling a friend who does not work in the facility that the nurse took care of the friend's aunt, without the aunt's consent or knowledge, is considered a violation of privacy. Another way a nurse could violate privacy is to access a patient's medical record when they are not actually caring for them. For example, if a celebrity has been admitted to a different unit, and the nursing assistant accesses the celebrity's electronic health record, then they are in violation of HIPAA. Those who are caught violating HIPAA could lose their jobs and face other punitive actions. Nurses should also ensure that other staff members, as well as patients, understand the confidentiality requirements of the facility, state, and country.

Continuity of Care

If one imagines a patient's illness as a road, what would the ideal road look like? Smooth, no potholes, appropriate signage to guide and direct the patient from illness to wellness, right? In the real world of health care, the road the patient travels from illness to wellness often has bumps and miscommunications. Things do not go as planned, missteps are taken, and unexpected events or miscalculations unfortunately do occur.

All members of the healthcare team should be striving to provide patients with a high quality of care over time, or **continuity of care**. The patient begins their journey with an illness at a doctor's office, convenient care clinic, or an emergency room. From there, the road proceeds through various tests and procedures to diagnose and treat the illness. Management teams that include doctors and nurses provide input into this process and contribute resources. The patient is at the center of the continuity of care model. In continuity of care, the whole patient is treated, not just an organ or an illness. Ideally, the community surrounding the patient is also involved in promoting good health and high quality of life.

The roots of continuity of care lie in a meaningful, long-term relationship between the patient and the healthcare provider. This relationship ensures that the patient is known. Their needs are anticipated through regular check-ups and follow-ups after the illness has run its course. The idea is to form a firm bond of trust between the healthcare provider and the patient. This trusting relationship and deep knowledge of the case allow the provider to better advocate for the patient.

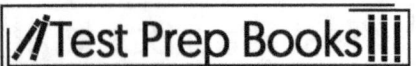

The physician or nurse practitioner coordinating care for the patient will look for ways to make the plan of care cost-effective for the patient. Tests and procedures are carefully weighed for their usefulness in the patient's case, looking for ways to eliminate wasteful healthcare spending.

The main idea behind continuity of care is to avoid what happens all too often in healthcare: **fragmentation of care**. The responsibility of the patient's case is often shifted from one entity to another over the course of an illness. Initially, the patient's case is handled in a primary care setting or perhaps an emergent care setting, depending on the illness. Then the patient may become hospitalized, at which point the hospitalist and various specialists step in and take over. At discharge, the patient's case is then handed over to their primary care physician and community centers. Due to this shifting of care, it becomes ambiguous as to who is overseeing the patient's care. The patient has a fragmented experience rather than a continuous one.

One issue faced by healthcare providers is not having the infrastructure to effectively coordinate patient care and avoid the problems associated with fragmented care. A case manager comes into play here because their role is perfect for coordinating the patients' care as they move through the system.

Primary care physicians face a hurdle when coordinating patient care because they have limited communication with the hospital team when their patient is admitted. Presently, there is often a team of healthcare providers called **hospitalists**, whose job it is to care for patients while they are in the hospital, but not pre- or post-admission. This is helpful because they know the ins and outs of the facility and have good communication with the hospital's specialists and surgeons. They can all work together to get the patient in and out of the hospital relatively quickly.

A **patient-centered medical home** (**PCMH**) comes into play pre-admission to prevent a costly hospital visit. The idea of a PCMH is to combat fragmentation of care and promote better continuity of care for the patient on their road to wellness. The PCMH is a model of care that is well-coordinated, proactive, and centered on the patient. In this model, a patient is paired with a personal physician to oversee their care. Their family and loved ones are recruited to assist in promoting a whole patient-focused wellness plan. The PCMH moves away from fee for service; instead, it focuses on fee for value, meaning the level of success in keeping the patient healthy determines how the healthcare team is reimbursed. The patient must regularly keep in touch with their primary care physician, a factor that has been associated with better patient outcomes.

Many communities are adopting the PCMH model of healthcare, attempting to promote a better continuity of care for patients on their road from illness to wellness.

Nurses are aware that the patient often requires continued reinforcement of the educational plan after discharge, which necessitates coordination with home care services. As facilitators of learning, nurses may be involved in a large-scale effort to educate all patients. The first step of any teaching-learning initiative is the assessment of the learning needs of the participants. Specific needs that influence the design and content of the educational offering include the language preference and reading level of the participants. Nurses must also consider the effect of certain characteristics, identified in the **Synergy Model**, on the patient's capacity to process information. Diminished resiliency or stability, as well as extreme complexity, are examples of characteristics that must be considered in the development of the educational plan. Nurses are also responsible for creating a bridge between teaching and learning in the acute care setting and the home environment. A detailed discharge plan, close coordination with outpatient providers, and follow-up phone calls to the patient may be used to reinforce the patient's knowledge of the plan of care.

Quality and Safety

Establishing Priorities

The ability to establish priorities is one of the nurse's most important skills. The nurse must be able to look at their patient load for the day, assess the needs of each patient, organize tasks in chronological order, and prioritize each task based on its importance and necessity.

When prioritizing the tasks for the day, the nurse must first employ their knowledge of the body, how it works, and what it needs to function. The nurse starts with **ABC**: airway, breathing, and circulation. Are any patients compromised in these respects? If so, they are immediately placed at the top of the list of priorities. If the patient cannot breathe, is hemorrhaging, or their heart has stopped beating, they require the nurse's immediate assistance. The ABCs are considered the first priority of patient needs.

Emergency Trauma Assessment
- A: Airway
- B: Breathing
- C: Circulation
- D: Disability
- E: Examine
- F: Fahrenheit
- G: Get Vitals
- H: Head to Toe Assessment
- I: Intervention

After the ABCs of patient needs are taken care of, the nurse can move down the scale to the next priority. A helpful acronym to remember is **M-A-A-U-A-R**. These are considered second-priority needs.

- M: Mental status changes and alterations
- A: Acute pain
- A: Acute urinary elimination concerns
- U: Unaddressed/untreated problems requiring immediate attention
- A: Abnormal laboratory/diagnostic data outside of normal limits
- R: Risks involving a healthcare problem such as safety, skin integrity, infection, and other medical conditions

Along with the ABC-MAAUAR methods of prioritization, the nurse may also utilize **Maslow's Hierarchy of Needs**. Maslow argues that physiological needs such as hunger, thirst, and breathing are among the first that must be met. This holds true for patients as well. For example, a patient in pain needs to be addressed before a patient who needs education on a procedure that is to happen tomorrow.

After the basic physiological needs have been met, the nurse knows that on the next level of the pyramid are safety and psychological needs. Mental health fits on this tier of the hierarchy and is a crucial step toward wellness. Love and belonging follow; for this part of care, the nurse can enlist the help of social services and family members. The next level of Maslow's hierarchy is self-esteem and esteem by others. In nursing terms, this level represents the patient's need to feel they are a respected and esteemed member of the care team. The final level of Maslow's hierarchy is self-actualization, in which a person reaches their fullest potential and highest level of ability. The nurse provides excellent patient care with the goal of helping them reach this level, do their best, and feel their best at all points in the care journey.

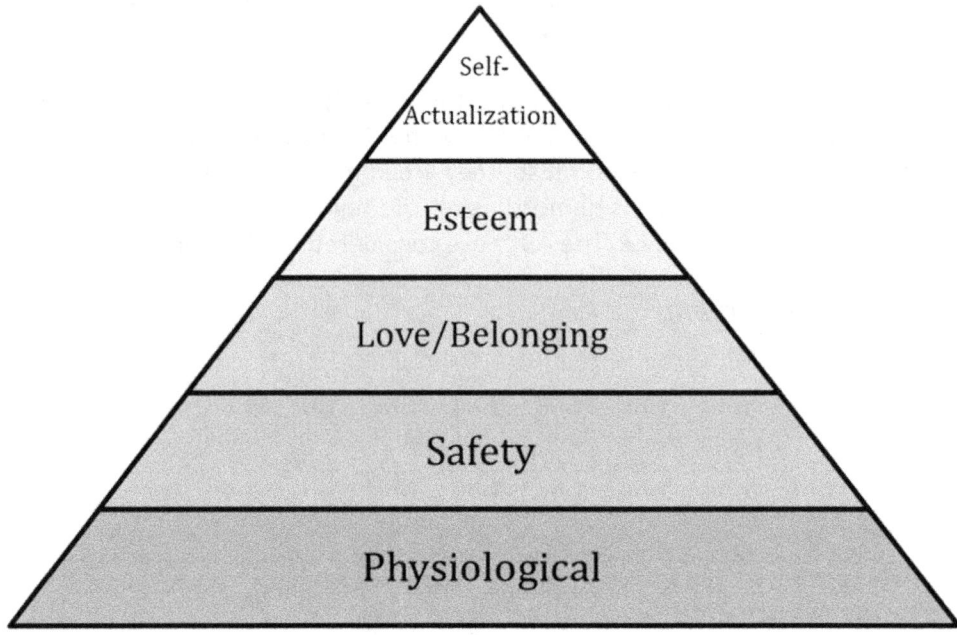

After recognizing the patient's needs and establishing priorities based on Maslow's hierarchy, the nurse can carry out patient care to meet these goals. Next, the evaluation stage begins. This step is ongoing, as the nurse must continually evaluate the plan of care for each patient. The plan may need tweaking and revision throughout the day, based on how the patient responds to interventions. Quality evaluation of interventions ensures needs are being met and proper care is being delivered.

Sound nursing judgment will guide the nurse as they endeavor to prioritize and adequately meet the needs of their patients in a timely manner.

Time Management and Work Prioritization

One of the most important skills a nurse must master in the busy healthcare environment is that of **time management** and prioritization of tasks. The workday is filled with tasks, scheduled activities, unexpected time conflicts, and constant interruptions.

In order to effectively meet the needs of each individual patient, nurses should have a way of planning the day. Many nurses create a written system to take notes and record vitals in between charting periods. Meal times can be the busiest times of day, so it should be accounted for in planning.

Countless interruptions will occur throughout the day, such as a call light going off when the nurse was planning to start a bath or a patient needing assistance to the bathroom when the nurse was planning on taking a break. It is vital that the nurse prioritizes tasks to make sure the most important ones are completed in a timely manner. It is easy to put off tasks for later that really should be done immediately, but that sort of procrastination can have adverse results. The day will be busy; that is a given. Developing one's time management and prioritization skills will help the day go a lot more smoothly.

Quality and Safety

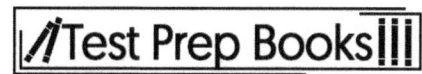

Ethical Practice

Healthcare providers routinely face situations with patients where they must analyze various moral and ethical considerations. In the emergency department for example, **ethical dilemmas** can arise without much time to process resolutions. Quick judgment and action are often necessary to care for patients who may not be fully sound in body or mind.

Nurses are held to the American Nurses Association's **Code of Ethics**, which outlines moral and ethical guidelines for nursing practice. Above all else, nurses have the responsibility to do no harm while serving as advocates, minimizing injury, and protecting the overall health and functioning of their patients. It is important to consider the patient holistically when applying these values. Holistic considerations may include how the patient views quality of life, their family values, affected family members, legal considerations, and logistical considerations, such availability of time and medical resources. When patients are unable to make decisions autonomously or provide consent to treatment, nurses should act from these responsibilities to make wise and compassionate decisions on the patients' behalf.

Dilemmas that can arise for nursing staff include situations where the patient may have cultural or personal beliefs that prevent lifesaving treatment. For example, a female emergency patient may not want to be treated by any male staff, or a patient that needs a blood transfusion may not accept this procedure due to religious beliefs. In cases where the patient is able to directly communicate their wishes, the nurse may need to defer to the patient's wishes in order to preserve the patient's autonomy.

Alternative means of care, such as finding available female medical providers to assist with the female patient who does not want to be treated by male staff, may be required in these scenarios. It may mean withholding treatment that the patient refuses. If the patient's life is in question and rapid medical action is necessary, nursing staff must consider the patient's wishes in the plan of care. Ethical considerations like these will vary by case and patient, and will depend on the severity of the case, the medical and personal history of the patient, and the judgment of the nurse in question. In all cases, it is ideal if the nurse and patient can communicate openly about the potential options to determine the best course of action.

Informed Consent

Before any medical procedure can be performed, the patient's consent must be obtained. Obtaining this consent requires educating the patient on what the procedure is, how it is performed, what types of outcomes are to be expected, and most importantly, why the procedure will be done. This process of educating the patient and getting their permission is called **informed consent**.

There are two key aspects of the term informed consent. The term "informed" implies that the patient has been given information pertaining to the procedure. This requires a conversation between the patient and their health care provider. Education must be provided to ensure that the patient has been given information about the procedure to be done as well as time to consider their options. If a patient signs a consent without having a proper understanding and comprehension of what's to be done, it is not a true informed consent.

The second part of the term is "consent." This means that the patient agrees with the plan and gives their permission for what is going to be done. Without consent, it is illegal or improper to perform certain healthcare procedures.

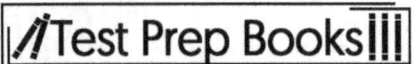

Consent can be given through three different avenues: implied, verbal, and written. **Implied consent** does not involve the patient signing a document or even verbally granting permission, but rather it is assumed that any reasonable person would consent to the health care interventions being performed. This can create the potential for gray areas to arise in certain situations. For example, let's say a patient drops to the floor in full cardiac arrest and becomes unresponsive. A nurse witnesses the fall, begins cardiopulmonary resuscitation (CPR), and activates the emergency response system. Although the patient was unable to issue verbal or written consent for CPR, consent is considered implied in this situation since the patient was in danger of death. On a much smaller scale, a patient coming into a doctor's office does not sign a document of consent to have their vital signs taken, yet they willingly comply with having their blood pressure taken. All parties present assume and agree upon certain procedures; thus, no formal consent is required.

Verbal consent is obtained by asking the patient verbal permission to proceed with a treatment or procedure. While more formal than implied consent, verbal consent is less formal than the signed legal document that is informed consent.

Written consent involves a formal conversation between the nurse, the physician performing the procedure, and the patient. It is vital that the patient is adequately educated on the procedure and has a full understanding before consenting. Obtaining consent without proper patient education is fraudulent and poor practice. Not properly informing the patient may lead to legal trouble down the road for both the nurse and the physician, in addition to potential complications following the procedure. Above all, it is a violation of a patient's rights to not be properly informed before giving consent.

While the physician is legally responsible for satisfying all elements of informed consent, nurses are ethically responsible for assessing the patient's ability to process and understand the implications of informed consent. After the physician's discussion with the patient, the nurse should ensure that the patient understands the information provided on the purpose of a procedure and any possible risks. The nurse should also be sure the appropriate person to provide informed consent for the patient has been identified and understands the procedure. This may be the patient, parent, their legal guardian, or other identified healthcare power of attorney. Nurses protect the patient's autonomy by raising these questions and concerns.

Legal Responsibilities

Nurses must uphold and answer to certain legal rights and responsibilities within their profession. From simple tasks like managing a patient's property, to more complicated issues such as reporting abuse and neglect, the nurse has a legal responsibility to act.

Nurses need a knowledge of the common legal terminology in their practice. The following is a list of terms the nurse should know:

- **Common law**: Based on legal precedents or previously decided cases in courts of law

- **Statutory law**: Based on a state's legislative actions or any other legislative body's actions

- **Constitutional law**: Based on the content of the Constitution of the United States of America

- **Administrative law**: Passed down from a ruling body, such as continuing education requirements mandated by each state's nursing association

Quality and Safety

- **Criminal law**: Involves the arrest, prosecution, and incarceration of those who have broken the law, including misdemeanors and felonies

- **Liability**: Involves accountability for one's actions from a legal standpoint

- **Tort**: Refers to nursing practice violations, such as malpractice, negligence, and patient confidentiality violations

- **Unintentional tort**: Examples can include negligence and malpractice in certain situations

- **Intentional tort**: Examples can include false imprisonment, privacy breaches, slander, libel, battery, and assault

A nurse is legally responsible for maintaining an active **licensure** according to their state regulatory board's laws. Failure to maintain licensure requirements, such as **continuing education** credits, will result in disciplinary action. Nursing licenses may be revoked or suspended because of disciplinary actions.

Nurses must report abuse, neglect, gunshot wounds, dog bites, and communicable diseases. Nurses are also legally mandated to report other healthcare providers whom they suspect may be abusing drugs or alcohol while practicing, because they are putting patients and themselves at risk.

Nurses have a legal obligation to accept the patient assignments given to them, given they are appropriate and contain duties within their scope of practice. However, if they are assigned tasks that they are not prepared to perform, the nurse must notify their supervisors and seek assistance.

Practicing nurses must comply with laws at the national, state, and local level. Examples include those in relation to the Centers for Medicare and Medicaid services, as well as local laws regarding the disposal of biohazardous waste.

Legal Reporting Obligations

Reporting critical patient information in a timely manner and using the correct order in the chain of command are legal obligations of nurses. Failing to report important information could result in serious ramifications and punitive action for the nurse, such as loss of employment and licensure. Furthermore, it can result in patient harm or unresolved conflicts that escalate into larger issues. Preventing patient harm and potential conflicts both start with accurate and timely reporting.

A basic definition of a **report** is the relaying of information that one has observed or heard. When this report is given to an authority figure who can intervene, it should contain the patient name, situation, time of event, and circumstances surrounding the event.

As one shift ends and another begins, there is a **handoff report** that is given from the outgoing team to the oncoming team. The nurse who has completed the shift will tell the nurse beginning the next shift all pertinent information related to each individual patient. Throughout the shift, the exchange of smaller pieces of information continues to take place to keep all members of the healthcare team equally informed.

In the handoff report, the nurse should strategically relay information in a simple, concise manner that is easily understood by the oncoming nurse. It can be easy to get carried away with reporting and include every little detail of the day, opinions about patients or other coworkers, and stories of particular conversations or interactions that occurred during the shift. These superfluous details should be limited, and the report should be kept to the essential items only.

Some organizations employ the **SBAR method** to help guide communication. SBAR is an acronym for situation, background, assessment, and recommendation. An SBAR report starts with the situation: why is this communication necessary? The background is a brief explanation of the circumstances leading up to the situation. The assessment details the present issue at hand, while the recommendation provides guidance on the best course of action.

In addition to reporting, the documentation of patient information and interventions is equally important. A patient's chart is a legal record of assessments and care measures. Most facilities use an electronic health record, with training provided during new employee orientation. Documentation may include timing related to observations, interventions, and patient responses.

There are various charting systems used by patient care facilities to document patient data. Documentation requirements will be dictated by facility policy and regulatory guidelines. Two methods are commonly used: charting by exception and comprehensive charting.

Charting by Exception
Charting by exception requires that only vital signs and abnormal findings are documented. This charting method is somewhat controversial since a great amount of information about the patient is usually left out. It is sometimes argued that this is the safer way to chart, as only what is deviant from normal is noted, and thus, there is less room for documentation errors. The normal is assumed, unless otherwise noted. This method also saves time, as less information needs to be documented, leaving more time for patient care.

Comprehensive Charting
Some facilities prefer a **comprehensive method** of documentation, charting everything about the patient—normal and abnormal—in a very thorough manner. This way, when the patient's chart must be reviewed, especially in the case of a safety incident (e.g., a pressure sore develops or a patient falls), all details surrounding the event should be present in the medical record. This method is effective if all information is properly charted, although it can be quite time-consuming and take away from patient care time.

Documentation provides a defense for healthcare workers and patients in the case of incidents, serving as evidence of the sequence of events. There is an adage that says, "If it wasn't charted, it didn't happen." The nurse needs to be mindful that the medical record is a legal document—a complete, thorough, and accurate documentation of care, according to facility policy.

Performance Improvement
Performance improvement is a mechanism to continuously review and improve processes in a system, ensure that work is completed in the most cost-effective manner, and produce the best possible outcomes. Healthcare facilities are constantly aiming to drive down cost and increase reimbursements while delivering the highest quality of healthcare and utilizing analytical methods to achieve this. These analyses and implementations may be done by top administrative employees at the organization and be executed across the healthcare system, or within a particular department. Leadership support is always crucial for positive change to occur and sustain itself.

Quality and Safety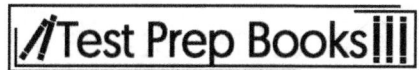

All processes should be regularly monitored for opportunities for improvement. Common opportunities include areas of reported patient dissatisfaction; federal, state, or internal benchmarks that are not being met; areas of financial loss; and common complaints among staff. While multiple opportunities for improvement may exist, focusing on one at a time usually produces the greatest outcome. When choosing a process to improve, it is important to select one that has the potential to be changed by the members involved (e.g., medical staff often do not have control over external funding sources). Processes where minimal resources are required for change, but that can produce positive end results, are also preferable to more costly improvements. Once the process has been selected, a group of stakeholders that are regularly involved in the process should map out each step while noting areas of wasted resource or process variation. From here, stakeholders can develop a change to test.

The **PDCA cycle** provides a framework for implementing tests of change. *Plan*, the first step, involves planning the change. This will include accounting for all workflow changes, the staff members involved, and logistics of implementation. It should also include baseline data relating to the problem. *Do*, the second step, involves implementing the change. During this step, data collection is crucial. For example, if a department believes that implementing mobile work stations will decrease nurses' wait time between patients, the department should keep a detailed record of the time spent with and between each patient. *Check*, the third step, involves checking data relating to the change with the baseline data and determining if the change improved the process. *Act*, the final step, involves making the change permanent and monitoring it for sustainability.

Evidence-Based Practice

Evidence-based practice (EBP) is a research-driven and facts-based methodology that allows healthcare providers to make scientifically supported, reliable, and validated decisions in delivering care. EBP takes into account rigorously tested, peer-reviewed, and published research relating to the case; the knowledge and experience of the healthcare provider; and clinical guidelines established by reputable governing bodies. This framework allows healthcare providers to reach case resolutions that result in positive patient outcomes in the most efficient manner. This, in turn, allows the organization to provide the best care using the least resources.

There are seven steps to successfully utilizing EBP as a methodology in the nursing field. First, the work culture should be one of a "spirit of inquiry." This culture allows staff to ask questions to promote continuous improvement and positive process change to workflow, clinical routines, and non-clinical duties. Second, the PICOT framework should be utilized when searching for an effective intervention, or working with a specific interest, in a case. The **PICOT framework** encourages nurses to develop a specific, measurable, goal-oriented research question that accounts for the patient population and demographics (P) involved in the case, the proposed intervention or issue of interest (I), a relevant comparison (C) group in which a defined outcome (O) has been positive, and the amount of time (T) needed to implement the intervention or address the issue. Once this question has been developed, staff can move onto the third step, which is to research. In this step, staff will explore reputable sources of literature to find studies and narratives with evidence that supports a resolution for their question.

Once all research has been compiled, it must be thoroughly analyzed as part of the fourth step in the process. This step ensures that the staff is using unbiased research with stringent methodology, statistically significant outcomes, and reliable and valid research designs. Furthermore, it includes verification that all information collected is applicable to their patient. For example, if a certain treatment worked with statistical significance in a longitudinal study of pediatric patients with a large sample size, and all other influencing variables were controlled for, this treatment may not necessarily

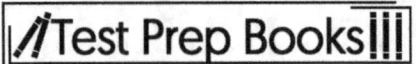

Quality and Safety

work in a middle-aged adult. Therefore, though the research collected is scientifically backed and evidence-based for a pediatric population, it does not support EBP for an older population. The fifth step is to integrate the evidence to create a treatment or intervention plan for the patient. The sixth step is to monitor the implementation of the treatment or intervention and evaluate whether it was associated with positive health outcomes in the patient. Finally, practitioners have a moral obligation to share the results with colleagues at the organization and across the field, so that it may be best utilized (or not) for other patients.

Evidence-Based Practice Flowchart

Specify Research Question
↓
Locate Potentially-Relevant Evidence
↓
Discard Poor Evidence ← Evaluate Evidence → Update Evidence
↓
Assemble Relevant Evidence
↓
Use Evidence to Inform Decisions

Referral Process

As patient advocates, nurses should be knowledgeable about referring clients when a need arises. The nurse is aware of many branches of the healthcare tree that are designed to assist with each patient's specific needs. A **referral** is a method by which the nurse contacts another member of the healthcare team to meet the patient's care needs in the most appropriate setting. This is part of care coordination and must happen throughout all stages of the client's continuum of care. Case managers play a key role in making appropriate referrals.

Referral occurs during the first stage of the nursing process: assessment. The nurse assesses the patient and identifies a need. For example, a school nurse may become aware of students who have learning or developmental disabilities. In these cases, the nurse may refer the child and their parents to a speech therapist, a language therapist, or a developmental therapist, depending on the case.

In the hospital environment, the nurse may recognize the need for an auxiliary team and refer the client to them. Such **auxiliary teams** include the palliative care and hospice team, respiratory therapy, physical and occupational therapy, and speech/language therapy. **Community resources** should be used when appropriate, such as extended-care therapy, social service support, and shelters for the homeless and disadvantaged. Patients may also need spiritual care, in which case clergy can be requested to make a bedside visit.

With any referral, the nurse must follow the appropriate protocols and remain within their scope of practice. Other members of the health care team, such as physicians and nursing management, should be consulted. Doctor's orders must be obtained where necessary.

After the referral has been made, it is vital that the nurse or case manager evaluates the patient for their response to care. Evaluation is a key component of the nursing process. Without evaluating for effectiveness, the process is incomplete. Only after evaluation has shown effectiveness and the patient is on their way to recovery can the plan of care be deemed successful.

Resource Management

As managers of client care, nurses must decide which supplies, materials, and equipment are necessary to fulfill the patient's needs as part of the preliminary and ongoing client evaluation. They do this by assessing and determining the patient's condition, at time of primary contact. This involves measuring and recording a patient's vital signs using healthcare tools such as stethoscopes, blood pressure cuffs and thermometers, as well as other patient care equipment, medical technology, and devices. After this initial determination, the next step is ensuring that the patient is supplied with the proper resources, such as patient lifts, ventilators, compression devices, or catheters.

Each nursing team member has varying skills and duties according to the training and degrees he or she received. These skill sets are matched with the client care requirements in the healthcare setting. Depending on the training received, a nurse will be licensed to handle a specific range of materials and supplies. **Nursing assistive personnel (NAPs)** are responsible for providing support services such as assistance with daily living activities, basic hygiene, and comfort care. It is important for all team members to understand how to utilize these associated materials efficiently and effectively.

Nurses should review each function of patient care materials with the NAPs. A good knowledge check is to quiz or question staff members on the various medical devices under their care. This provides an extra level of patient safety, ensuring that all team members are aware of the required equipment and how to utilize it correctly.

The term **cost-effective** means that the cost of a product or service is not too high for what is being purchased. Therefore, a **cost-benefit ratio** refers to weighing the value or likely costs of a project or plan with its desired benefit. Both effective patient care and cost-benefit ratios must be weighed to determine care standards. For example, it has been shown that the length of time between some routine tests could be altered, such as a Pap smear screening, which has been determined to be just as effective to get checked once every three years instead of annually for most women. Regardless, patient care and services must be as cost-efficient as possible while still maintaining high quality standards and client needs requirements.

As a result, providing cost-effective healthcare is often a balancing act performed by all involved. Client care planning by nurses and other members of the healthcare team is determined according to what they deem suitable, economical, and cost beneficial without sacrificing optimal care quality and results. Therefore, the nursing team must carefully select therapies, interventions, and resources that are not only cost-effective, but also the most useful and applicable based on the patient's needs.

For instance, nurses could determine the costs of patient falls within their facility and show how nursing assistance could help prevent them. Another example would be to use cost-analysis data to determine the cost benefit and birth outcome (premature vs. full-term births) for pregnant teens who received prenatal care in a school setting compared those who received routine care. A third example would be to assess the rate of various community health issues, such as smoking, car accidents, elderly injuries, teen drinking, and drug usage, and determine how nursing intervention could improve these outcomes, ultimately decreasing the rate of admissions at their facility.

Safety and Infection Control
Accident/Error/Injury Prevention
The safety of both patients and team members is a major concern for healthcare organizations. Nurses must have an understanding and the necessary skills to prevent accidents, errors, and injuries.

The majority of accidents that occur in the older population happen in their homes, with falls being the most common accident. **Accident prevention** involves maintaining a clean home and living area and recognizing potential hazards. In addition, individuals should be aware of their own body's level of health, capabilities, and weaknesses. Keeping regular appointments at the physician's office and following any medication regime correctly will keep one's health in check. It is important for patients to have understanding and awareness of potential side effects of their medications. Recognizing a **side effect** could be a way to prevent an accident, especially if it relates to mental status or mobility. For example, blood pressure medications have the potential to cause lightheadedness and increase the risk for a fall. Informal caregivers such as family members should check on elderly family to ensure they are able to continue taking care of themselves and to survey the home for safety hazards.

If an older adult is still living in their home, the following measures should be addressed to avoid accidents related to poisoning, burns, hypothermia, and falls. The main causes of poisoning in adults aged sixty-five and older are medicines and gases. Gases would include carbon monoxide and pipeline gases, such as propane or natural gas for heating the home. Fuel-burning devices should be checked regularly for proper functioning. Chimneys and flues should be cleaned once a year.

Older adults are often on a complicated medication regime involving multiple pills, various dosages, and schedule requirements of different administration times and days. Medicines should be taken exactly as prescribed, and an organized schedule should be in place to prevent mistakes. One example for organizing medications is a pillbox that has individual compartments for each day of the week.

Burns and scalding in the home can be prevented if water heaters are not set too high and the cold water is turned on first. Kettles should be avoided if possible. If necessary, spout-filling kettles, cordless kettles, or wall-mounted heaters can be used instead. Items in the kitchen and the flow of the kitchen should allow for the least amount of distance for carrying hot food or beverages. On the stove, rear burners should be used, and handles should be kept away from the edges to avoid accidentally knocking a pan off the stove.

An additional accident not often thought of in the older population is hypothermia, which means the body's temperature drops below 95 degrees Fahrenheit. Strategies to prevent hypothermia in the elderly include making sure the home is heated properly in colder weather, providing several layers of clothing, encouraging movement and exercise around the home to increase body heat, and making sure there is enough food and drink available.

Quality and Safety

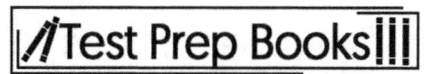

As previously discussed, **falls** are the most common accident in the older adult population. Whether the person lives in their home or in a care facility, there are preventative measures that should be put into place.

Fall prevention interventions include:

- Identification of patients at high risk for falls
- Assessment of the patient's room or environment for hazards that can be removed, such as:
    - Rugs
    - Slippery floors
    - Clutter
    - Poor lighting
- Use of assistive devices, such as:
    - Canes, used for stability
    - Walkers, used for balance because of their wide base
    - Reachers or grabbers, used to pick up items off the floor or reach items on a shelf
    - Gait belts, used with an aide or caregiver and placed around the patient's waist to assist in walking or when standing up from a sitting position
    - Railings in bathrooms, hallways, and tubs
- Use of proper footwear, such as rubber-soled shoes
- Staff, family member, and patient education on fall prevention strategies
- Assistance for patients with daily activities and routines if necessary
- Stairways that are well-lit, have railings, and are lined with nonslip flooring

Fall prevention specifically for bedridden patients includes:

- Keep two side rails up when a patient is in bed
- Keep the call light and personal items on a table within reach of the patient's bed
- Place bed alarms on the patient's bed to alert the staff of any attempt to get out of bed
- Offer toileting at least every two hours to prevent patients from getting up without assistance

Falling with a Patient
Sometimes it becomes necessary to assist a person to the ground safely if it becomes clear that they are about to fall. When standing in front or behind the falling person, spreading one's legs shoulder width apart allows for a wide base of support. Try to keep an arm under their shoulders or under their arms and ease them to the floor. Always attempt to protect their head first, and try to direct them away from hard objects, such as furniture.

Healthcare facilities should identify which patients are at a higher risk for falls, as these patients will require special **fall precautions**. Many facilities have door signs and certain color bracelets that indicate the patient is a fall risk as a reminder to staff and family. Keep in mind that all patients are at risk for a fall, especially if they are elderly. Staff will be educated regarding how much assistance is needed for each patient. For example, one patient may be able to walk with assistance or walk with stand-by assistance. Another patient may need assistance x 2, or two staff persons, to help transfer.

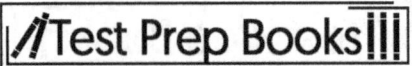

Quality and Safety

Assistance for Ambulation
The types of assistance needed for ambulation are as follows:

- **Stand-by assistance** (SBA): This patient does not require any assistance to move and can walk independently, though someone should be standing by to monitor. A gait belt is not required.

- **Contact-guard assistance** (CGA): This patient requires an assistant to place one or two hands on the patient to assist with balance rather than movement.

- **Minimum assistance** (MIN): This patient needs a little support when moving about, such as the use of a gait belt.

- **Maximum assistance** (MAX): This patient is unstable and may not be able to walk or stand without help. At least two staff persons are needed for assistance.

Patients who use assistive devices for ambulation need instruction on how to use them and may need reminders to ensure they are still using the device properly. It is important to stay with a patient who is learning to use an assistive device. A **gait belt** should be used while the patient is learning to use a walker.

Canes
The purpose of the **cane** is to help stabilize a leg that is weak. Steps for using a cane are listed below:

- Have the patient place the cane in their strong hand and move the cane out one step while stepping the weak leg out with the cane.

- With their weight on the cane, have them step out with their stronger leg.

- After each step, the patient can rest to ensure they feel balanced.

A Walker Without Wheels
A **walker** is used to give the patient extra stability when a patient is weak in both legs or has trouble with balance when walking. Steps for use are listed below:

- Instruct the patient to stand inside the walker while holding onto the walker with both hands.

- Have the patient lift and move the walker forward so that the back legs of the walker line up with their toes.

- With their weight on their stronger leg, have the patient take a step with their weaker leg while gripping the handrails of the walker. They should step into the center of the walker.

- Finally, their stronger leg steps up to evenly meet their other leg. They may rest in between steps if necessary.

Care must be taken to ensure that the flooring surface is flat when using a walker or a cane. Trips or falls can occur if rugs or thick carpet get caught in the walker or cane. Some walkers have wheels on the bottoms of the legs so that a patient can push the walker while walking. The wheels may be on all four legs or just the front two legs. The patient's weight is placed on the walker with their hands, with provides extra support as they lean forward. This type of walker is not lifted during walking to allow for a slightly faster pace. It is important to ensure that the walker does not move too far ahead of the patient while in motion.

Here are steps for moving from a chair to standing with a walker:

- Place the walker in front of the patient and have the patient place their hands on the arms of the chair.
- Assist the patient with standing up.
- Encourage the patient to place one hand at a time onto the handgrips of the walker.
- Ensure the patient feels steady and is not dizzy before walking.

Use of Crutches

Crutches can be used on a short-term basis when a patient has limitations for weight bearing on a leg. An example would be a patient that has a cast or a splint on their ankle, foot, or leg. Putting weight on an injured leg may interfere with healing and may be painful. A physical therapist will be responsible for fitting the crutches to ensure they are the appropriate length for the patient. The armpit, or axilla, rests should fit into the patient's armpit without lifting the shoulders and without causing stooping. The pads should be one to one-and-a-half inches below the axilla. If the crutches are too tall, the patient could trip over the crutches and too much pressure will be placed in their armpits. If the crutches are too short, leaning over will put unnecessary strain on the patient's back. The handgrips should also be adjusted so that the arms are slightly bent at the elbow. The grip should be comfortable.

Crutch Gaits

The **three-point crutch gait** helps with an inability to bear weight on one leg, such as with fractures, pain, or amputation.

- Move both crutches and the weaker leg forward.
- Place all weight down on the crutches and move the stronger or unaffected leg forward.
- Repeat this pattern.
- Good balance is required for this type of gait.

The **two-point crutch gait** is used for weakness in both legs and poor coordination.

- Move the left crutch and right foot together.
- Then move the right crutch and left foot together.
- Repeat this pattern.
- This is a faster gait but difficult to learn.

The **swing-through crutch gait** helps with an inability to bear full weight on both legs.

- Move both crutches forward, then swing both legs forward at the same time. The legs must swing past the crutches.
- This is the fastest gait but requires a lot of arm strength and energy.
- It will not be used in the elderly.

The **swing-to crutch gait** is used for patients who have weakness in both legs.

- Move both crutches forward.
- Put weight on both crutches and swing both legs forward together to the crutches. The legs must not swing past the crutches.
- This requires good arm strength, so it most likely will not be used for the elderly.

Standing up with crutches:

- Have the patient hold both crutches on their injured side.
- Have the patient lean forward while pushing off with their arm from the chair.
- Once standing, place the crutches under the arms.

Sitting down with crutches:

- Have the patient place both crutches on their injured side.
- Holding the handgrips in one hand, they can use their other hand to brace on the chair as they sit.

Using crutches on stairs should not be attempted until the patient is confident on level ground. Until then, or at any time, the patient can also slide up or down the stairs on their bottom. Also, the railing of the stairs can be used with one hand while holding the crutches in the other arm.

Going up steps:

- The crutches should stay on the step the patient is standing on.
- The good leg is brought up to the next step while letting the injured leg lag behind.
- As the patient straightens up to their good leg, they should bring the crutches and their injured leg up onto the step.

Going down steps:

- Have the patient place the crutches on the next step lower and bring their injured foot forward.
- The good foot is moved down to meet the crutches on the lower step, keeping the weight on the crutches.

Transfer Devices

Nurses will be educated on the lift and transfer equipment available in their facility, and this equipment will be used every day to ensure the safety of patients and staff. Using **transfer devices** will greatly reduce the risk of lower-back stress and injury. Transfer devices eliminate manual methods of lifting and transferring patients from one location to another. Additionally, they reduce the number of transfers needed per task. For example, it may normally take three steps to move a patient without a transfer device. With a transfer device, however, the task can be completed in only one step. Types of protective transfer devices include hoists, walking belts with handles (called gait belts), shower chairs, repositioning devices, and weighing devices that use slings. Examples of **repositioning devices** may be a draw sheet, a roller board, or a sliding sheet. Beds can have scales built in so that a patient can be weighed while staying in their bed. Also, scales that are larger in size and width are available to accommodate a wheelchair-bound or morbidly obese patient.

Fire Hazards

Recognizing **fire hazards** in the workplace is important in the prevention of fires and the promotion of safety for patients and employees. Staff will be trained on the fire policy and regular drills should be performed so that each staff person's role is known and practiced. Below are some potential workplace fire hazards:

- Candles may not be allowed in certain facilities. If they are allowed, make sure they are never left unattended, are not within reach of children or pets, and are not placed near windows or material that could burn.

- To mitigate electrical hazards, unplug appliances when not in use and keep them clean and in good working order. If there is concern about a piece of electrical equipment that is not working properly, report it and stop using it. Keep three feet of space around heaters. Do not overload outlets with too many cords, pinch cords behind devices or furniture, or use cords that are cracked or broken.

- Use of a stove and cooking appliances may not be allowed in certain facilities, but these guidelines are useful for anyone that may be cooking:

    o Never leave cooking unattended.
    o Don't cook if too sleepy or if taking medication that causes drowsiness.
    o Use back burners on the stove to prevent spills and burns.
    o Turn handles away from the front of the stove.
    o Don't leave towels or potholders laying on the stovetop.
    o Keep the oven and stove clean and wipe up spills.
    o In case of a grease fire, do not use a fire extinguisher. Smother the fire in the pot or pan with a lid and turn off the burner.
    o For an oven fire, turn off the oven and leave the door closed.
    o For a microwave fire, leave the door closed, turn off the microwave, and unplug it.

- Healthcare facilities are smoke-free, but there may be designated smoking areas outside. Ensure that guests or employees use the appropriate area and extinguish the cigarette completely.

- Do not allow smoking near someone who is using oxygen because oxygen can increase the strength of a fire.

Each year, there are many structure fires in health care facilities. These fires happen in nursing homes, hospitals or hospice houses, mental health facilities, and doctors' offices or clinics. Cooking equipment is the primary cause of fires. Other causes of fires include clothes dryers or washers, intentional fires, smoking materials, heating equipment, electrical distribution or lighting equipment, and playing with a heat source.

Employees will be educated on the location of fire alarms, sprinklers, fire extinguishers, and any additional **alarm systems** that are in place. The danger of a fire is mainly from the smoke it creates. Smoke can travel quickly in a fire and affect areas in a building that are not close to the fire itself. With elderly and sick patients, lack of mobility inhibits a quick escape; therefore, proper evacuation and rescue planning is essential. When responding to a fire or an alarm, always treat it as a true emergency.

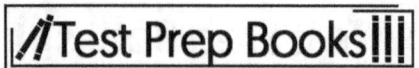

Quality and Safety

Call 911, even if an alarm system is monitored and activated, to ensure that help is on the way. If it is a false alarm, the fire department may still search to make sure everything is safe.

Facilitating Correct Use of Infant and Child Car Seats

As per the **National Highway Traffic Safety Administration (NHTSA)**, car seats that are used and fitted appropriately can considerably lower infant and child death and injury in motor vehicle accidents. Estimates state that the proper use of infant and child car seats can prevent infant death by 71% and the death of toddlers and young children under 3 years of age by 54%.

It is imperative that infant and child car seats are not only properly installed, but also the correct size in order to be effective against injures and death. For instance, rear-facing infant seats should be mounted in the back seat facing the rear of the automobile until the child is at least 2 years of age, or longer depending on the weight limit of the car seat and specific laws in each state. Convertible safety seats can be installed as either rear or forward facing. In most cases, regular car seat belts can be used when the child reaches at least 40 pounds and about 4 years of age, ideally in combination with a booster seat. Nurses should review these various safety regulations with patients who are parents-to-be or caring for infants or young children to make sure they are aware of the correct ways to install and use car seats.

Mental Health Factors That May Contribute to the Potential for Accident or Injury

A variety of issues related to a patient's mental status can influence the potential for injury. The American Psychiatric Association's (APA) *Diagnostic and Statistical Manual of Mental Disorders (DSM) V* recognizes four main **mental illness** categories: thought disorders, mood disorders, behavioral disorders, and mixed mental health disorders. Agitated and altered thought processes can result from a variety of etiologies, such as hallucinations, dementia, concussions, tumors, or trauma.

It is important for nursing team members to recognize the signs and symptoms of impaired cognition, such as memory loss and poor hygiene, as well as those of acute and chronic mental illness, such as schizophrenia, depression, and bipolar disorder. Impaired cognition, also known as a disturbed thought process, interrupts and distracts a patient's mental and thought abilities, processes, and activities. Attributes that could impact safety include short or long-term memory loss, mental conflict, aphasia, confusion, disorientation, a lack of good judgment and insight, and inability to perform basic life skills and activities.

For patients with acute and chronic mental illness, it is important to be aware of changes in their mental status and behaviors to adjust safety precautions as needed. To evaluate the patient's **mental capacity**, complete an assessment of their appearance, behavior, mood, alertness, memory, and signs of odd thoughts or viewpoints, such as delirium or delusions. Assessments should be completed as often as the nurse deems necessary based on the patient's past and present mental condition. For example, during the manic phase of bipolar disorder, the patient will require safety precautions when experiencing hallucinations or delusions.

Utilizing Facility Client Identification Procedures

Failing to identify patients correctly can cause mistakes and miscalculations regarding medication, transfusions, test procedures and results, procedures involving the wrong person, and discharging infants to the wrong families. It is essential to utilize two **patient identifiers**, which allows for the patient to be involved in the identification process and ensures dependability and consistency in the process.

Quality and Safety

Using two identifiers also helps guarantee an accurate match between the service or treatment and the patient, helping to prevent mistakes and improve patient care.

There are a number of patient identifiers depending on the healthcare facility. Some examples include patient name, birthdate, address, phone number, Social Security Number (SSN), photograph, or their medical record number.

The nursing team must make sure that two of these above identifiers are assigned to each patient according to the facility's policy. Additionally, these same two identifiers must be linked to the patient's medication, blood product, treatment, procedure, or specimen container via an attached label. It is imperative to always check a client's ID band to verify it matches the name on the chart and the orders being performed. These identifiers must be used to verify a patient's identity when admitted or transferred to another hospital or care location and prior to caring for the patient. It is important to avoid using the patient's room number, which could result in a patient misidentification. The nursing team also needs to be aware of how to integrate automated systems into the patient identification process if used in their facility. These are utilized in order to decrease the likelihood of identification inaccuracies and reduce **medication errors**. Some examples include the following:

- **Computerized provider order entry (CPOE)**: A system that allows healthcare personnel to enter and send treatment orders electronically.

- **Barcoding**: Computerized reference numbers that contain descriptive and other essential data.

- **Radio Frequency Identification (RFID)**: Wireless technology utilizing radio waves and signals to communicate data.

- **Biometric identification**: The measurement and statistical analysis of a patient's individual features for the purpose of identification.

Identifiers should be listed on an **identification band (ID)** applied to the patient's wrist. A separate band must also be worn to indicate any known allergies and, if the patient is predisposed towards falling, a fall risk band should be added. Facilities typically assign a specific color for each type of ID band. Often, name bands are white, allergy bands are red, and fall risk bands are yellow. Examples of facility-specific requirements include the exact location of each band on the patient's arm and whether a do not resuscitate (DNR) order is also noted on a specific ID band. Since these ID bands are imperative to patient safety, they are designed to be waterproof and difficult for the patient to remove.

Protecting Clients from Accident/Error/Injury

Healthcare providers and facilities must ensure that patients, visitors, and employees are safeguarded from injury. Examples of injuries that happen most frequently include burns, falls, electrical shock, accidental poisoning, and disaster incidents.

Injuries involving heat can result from defective heating and cooling devices, as well as when these devices are incorrectly applied to the patient. Patients with sensory or neurological issues, which impedes their capacity to recognize and feel bodily harm, are at an increased risk of injury resulting from hot or cold therapy. Falls, both with or without injury, are a frequent and expensive accident that affect nearly every healthcare facility. As a result, all patients should undergo fall risk screening on admission and after substantial changes in physical, psychological, or cognitive attributes.

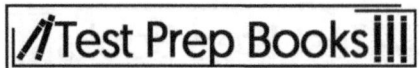

After undergoing the screening process, any patients deemed to be at risk for falling should receive a fall risk band along with special instructions and procedures to prevent incidents. These fall risk interventions should also be documented in the patient chart.

There are several risk factors related to falls that are often included in a **falls risk screening** and assessment. These include:

- *Incontinence*: Patients with incontinence issues are more likely to fall, usually due to slipping and rushing to get to a toilet.

- *Confusion:* Patients who are confused may experience judgment issues and be unaware of environmental hazards that could cause them to fall.

- *Poor vision*: Those patients with vision issues are more likely to trip over items, especially when in an environment that is new or different. It is important that clients have their eyeglasses nearby and are urged to utilize them.

- *Reaction time*: Patients who experience reaction times that are slow or delayed are more likely to fall. This occurs more often with elderly patients, who may not react in time to steer clear of something that could cause them to slide or fall, such as a floor that is wet or slippery.

- *Age*: Patients that are at the greatest risk of falling include the elderly and young children.

- *Medications*: Patients taking painkillers or other tranquilizing drugs may have side effects causing them to feel disoriented due to sleepiness, dizziness, muscular weakness, or orthostatic hypotension, therefore increasing the chance of falling.

- *Poor muscular strength, balance, coordination, gait, and range of motion (ROM)*: Patients with deficits in these areas should work with a physical therapist to strengthen these functions and prevent falls.

- *Environmental hazards*: The room or area occupied by the patient should be free of clutter and glare, kept dry and clean, and have adequate lighting as well as a working nurse call bell. These are all dangers that could exacerbate the chance of a fall. The entire healthcare team should work to make sure the patient's environment remains free of these types of environmental hazards.

- *Past incidence of falls*: Patients who have exhibited a prior history of falls, especially those who have fallen more often and in the recent past, are more likely to fall again.

- *A fear of falling*: It has been found that patients who have indicated they are afraid of falling are at a greater risk of a fall occurrence.

- *Certain diseases and disorders*: Examples of disease processes that increase risk for falls include those involving the musculoskeletal and neurological systems, such as muscular dystrophy, Parkinson's disease, and seizure disorders.

In addition to these fundamental patient-related factors, there are external and environmental influences that should be considered risk factors and corrected as soon as possible:

- *Insufficient patient footwear*: Shoes, slippers, and other footgear that do not fit properly or are slippery can increase the chance of a fall occurring. The items worn by patients on their feet should be skid proof, durable, safe, and the correct size. Skid proof socks are highly recommended to help prevent falls.

- *Nonworking and/or incorrect usage of patient equipment*: Medical equipment that is not in proper condition, such as a broken wheelchair or cane, can lead to falls. Damaged equipment should be immediately reported and sent off for repair until they are authorized as safe to use again. Nurses also need to make sure they are aware of the correct usage of all patient equipment. For example, a patient can fall if a mechanical lift is used improperly.

- *Delayed response time to calls for help*: Nurses must answer patient calls quickly to avert the chance of a patient falling or suffering from injury.

Besides patient risk assessment, other procedures that nurses can follow to avoid falls and decrease the level of harm caused by a fall include:

- Using supportive equipment, such as walkers and canes
- Wearing padded clothing and/or placing padded gym mats next to a patient's bed
- Keeping the patient's bed in the lowest and locked position
- Equipping a bed or chair with an alarm to signal staff when a patient is getting up
- Increasing the level of patient monitoring and frequency of observation
- Making sure the patient has high toilet seats and grab bars in the bathroom

Providing Patients with Appropriate Methods to Signal Staff Members

One of the best ways to prevent accidents and injuries is to ensure patients have a device nearby to alert nurses when they need assistance. At the same time, it is the responsibility of the healthcare team to answer calls for assistance as soon as possible so that the patient is quickly addressed and safeguarded from injury. The types of **signal methods** available vary by facility, patient, and situation. Nurses need to be aware of the various types and provide the best option for clients under their care.

For example, although most patients can contact a nurse with a call light, there may be some patients who can only vocalize their calls. In this case, they should be positioned near the nurses' station or another high traffic area so that they can be heard when needs arise. Other patients may not be able to alert the nurse on their own at all. Those who are unable to alert the nurse by pressing a call light or shouting out for help also need to be located near the nurses' station, which allows them can be checked frequently. In the case of a power failure or system breakdown that renders call lights unusable, patients should be equipped with handheld bells or buzzers to converse with the nursing staff.

Evaluating the Appropriateness of Healthcare Provider's Orders for a Patient

Nurses are responsible for executing two types of tasks: independent and dependent. Those considered independent are patient duties that do not require a doctor's order; those that are dependent are patient duties that can only be administered as per instruction from a doctor or other independent licensed practitioner.

When receiving an order, the nurse is required to make sure it is thorough, appropriate, and executed quickly. Nurses should never act on any orders from a healthcare provider that are unclear or inappropriate. Instead, the nurse should follow up on any order that seems uncertain by contacting the provider right away for an explanation.

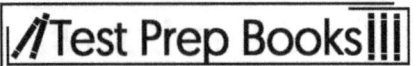

Quality and Safety

For an order of restraints to be considered complete, it must at least include why the order is needed, the kind of restraint required, the length of time it should be used, patient actions that necessitate its usage, and the signature of the person who ordered it. Medication orders must designate the name of the patient along with the drug name, dosage, administration instructions, frequency, indication, and a signed confirmation of the person who ordered it. Any part of this process that deviates from these requirements or seems incorrect requires intervention from the nurse.

Ergonomic Principles

Ergonomics is the science of matching the physical requirements of a job to the physical abilities of the worker. Musculoskeletal injuries can occur if physical demands are greater than the employee's physical capabilities. **Body mechanics** refers to how the body moves during activities of daily living. Understanding and practicing the use of proper body mechanics is imperative to preventing associate injury. The physical requirements of a job are explained during the interview process, and the physical capabilities of the associate are assessed during the pre-employment physical examination. Education on the use of proper body mechanics begins in nursing school and continues during employment. New associate orientation should include validation of proper body mechanics.

Principles of Body Mechanics

One way the nurse can take care of themselves is to employ proper body mechanics since the job is often highly physical in nature. Common physical tasks include turning patients in bed, transferring them to the chair or bedside commode, and assisting with ambulation to the bathroom or around the unit. Moving another person, especially one with limited ability to assist, can be extremely difficult and taxing on the body.

Depending on the facility in which the nurse works, different equipment will be available to assist with moving patients. Becoming acquainted with how and when to use this equipment will be part of the nurse's training in that facility. The nurse should use this equipment whenever possible, even if it takes a little more time to do so.

Basic **safe lifting techniques** include lifting with the legs, avoiding twisting and awkward positions, and keeping the back upright as much as possible to avoid straining. The individual should make sure to keep their feet as balanced as possible and not rush lifting or moving a patient. The nurse should ask for help from other nurses whenever needed to avoid injury.

The medical environment can present potential hazards that increase risk of injury to the nurse. Examples of these situations include transferring the patient from the stretcher to the operating room bed, positioning the patient, and standing for prolonged periods of time. Repetitive motions, such as turning the head to one side for visualization of monitoring equipment and holding a retractor for an extended time period, can also present ergonomic hazards. Proper body mechanics should be consistently followed to prevent injury. There are three foundational principles of proper body mechanics that should be followed by nurses. First, bending at the hips and knees, instead of at the waist, uses the large muscle groups of the legs to prevent back injury. Second, standing with feet at about shoulder-width apart helps to reduce risk of injury by providing foundational support. Finally, the nurse should keep the back, neck, pelvis, and feet aligned when turning or moving. Twisting and bending at the neck and waist can increase risk of associate injury.

As a standard of care, many healthcare institutions have mandated use of **safe patient mobilization (SPM)** equipment to reduce associate injuries and promote patient safety. SPM equipment in the medical environment can be used during patient transfers and positioning. For example, slide sheets are

Quality and Safety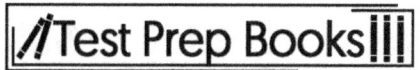

often used in patient transfers. These sheets are placed underneath the patient prior to lateral or vertical transfer. They decrease the surface tension, making transfers easier for the associates. However, since the slide sheets decrease surface tension, they must be removed after use to prevent the patient from sliding off the operating room bed.

Inflatable blankets can be placed under the patient to assist in lateral transfers as well. When engaged, the forced air blanket helps to support the weight of the patient, making lateral transfers easier. The mattress should be deflated after completion of transfer. Another type of SPM equipment is lift equipment. **Lift equipment** works by placing a sling under the patient's limb or underneath the entire patient, connecting the sling to the lift machine, and programming the machine to lift the body to the desired height. The weight limits of these machines vary, so the nurse must ensure the patient's weight does not exceed the weight limit set by the manufacturer.

Injury Prevention

Team members who are not careful to follow guidelines increase their potential for injury, which can result in physical harm, missed days of work, lost wages, and medical bills. Nurses are at high risk for injury due to the amount of lifting required during a shift. Using the appropriate lifting techniques can prevent back injuries and joint strains or sprains. The nurse should employ assistive devices, such as gait belts and mechanical lifting devices, whenever possible. It is important to ask for help whenever necessary to prevent injury. The following list details eight steps to use when lifting a heavy object:

1. Plan for lift and test the load
2. Ask someone for help
3. Get a firm footing
4. Bend knees
5. Tighten stomach muscles
6. Lift with legs
7. Keep the load close to the body
8. Keep back straight

Handling Hazardous and Infectious Materials

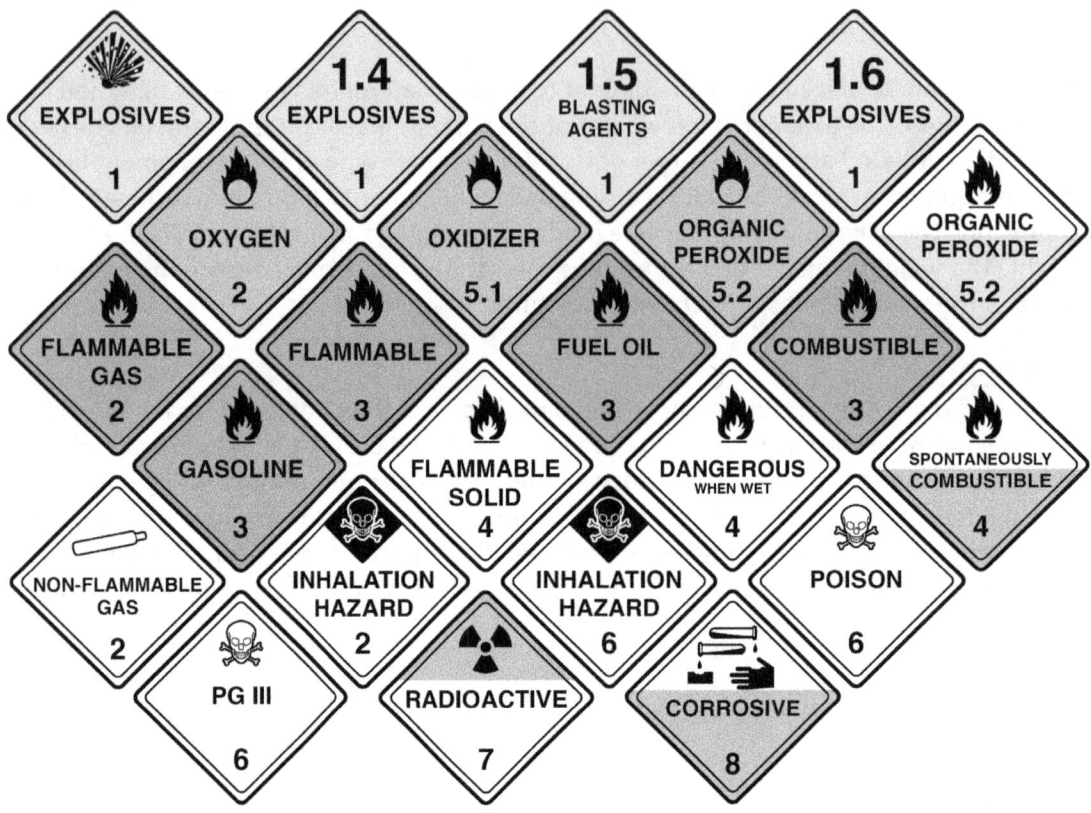

According to the **Institute of Hazardous Materials Management (IHMM)**, a hazardous material is defined as "any item that has the potential to cause harm to humans, animals, or the environment, either by itself or through interaction with other factors." A hazardous item may be biological, chemical, radiological, and/or physical in nature. Agencies such as the United States **Environmental Protection Agency (EPA)** and the Occupational Safety and Health Administration (OSHA) provide regulation and guidelines as to how hazardous materials are handled.

Biological hazardous materials are commonly referred to as **biohazards**. These are materials that present a threat to the health of living things, primarily humans. Biohazards are typically introduced into the medical environment in the form of patient body fluids and excreta. Examples of biohazardous materials are blood, body fluids, viruses, and bacteria. Items in the medical environment that have been exposed to biohazardous materials are considered biohazardous as well, until the decontamination process is completed. For example, used surgical instruments are considered biohazardous until they have been cleaned of bioburden and sterilized.

Chemical hazardous materials in the medical environment include solid, liquid, or gas materials that pose a threat to health. Primarily, solid and liquid chemical hazards include materials used to clean, disinfect, and sanitize the medical environment. They may also include cytotoxic and chemotherapy medications. Gas chemical hazards are primarily anesthetic gases. Containers for chemical hazards are labeled with symbols representing the type of potential hazard, along with instructions for steps to take in the event of exposure.

Radiological hazards found in the medical environment are seen in the forms of thermal, radioactive isotopes, and electromagnetic radiation. The most common thermal radiological hazard is in the form of laser. The use of **lasers** exposes the patient and the healthcare team to risk of eye damage, as well as increasing the risk of fire in the operating room. Laser operators must be trained on the correct usage of the laser, along with indicated safety precautions. Radioactive isotopes are used in brachytherapy. Brachytherapy is a form of cancer treatment where radioactive beads are inserted near or inside a cancerous tumor, delivering a high dose of radiation to the tumor while sparing the surrounding healthy tissue. **Electromagnetic radiation** is seen in the form of X-ray and ultraviolet radiation. During a procedure where electromagnetic radiation is used, the patient is protected by shields and/or drapes specifically designed to minimize exposure to the radiation. The perioperative team utilizes shields, gowns, and eyewear to minimize radiation exposure.

Physical hazards also exist in the medical area. Autoclaves are used to steam sterilize surgical instruments, and this steam can potentially cause burns. Removing surgical instruments straight from the autoclave can cause burns to the hands if the proper gloves are not used. Liquid on the floor can cause someone to slip or fall, causing injury. Handling carbon dioxide tanks or cryogenic material can cause severe burns to the hands if gloves are not worn.

The types of hazards should be discussed at the beginning of employment in the medical environment. This should include identifying the potential hazards and known hazards, steps to minimize exposure to them, and discussing the necessary steps to take in case of exposure. Healthcare facilities are required to provide **Safety Data Sheets** (**SDS**) and keep them in a central area. For most healthcare facilities, education on hazardous materials management is done on an annual basis.

Least Restrictive Restraints and Safety Devices

Restraints can be defined as anything that is used, done, or said to intentionally limit a person's ability to move freely. Restraints, when applied properly, cannot be easily removed or controlled by the person. In addition to physical form, restraints can also be emotional, chemical, or environmental. Use of restraints is very controversial due to the ethical issue of personal freedom. These are a temporary solution to a problem and must always be used as a last resort. Restraints are used to limit a patient's movement to prevent injury to themselves or others and always require a physician's order.

Types of restraints include:

- *Physical*: vests, wrist restraints, straps, or anything that confines the body
- *Emotional*: verbal cues or emotions used to coerce the patient to act a certain way
- *Environmental*: side rails, locked doors, closed windows, or locked beds
- *Chemical*: any medication used to restrict a patient's movement

The medical doctor or practitioner is responsible for ordering the use of restraints. Nurses and caregivers are responsible for applying restraints safely and for the management of a patient with a restraint. After an order is given, the physician must visit the patient within twenty-four hours of placing the order to assess its further necessity.

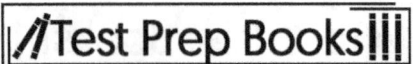

Quality and Safety

Alternatives to Restraints
Other methods must be tried before restraints. Examples include:

- Talking with the patient about being cooperative
- Using distractions such as television, music, knitting, and folding towels or cloths
- Placing the patient within view of a caregiver, such as near the main desk
- Having someone sit with the patient
- Moving the patient to a quiet area
- Ensuring that the patient's bathroom needs are being met
- Ensuring personal items are within reach

When to Use Restraints
Each facility will have a specific protocol that must be followed for restraint use. Circumstances under which restraints are used include:

- Signs of patient aggression toward self, staff, or other patients
- Interference with important medical devices, such as an IV or a catheter
- Patient movements that are potentially harmful to their health or may cause further injury
- Potential for a patient to interfere with a procedure

Applying Restraints
If the situation arises where the use of restraints is necessary, it is important to keep in mind the following:

- Always follow the facility's restraint policy.

- Obtain an order from a physician or medical practitioner unless it is an emergency situation.

- Obtain consent from the patient or their legal representative if the patient is not capable of understanding.

- Explain to the patient what is going to happen, even if the patient is unable to understand due to confusion or dementia.

- Always monitor the patient per facility policy, such as checking the positioning of the restraint every thirty minutes and removing every two hours for range of motion.

- Remember to reposition the patient and offer toileting every two hours.

- Explain the need for restraints and how long the restraints will be used.

Applying Physical Restraints
Vests have holes for the arms and the opening crosses in the back. The straps will be secured on either side of the bed or chair, depending on the patient's location. Tie it in a **quick-release knot** to a lower part of the bed that does not move. Make sure that two fingers fit underneath the vest on the patient's chest so that it is not too tight.

Wrist or ankle restraints are cloths that wrap around each wrist or ankle. They have a strap that is tied to a lower, immovable part of the bed or chair. Tie it in a quick-release knot. Ensure the restraints aren't

Quality and Safety

too tight and that the patient's arms or legs aren't in an awkward position. To prevent **pressure sores**, a pillow will be placed under the arms and/or the knees and heels.

Legal Implications in the Use of Restraints
If restraints aren't used correctly or are used for the wrong reasons, the patient's family can take legal action against the facility. A patient in restraints becomes completely vulnerable and may feel helpless. They are at a greater risk of sexual abuse, elder abuse, psychological abuse, or violence from other patients.

Possible injuries from restraints can include:

- Broken bones
- Bruises
- Falls
- Skin tears or pressure sores
- Depression or fear due to lack of freedom
- Death from strangulation

Incident Reporting (Event, Irregular Occurrence, or Variance)
If there is an unanticipated or **adverse event**, the nurse should follow the facility's policies and procedures for reporting and documentation. One of the first activities after the patient is stable should be to inform the respective manager or charge nurse of the event. The facility may also have internal processes to follow that serve to mitigate any potential legal consequences.

One of the more common reportable events that the nurse will be involved in is an **incorrect count**. In the event of an incorrect count, the circulator should make attempts to recover the missing item. The circulator should also follow the facility's policies and procedures; at some facilities, X-ray may not be required for needles smaller than a certain size because they are typically not visible on the X-ray. If an intraoperative X-ray is required for a potentially retained object, the team should ensure that the integrity of the sterile field is maintained because the X-ray may be performed prior to full closure of the incision.

Following reasonable attempts to recover the potentially retained object, the circulator should complete the necessary documentation in the patient's chart, such as which count is incorrect, what actions were taken to recover the object, and who was notified. In addition to the documentation in the patient record, the facility's policies may require reporting of the incident in an internal system. This allows the facility to gather additional data that may not be appropriate for the patient record. In the event of a retained foreign object, the facility can use this information to determine if all appropriate actions were taken.

Safe Use of Equipment
Nurses should ensure that all equipment that is to be used is safe and functioning properly. The use of medical devices is regulated by the United States **Food and Drug Administration (FDA)**, **The Joint Commission (TJC)**, and the **Centers for Medicare and Medicaid Services (CMS)**. Both TJC and CMS require the presence of **manufacturer's instructions for use (IFU)** to be present in areas where the equipment is used. Prior to medical equipment being used on patients, the IFU are established by the device manufacturer. It is important for care providers to use the equipment only per manufacturer guidelines, since these guidelines are the ones tested and approved as safe for patient use by the FDA. If

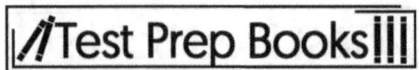

a safety concern regarding the equipment arises, the FDA recalls the product until the safety issue is resolved. For example, if a specific type of surgical guidewire breaks off at the tip and causes patient harm, the product may be recalled and pulled from circulation until further investigation.

The product manufacturer's IFU indicates if the equipment poses a fire, electrical, laser, or radiation hazard. If the product does pose one of these hazards, the IFU indicates the type of hazard and recommendations for protecting the patient and equipment users. For instance, if the product poses a fire hazard, the IFU contains information stating which type of fire extinguisher should be available. Also, the IFU advises if liquid, such as sterile water or sterile saline, should be available on the surgical field as a precautionary measure.

TJC and CMS observe **infection control** practices, such as chemical disinfection and sterilization of surgical instruments, during site visits to ensure healthcare facility compliance. If disinfection and sterilization are not performed according to manufacturer guidelines, the cleanliness and sterility of the surgical equipment cannot be verified. Manufacturer instructions for use should be available in each area where surgical equipment is used. Many healthcare facilities utilize **OneSource**, an online database of manufacturer instructions for use. Since OneSource is an electronic database, the contents are updated automatically, eliminating the need to update unit-based binders.

Security Measures

Within the healthcare facility, maintaining a strong **security system** is vital for patient and staff safety. The nurse executive will likely be trained in and involved with the hospital's security team, playing an active role in promoting a safe environment.

There are many ways a hospital can be threatened. Examples include infant abductions, secure information breeches, violent person alerts, runaway patients, or bomb threats. For each type of threat, the facility will likely have a plan in place to act quickly and eliminate the potential for danger.

The nurse executive may be involved with a hospital security planning team, which meets to discuss potential threats and devise appropriate plans. This allows the nurse executive to voice their opinion and contribute helpful ideas for each potential situation. The security team can share key tips with the rest of the staff based on their training and experience, which is beneficial to the overall security of the facility. Planning, training, and drills all ensure that if a threat were to happen, the team is ready to respond.

Within the hospital, there are various methods of alerting the staff to a security breach. There may be alarm systems, announcements made over a PA system, or a text alert system on the staff's phones that notifies everyone of the situation. Many hospitals have **closed-circuit television security monitoring systems** that employ cameras and video screens to monitor high-risk areas, such as entrances and isolation rooms for violent patients. Certain security doors may be used to keep areas of the hospital off-limits to visitors or can close off areas of the hospital as needed.

Many hospitals use identification badges and bands to ensure only authorized persons and personnel are allowed in certain areas. For example, the parents of a newborn receive a special ID band identifying them as such, which ensures that no one else is permitted access to the baby and prevents abduction.

If the nurse receives a bomb threat over the phone, they should attempt to stay on the line with the person making the threat as long as possible. The nurse may alert other staff of the bomb threat to get the security team in action, while trying to collect as much data on the perpetrator as possible. This information can include sound of their voice, male or female gender, their location, the bomb location, and their motive. The nurse may even be able to deescalate the situation over the phone if they remain calm and collected, but the situation should be handed over to the experts on the security team as soon as possible.

Standard Precautions/Transmission-Based Precautions

Infection prevention is an important focus in all patient care areas to protect patients and staff from transmission of infectious organisms. Standard precautions are practiced during direct contact with the patient and their environment. Followed universally by healthcare providers, **standard precautions** are the foundation for preventing disease transmission in all patient care settings. Included in standard precautions are hand hygiene, **personal protective equipment** (PPE), environmental control, and sharps safety. **Hand hygiene** is the gold standard for preventing disease transmission. In compliance with standard precautions, the nurse performs hand hygiene before and after patient contact, before and after applying exam gloves, after touching anything in the patient's environment, before eating, and after using the restroom. PPE protects the nurse from coming into contact with the patient's bodily fluids and other potentially infectious material.

Examples of PPE are gloves, masks, gowns, shoe covers, and eye shields. Surfaces in the patient environment are laden with bacteria and other infectious agents. Environmental contamination is directly linked to pathogen transmission and **hospital-acquired infections** (HAIs). Reusable laundry and textiles should be changed and laundered between each patient in a healthcare-accredited laundry facility. Syringes and needles should be limited to single-patient use in compliance with evidence-based care related to infection control. **Sharps** should include safety devices, when possible. Angiocaths (IV needles) and surgical blades are available with built-in safety features that cover the sharp when not in use, decreasing the chance of needle-stick exposure to patient body fluids. In addition to standard precautions, transmission-based precautions are to be used for patients with known or suspected infection of highly transmissible pathogens.

Transmission-based precautions are classified in three ways: contact, droplet, and airborne. **Contact precautions** are used with patients infected or colonized with microorganisms transmitted by direct or indirect contact. These include *Clostridium difficile (C. diff)*, methicillin-resistant *Staphylococcus aureus* (MRSA), and vancomycin-resistant *Enterococcus* (VRE). When caring for these patients, the nurse dons a gown and gloves prior to entering the patient room. The PPE is discarded just prior to leaving the patient room, and hand hygiene is performed immediately. **Droplet precautions**, in addition to standard precautions, are used if a patient has a confirmed or suspected infection transmissible through respiratory droplets. PPE associated with droplet precautions are gloves, gown, and mask. The patient is also placed in a single-patient room. Influenza and respiratory syncytial virus (RSV) are indications for droplet precautions. **Airborne precautions** are taken when providing care to a patient with known or suspected infection transmissible via airborne route. The patient's respiratory particles are airborne for prolonged time periods and are carried by normal air currents. PPE for these patients an appropriate respirator with a level of N95 or higher. The most common airborne-transmissible infections are tuberculosis, measles, and varicella.

Spread of Disease-Causing Organisms

Microorganisms that cause infection can be spread by touching surfaces, equipment, people, and bodily fluids, as well as by breathing in airborne droplets, such as those that exit the nostril when a person sneezes. Touching infectious microorganisms, followed by contact with one's hands, face, mouth, eyes, or food, can spread the germs. A clean environment and good handwashing are protective measures for both patients and healthcare workers. Infections can spread from patient to patient, from caregiver to patient, and vice versa.

There are three types of infections: viral, bacterial, and fungal. **Fungal infections** are caused by spores of fungus that usually affect the skin, but they can also be inhaled and cause respiratory infections. Examples of fungal skin infections include Athlete's foot, ringworm, and yeast infections. Fungal infections can be spread by touching the lesion or skin area that is infected.

Bacterial infections and **viral infections** are caused by microbes, or microscopic organisms. Both types of infection can produce similar symptoms, including:

- Coughing and/or sneezing
- Inflammation (swelling)
- Fever
- Vomiting
- Diarrhea
- Fatigue

Bacteria and viruses are both too small to see without a microscope, but they differ in how they infect the body. Bacteria are complex and can reproduce or multiply on their own. They can live in extreme environments, such as heat and cold, and can infect both the bodies of animals and humans. Bacterial infections are usually localized or found in contained areas of the body, such as the sinuses. Most bacteria are harmless and, in some cases, necessary for the body. One example is the bacteria in our gut, which is important for digesting food. Bacterial infections are treated with antibiotics, which will either kill the bacteria or stop the growth of the bacteria that has entered the body.

There are many different types of bacterial infections. Some common bacterial skin infections include cellulitis, folliculitis, impetigo, and boils. Foodborne bacterial infections usually cause vomiting, diarrhea, fever, chills, and abdominal pain. Harmful bacteria may be found in raw meat, fish, eggs, poultry, and unpasteurized dairy products due to unsanitary food preparation and handling.

Sexually transmitted bacterial infections include chlamydia, gonorrhea, syphilis, and bacterial vaginosis. There are many additional types of infections, such as otitis media (ear infection), urinary tract infections, and respiratory tract infections. Infections in the respiratory tract can be bacterial or viral and can cause a sore throat, bronchitis, sinus infections, tuberculosis, or pneumonia.

Viruses are different from bacteria in that they need another cell in order to reproduce, or multiply. They attach to a cell in the body and change the cell to make more of the virus. Eventually, the original body cell dies. Viral infections do not respond to antibiotics and are more difficult to treat. Unlike bacteria, most viruses cause infection. The common cold is most often caused by a virus in the rhinovirus family and is an example of a mild virus. An example of a life-threatening virus is the human immunodeficiency virus (HIV). Vaccines are an effective prevention measure against viruses such as polio, chicken pox, influenza, and measles. Additionally, antiviral drugs available to treat certain viruses, such as herpes simplex virus.

Quality and Safety

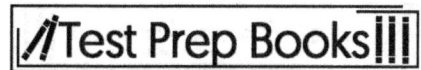

Common types of respiratory viruses include influenza-causing viruses, respiratory syncytial virus, and rhinoviruses, which are most often the cause of the common cold. Viral skin infections can include molluscum contagiosum (small, harmless bumps on the skin), herpes simplex virus-1 (cold sores), and varicella zoster virus (chicken pox and shingles). Foodborne viral infections are the most common cause of food poisoning and can include the hepatitis A virus, norovirus, and rotavirus. Viruses that are transmitted sexually include human papilloma virus, hepatitis B, genital herpes (herpes simplex virus-2), and HIV. Other types of viruses include Epstein-Barr, West Nile, and viral meningitis.

Bacteria and viruses can be spread by:

- Droplet contact from coughing and sneezing
- Contact with infected individuals
- Contact with infected animals, such as livestock, pets, fleas, or ticks
- Contact with infected surfaces, such as tabletops or railings
- Contact with contaminated food or water

Microbes can cause acute infections, chronic infections, or latent infections. **Acute infections** last for a short period of time, while **chronic infections** can last for weeks, months, or years. **Latent infections** may not show any symptoms at first; then, they may reappear after months or years.

Handwashing with soap and water is the number one way to prevent the spread of germs. The soap removes the visible dirt and invisible germs from the hands, and the water rinses them off.

Handwashing steps:

- Remove any jewelry or watches and pull long sleeves up past the wrists.
- Turn on warm water.
- Place soap in one hand and rub hands together for at least twenty seconds.
- Make sure to rub the top and palms of the hands, between the fingers, and around the nails.
- Wash above the wrists.
- Handwashing should occur for at least 20 seconds. If there was contact with bodily fluids, wash for at least one minute.
- If the sides of the sink are accidentally touched, repeat the washing process.
- Rinse hands with fingers facing down so that the soap and germs run off rather than back up the arms.
- Dry hands with a paper towel or clean hand towel.
- Use the towel to turn off the faucet.

When to perform handwashing:

- After using the bathroom
- After sneezing or handling tissues

- Before and after eating
- Before entering and after leaving a patient's room
- Before and after feeding a patient
- Before and after performing a procedure on a patient
- Before and after coming in contact with a wound
- After coming in contact with dirty linens or clothes
- After coming in contact with bodily fluids of any kind (blood, urine, vomit, mucus, or stool)
- After leaving a patient's room

Cleansing the hands with an **alcohol-based hand sanitizer** is also available in healthcare facilities, but it is best to wash with soap and water. Hand sanitizers can get rid of many, but not all, microbes. For example, *Clostridium difficile*, commonly referred to as *C. diff*, is a microbe that is not killed by alcohol-based sanitizers. A *C. diff* infection causes a patient to have copious amounts of watery diarrhea. In addition to standard infection prevention precautions, the nurse must wash hands with soap and water before and after caring for a patient with *C. diff*.

Hand sanitizer should not be used when the hands are visibly soiled or if bodily fluids have been touched. After several uses of hand sanitizer, oils build up on the hands and should be removed by washing with soap.

Educating patients about cleanliness and proper handwashing will also help prevent the spread of disease. Make sure to assist patients with washing their hands with soap and water or a soapy washcloth throughout the day, especially after toileting and prior to eating. Proper handwashing in the community reduces the number of people who get sick with diarrheic illnesses and respiratory illnesses, such as colds.

Isolation Techniques

One unfortunate downside of staying in a healthcare facility is the chance of contracting a healthcare-associated infection. According to the **World Health Organization (WHO)**, many of these can be prevented by using appropriate isolation techniques.

The types of infections that necessitate isolation are those that are easily transmitted and accessible to those with compromised immune systems, making it difficult for them to fend off the infection. Some of the most common types of illness transmitted in healthcare settings include MRSA, *C. diff*, and **ventilator-associated events (VAEs)**, such as pneumonia. Therefore, nurses should be especially aware of vulnerable patient populations, such as those with HIV, hepatitis B, or tuberculosis. In these cases, isolation safeguards may be necessary to prevent exposure to common pathogens that can lead to more serious infections.

Isolation techniques are categorized into one of five types:

- **Contact precautions**: Conditions with a high risk of contact transmission that often warrant isolation include *C. diff*, HSV, scabies, MRSA, and fungal infections. This technique includes wearing gloves and a gown, followed by immediate handwashing.

- **Droplet precautions**: These involve diseases spread by coughing or sneezing, such as influenza, rhinovirus, pertussis, and group A streptococcus. Precautions include wearing a mask and goggles, followed by removal of protective gear just prior to and handwashing after leaving the patient's room.

Quality and Safety

- **Airborne precautions**: Airborne infections, such as *Aspergillus* or tuberculosis, involve spread through airborne particles that are smaller in size and remain in the air for longer periods of time. Patient isolation involves utilizing a negative-pressure room, which has a lower pressure ventilation system that prevents airborne pathogens from escaping. Precautions include wearing an appropriate N-95 respirator and disposing of protective gear in an adjacent room.

- **Neutropenic precautions**: Patients with compromised immune systems, such as those with AIDS or taking immunosuppressants, may suffer from decreased neutrophil counts. It is important to keep contaminants out of these patient's rooms, which may involve donning protective gear, washing hands prior to entering, and screening any items such as food or gifts.

- **Radiation precautions**: Radiation safeguards are comparable to neutropenic precautions because they also involve the possibility of a compromised immune system. When a patient is undergoing radiation therapy, time limits may be enforced for both visitors and healthcare staff to limit their exposure. The use of gowns, shoe covers, or other protective gear may be required. An exposure-guideline chart should be placed on or near the patient's door.

Skills

Continuous Process Improvement

Continuous process improvement applies broadly to operations across healthcare, business, the public sector, nonprofits and beyond. Process improvement can occur incrementally over time or happen in a discrete breakthrough; however, continuous process improvement is the paradigm of viewing such improvements as part of a repeating cycle for the development of better work processes. Three central concepts to continuous process improvement are the Plan-Do-Study-Act (PDSA) cycle, "Lean Leadership" business planning, and responding to system failures through root cause analysis.

PDSA

Fundamental to the paradigm of continuous process improvement is the **Plan-Do-Study-Act cycle**, sometimes also referred to as Plan-Do-Check-Act (**PDCA**). Healthcare leaders can use this method to implement change in a systematic way. It allows for testing, assessing, and adjusting changes on a limited scale to maximize the chance of success once the change is rolled out broadly.

Plan

Healthcare leaders assess the need for change, the conditions surrounding the process, and the desired outcomes. They may interview staff, collect data, and reach out to peers at other organizations to learn from their experiences and methods. They may also observe the different systems within the healthcare environment (e.g., nursing, pharmacy, respiratory therapy, and environmental services) to learn the way they interact, contribute to, or hinder the process in question. Then, leaders begin to form a plan for improvement, usually targeted to an initially limited scope that will be implemented in the "Do" step.

Do

Healthcare leaders then implement the plan in the "Do" stage of the PDSA cycle. In this phase, it is important to stay in communication with stakeholders, staff, and other allied health colleagues to monitor for any safety issues and to check on participation and staff buy-in.

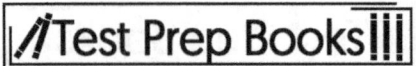

Quality and Safety

Study (or Check)
This is the phase during which healthcare leaders step back and assess the results of the process change. Was it a success? Were the desired outcomes achieved? Again, this may involve data collection, discussions with staff, and considerations of any safety implications. In this step, healthcare leaders can make adjustments and may consider issues involved in scaling up the change.

Act
Actions taken in this last step depend on what was learned in the "Study" step. If the change was unsuccessful, the cycle begins again with an adjusted or even entirely new plan. If the attempted change was successful, the "Act" step allows healthcare leaders to make minor adjustments and consider issues involved in scaling up the change. If the change was successful, this is the step during which the change is rolled out to a larger audience. Additionally, measures are taken toward permanent implementation and ongoing assessment of outcomes.

Lean Leadership

"**Lean**" is a system of thinking and practicing that originated with the Toyota car company. It aims to produce maximum value with minimum waste. "**Lean leadership**" relies on respect for the people who carry out the daily operations of the organization and employs a continuous learning cycle to deliver process improvement. The "**lean approach**" in healthcare focuses on the patient and what is of value to them, such as reduced wait times, a quiet sleep environment, reduced readmission rate, and on-time discharge. However, the lean approach can be targeted toward any group, such as frontline nurses or physicians, and attempt to deliver value to that group in the most resource-efficient manner possible.

The lean approach pursues continuous process improvement on a granular and incremental level, aiming for ever increasing efficiency, flow, and elimination of waste. It does this by first determining a valuable measure, such as a reduction in medication errors or increased patient satisfaction. The next steps involve identification of a purpose or problem to be solved, the work necessary to solve that problem, and the capabilities required for the desired solution. These capabilities can include management and leadership actions, both material and human resource needs, and developing awareness and buy-in among staff. The lean approach attempts to remove barriers or workflow steps that do not contribute to producing the maximum value.

Standard work is an example of a lean-based practice that has been widely adopted in hospitals and healthcare systems. Standard work protocols aim to add value to the patient experience by training staff in best practices to reduce many healthcare-related risks, such as infection, transfusion reaction, and falls. The lean approach identifies the value being delivered (e.g., reduced healthcare risks), a problem to be solved (e.g., inconsistent use of best practices), and what capabilities are required in the effort to produce maximum value with minimum waste (e.g., standardization, ease of use, and ease of access). The result is that best practices for many different procedures are available for use in front-line practice, and are easy to update, disseminate, and access.

Root Cause Analysis

A **root cause analysis** is a powerful tool to address individual incidents of system failure in a way that creates broad and lasting change. Root cause analysis assesses all factors that contribute to the system failure and attempts to identify the fundamental cause or causes of the failure. This singles out the most effective target for change to prevent future failure.

Quality and Safety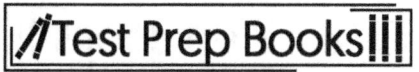

Root cause analyses are non-punitive. They address the *why* and *how* of a problem, approaching the problem within its system rather than as the failure of an individual. A non-punitive leadership response to errors is vital in healthcare because it fosters transparency and reporting of errors and near-misses. If a staff member is afraid of punishment or retribution, they will have a greater incentive to remain quiet or even cover up errors, which is a serious threat to patient safety.

Root cause analysis involves individuals at all levels and in all systems at the point of failure. The participation of the individual or individuals most closely involved with the actual system failure is crucial, as they will often have the clearest view of the causes that need examination.

Root cause analysis may, and often does, identify more than one root cause. The goal of the process is to identify a clear cause-and-effect chain between the root cause and the failure. This information can be presented as insight to help leaders and staff take action to prevent similar system failures in the future.

In a root cause analysis, healthcare leaders must use flexible and holistic thinking to go beyond what may seem obvious. They must resist the inclination to assign blame and consider the implications of all contributing factors, including those that are outside their scope of expertise or practice.

Healthcare is a highly complex enterprise. Potential for error is ever-present, and healthcare leaders cannot rely solely on the vigilance of individual staff members to prevent errors.

Research and Evidence-Based Practice Methods

Literature Review

A **literature review** is an analysis of publications related to a specific topic. It is a way to investigate and study work that has already been developed, gain understanding of a topic, and learn how the topic can be progressed through future work. The literature review is an essential component to researching disease because it gives those involved an idea of the current understanding of the disease and prevents conducting experiments that have already been performed and published. Conflicting theories can also be examined to determine the best course of action in disease prevention strategies. Literature surveyed can include books, published articles from journals, theses from universities, and past medical surveillance data to help form a full understanding of the disease or situation as it currently stands. The literature review then organizes this data and presents an analysis of how it may relate to the situation that needs to be addressed.

The first step in developing a complete literature review is to define a set of goals or objectives that need to be accomplished. This will provide insight on where to look for relevant literature and the type of information that will be most useful when conducting research. The next step is to complete the proper research, including selection of the articles or information that are the most relevant and useful to accomplish the goals. It is important to read as much information on the topic as possible to obtain an understanding of the type of data that is the most useful. Also, vetting sources for authenticity and credibility will guide which ones are known to be used frequently and are the most reliable. Once the best sources have been selected, a summary of each source that examines its credibility and suggestions to further the research should be written. Then, it will be possible to select the sources that are the most helpful to the current problem and document this reasoning to formulate the literature review.

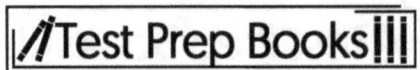

Critically Appraising Literature

When performing a literature review, it is important to be able to identify what sources have the most useful information related to a current problem. Not all sources are trustworthy, and not all trustworthy sources are relevant. It is up to the researcher conducting the literature review to determine which sources contain the most useful, credible data. When critically appraising literature related to healthcare and disease prevention, it is important for each source to be free of errors that might steer the course of further research in the wrong direction. Literature should be appraised based on credibility, relevance, and date of publication.

The most **credible literature** comes from academic sources that have been peer reviewed by professionals before publication. For disease prevention, scientific and healthcare-related medical journals are the best source for finding data and articles that have been well researched and cross-examined by multiple parties. Information that has already been confirmed by those in the same industry will have the least chance of containing misleading errors or too much unrelated or opinionated information. The relevance of the literature also needs to be compared with the problem that is being researched. Before conducting research, it is important to set goals and write questions that need to be solved to help the situation. The most relevant data is the data that directly solves these goals and answers the questions that have been laid out in relation to the current problem.

Literature that includes too little or too much data that may be hard to interpret should be avoided. Also, it is important to pay attention to when the literature was published to avoid using data that may be out of date or proven to be ineffective. The most recent articles are the most helpful because they contain the most up-to-date data collection methods and pertain to more modern health problems than those published before newer advancements in modern science were made.

Research Findings

Once relevant sources have been found and applicable research has been studied, the research needs to be put into practice. However, to determine how to best use the research, the goals and needs of the current situation should be assessed and developed. It is important to decipher the most effective methods of disease prevention and transmission. This will help develop a strategy of containment and provide focus in the research process to narrow the amount of information. Starting by developing a goal is an effective way to look for past works that have attempted to accomplish the same goal. If no such information exists or the past documented cases have been exhausted, it will be necessary to move on to commonalities that may exist in other areas, such as locations or specific symptoms. Comparisons between related reports can also help establish how others used similar findings. The research process will then follow a linear progression of studies, until reaching the most current one, to learn both the past and present status of the case.

Although prior research can lead to the development of a plan of action, previous experiments should not be entirely recreated; this will only lead to more of the same results if the source of the research has been peer reviewed. A more effective approach would be to determine where the research may have fallen short or how it can be updated to relate more to the current situation. It is important to take note of any technological updates that may have occurred since the research was conducted or how a disease may mutate to change the outcome of the published results. Then, current practice can aim to progress past research in a way that continues the discussion, provides new data, and be compared with data collected in the past. This allows the applicable research to be used to complement new findings, highlight how a disease or health crisis may have developed over time, and how it might continue to develop.

Research Related to Performance Improvement

Performance improvement is influenced by the collection and analysis of data. **Data** can be collected on a grand scale or on a more specific level. For example, HAIs in hospitals produce high morbidity and mortality. Acute care facilities track data on HAIs to determine areas of improvement. On a grand scale, the data is captured from the hospital as a whole, meaning all areas of patient care are included. Typically, critical care areas contain the highest risk for HAIs due to the acuity of patients and the complexity of treatment. However, the data may be offset by lower-risk patient care units, such as labor and delivery. When identifying opportunities to improve performance and avoid negative outcomes, it is important to research the data from independent levels.

For example, the infection control department of a hospital is tasked with researching an increasing rate of *Clostridium difficile* (*C. diff*) infections in patients. The first step would be to analyze the data and determine the problem areas. Should the data reveal that most *C. diff* infections are occurring in a specific patient care area, such as the intensive care unit, the infection control team would primarily focus their implementation strategies there. As part of the research, the team would identify the current infection control practices, such as hand washing, antibiotic use, cleaning practices, and staff education. Any deficiencies identified for any of the factors would prompt the infection control team to establish an implementation strategy. For example, further research revealed that the patient care rooms were being cleaned with a disinfectant not specifically approved to eliminate the bacterial spores associated with *C. diff*. Improper cleaning practices increase the risk of illness transmission. Should another patient be placed in the same room, the risk of acquiring *C. diff* would be increased. The infection control team may use this data to introduce a new cleaning product. Ongoing research would include the impact of the new product on the HAI rates within the hospital.

Evidence-Based Practice and Dissemination of Findings

As previously discussed, evidence-based practice (EBP) is a healthcare delivery framework that uses findings from rigorously performed research, relevant practitioner expertise, and patient preferences to develop and implement a medical treatment. EBP is a systematic approach that aligns closely with the scientific method to plan and test a medical intervention. The approach begins with a clinical question, which is generally focused on the patient's health concern and how to resolve it.

Once the clinical approach has been developed, the provider should review high-quality literature to find information. High-quality literature sources include manuscripts published in peer-reviewed journals, textbooks, and case studies from reputable sources (e.g., a university or health care system). Reputable research in EBP should be current, pertain to the same demographic as the patient, and have high levels of reliability and external validity. Anecdotes from the general population or from non-expert sources, opinion pieces, editorial pieces, and crowd-sourced encyclopedia sites are low-quality information sources and should not be used in EBP. Once this literature review is complete, consultation with field experts can add more information to the evidence pool. Field experts should be reputable, respected, and seasoned in their field; ideally, they have worked with large numbers of patients whose conditions and treatments are relevant to the clinical question that has been formed.

Finally, this evidence should be presented in a transparent and easily understood manner to the patient who will receive the intervention. It is important that the patient understands the evidence and treatment recommendations so that they can make an informed decision about their health plan. If a patient is distrustful of their provider, does not understand the treatment recommendation, or otherwise has a personal barrier to treatment, a successful intervention is unlikely. As a result, the patient may experience harm and the medical facility may have wasted organizational resources. When presenting information to the patient, the provider should be mindful of any possible biases or bedside manner that could sway the patient. Once the patient and provider have collaborated on the treatment plan, the intervention can begin. The patient should be monitored and evaluated with respect to the intervention, and findings should be documented and disseminated as appropriate. If the intervention is not successful, the practitioner should plan to go through this process again and design another intervention to test.

Practice Quiz

1. The manager of a nursing unit is conducting a root cause analysis of a serious medication error. Which of the following should the manager consider the goal of the root cause analysis?
    a. The identification and removal of the individual responsible for the error
    b. The addition of safety checks to prevent this medication error from happening again
    c. Identifying the underlying cause of the error to guide process change, which will prevent it from happening again
    d. Agreement among senior leaders on a risk-management strategy

2. The physician has made a treatment plan for a cancer patient and communicated it to the interdisciplinary team as well as the patient, who is awake and alert. Which principle states that the patient should make the final decision to accept or reject the plan?
    a. Moral agency
    b. Power of attorney
    c. The Health Insurance Portability and Accountability Act (HIPAA)
    d. Right to self-determination

3. What is the first stage in effective resolution of staff conflict?
    a. Agreeing on a solution that will prevent the conflict from reoccurring
    b. Clarifying the topic of disagreement with the affected parties
    c. Determining who started the conflict
    d. Defining barriers to reaching a common goal of resolution

4. The nurse executive is discussing process changes with their team based on the lean approach. Which statement should the executive use to best explain the goal of lean management?
    a. Lean management aims to deliver maximum value to the patient with minimum waste and wait.
    b. Lean management helps reduce staffing and spending as much as possible.
    c. Lean management ensures that every step in a workflow is covered by a policy or protocol.
    d. Lean management addresses the healthcare system's legal and financial exposure to risk.

5. When developing evidence-based practice protocols for a perioperative unit, the nurse executive should rely primarily on which type of source?
    a. Up-to-date patient satisfaction data
    b. Opinions of surgeons and senior medical officers at the organization
    c. The bedside practice of veteran staff nurses
    d. Peer-reviewed research and published guidelines from reputable governing bodies

See answers on the next page.

Answer Explanations

1: C. The goal of a root cause analysis is to identify the underlying cause of a system failure and gather information to guide practice change aimed at preventing the error from happening again. Choice A is incorrect because root cause analysis is a non-punitive process and does not aim to single out an individual or assign blame. Choice B is incorrect because root cause analysis is a holistic, investigative process and does not start with a pre-determined solution. Choice D is incorrect because root cause analysis involves all levels of staff and is not a risk-management effort.

2: D. The right to self-determination means that patients have the right to make decisions regarding their healthcare. Moral agency, Choice A, refers to a person's ability to determine right and wrong actions. A power of attorney, Choice B, is not relevant for a patient who is awake and alert and capable of making decisions. Choice C, HIPAA, covers the privacy of a patient's medical information, not their decision-making ability.

3: B. The first stage in staff conflict resolution is to clarify the disagreement or conflict and make sure the involved parties agree on what the problem is before moving forward. Choice A, agreeing on a solution, is the last stage of conflict resolution. Choice C, determining who started the conflict, is blame-based and not part of effective conflict resolution. Choice D, determining barriers to resolution, is a stage of conflict resolution, but is not the first stage.

4: A. Lean management aims to deliver maximum value to the patient with minimum waste and wait. All other choices are incorrect because they do not represent the goals of lean management. It doesn't aim to reduce staffing or spending as much as possible, Choice B. While it is important to know if a workflow is covered by a policy or protocol, Choice C, that is not the goal of lean management. Being aware of exposure to risk is not part of lean management, making Choice D incorrect.

5: D. Evidence-based practice refers to a methodology based on peer-reviewed research, clinical practice statements, and guidelines published in reputable medical, nursing, and allied health publications, as well as other scientific sources. It does not rely on consumer or practitioner opinion or defer to traditional practice. While Choices A, B, and C are important factors to consider in creating protocols, they are not the primary source for evidence-based practice.

Business Management

Knowledge

Reimbursement Methods

<ins>Payor Systems</ins>
As is the case with any business, a healthcare company looking to provide an effective and quality service to its customers must first have a thorough understanding of the various methods through which a healthcare company is reimbursed for its services. One useful method to discuss the multitude of ways in which healthcare providers are reimbursed is by identifying the individual or entity who is ultimately responsible for paying for the cost of a patient's care. This individual or entity, commonly called the **payor**, can usually be categorized into one of four groups. First, there are commercial insurance companies, the largest of which are companies such as UnitedHealth Group, Cigna, and Aetna. A government program may also be considered the payor in certain circumstances. **Medicare** and **Medicaid** are two examples of government programs that serve as payors in many cases. Many patients will also receive financial coverage from their employers, and in those cases the employer is considered the payor. Finally, there are circumstances in which a patient may be paying for their treatment directly, and therefore the patient can be considered the payor.

Although the categorization above may be sufficient for a client's understanding, a more complete picture of payors and payor systems is necessary for any individual seeking to adequately direct and manage patient care as a provider. In addition to the exact payor for a client's care, there are several other factors that need to be considered, such as those that vary between payors and impact the care a patient receives in a variety of ways. Examples of these factors include the specific laws that apply to care and reimbursement, which terms of payment are negotiable versus fixed, and the objectives of the relationship between patient, payor, and healthcare provider. For example, a major distinction that exists between different commercial insurance companies is the degree of flexibility they offer their customers in terms of which healthcare providers' services they will cover. A **health maintenance organization (HMO)** is a type of commercially available insurance plan, which is generally seen as one of the more affordable types of health insurance plans. Under such a plan, the insurance company negotiates with a network of healthcare providers, and care is only covered if that care is provided by one of those providers. Although a higher premium is required, a **preferred provider organization (PPO)** is a health plan that allows customers to see out-of-network doctors without a referral. Most PPOs have lower co-pays for in-service providers than HMOs, which are likely to have a fixed rate. Both HMOs and PPOs can also be compared with **point-of-service (POS)** and **exclusive provider organization (EPO)** plans, both of which seek to strike more of a balance between the cost of premiums and degree of choice customers have in seeking out healthcare providers.

Another aspect of the healthcare payor system that should be well-understood by nurse executives is the various methodologies that exist to reimburse a healthcare provider for a patient's care. Historically, the norm in the healthcare industry has been what is called a **fee-for-service (FFS)** model. As the name suggests, the focus of the FFS model is the services provided by a healthcare provider in their care of a patient. Under an FFS, a healthcare provider negotiates specific fees for specific services and then bills according to which services a patient received during their care. Notably absent in the FFS model is any consideration of the effectiveness of the services provided. This has led, in some cases, to the practice of overprovision by healthcare providers. **Overprovision** occurs when healthcare providers prescribe a

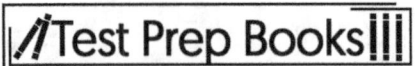

patient more services than might be entirely necessary, therefore increasing the amount they can bill the payor. It has been argued that overprovision, often associated with inefficiency and increased healthcare expenditure, is directly incentivized by the FFS model. Consequently, many in the healthcare industry have shifted away from using FFS models. However, FFS reimbursement does still exist for some services under certain conditions and largely depends on the health plan of the patient.

Value-Based Purchasing

The shift away from FFS reimbursement models has led to the usage of a variety of models and programs, all funded and overseen by the Centers for Medicare & Medicaid Services (CMS), which collectively are called **value-based purchasing** (**VBP**). VBP refers to any reimbursement system in which the healthcare provider is reimbursed not by the number of services they conduct, but by the quality of those services and/or the health outcomes of their patients. VBP models can usually be further categorized as either a value-based payment model or value-based insurance design. As the name might imply, **value-based payment** uses various measurements of patient outcomes and experiences in order to directly determine the cost of a particular service.

Value-based payment models focus largely on **patient throughput**, or how effectively a patient goes through the process of entering, being treated, and leaving a healthcare facility. Therefore, the quality of the patient's care— from check in, to treatment, to follow up care —is extremely important. Patient throughput can be measured in a variety of ways, but it mainly focuses on the amount of time that a patient spends at each step in the process of visiting a healthcare facility. If the healthcare facility is operating more efficiently or providing a higher quality of care, their reimbursement level will increase. For example, the VBP-based model of quality incentives operates by providing additional reimbursement if it can be shown that a provider has achieved certain quality of care metrics with respect to a certain population. Such metrics are set prior to an agreement between a payor (in this case, almost always a larger insurance provider, whether public or private) and the healthcare provider, allowing everyone full transparency on the expectations for reimbursement.

With **value-based insurance** design, the emphasis is similarly placed on **return on investment** (**ROI**) for various medical interventions and services; however, there is an important distinction between this design and value-based payment. Whereas value-based payment methods directly link patient outcomes to reimbursement, value-based insurance design seeks instead to restructure the entire insurance system, with a specific focus on treatments and medical services that are proven to be effective. Essentially, the payor responsible for the program will set lower rates for treatments or services shown to be broadly effective in an attempt to encourage its customers to seek out such treatments. Often, value-based insurance design will also specifically target low-cost programs shown to decrease future healthcare costs (e.g., diabetes treatment and prevention, tobacco cessation). Value-based insurance designs may also assign higher costs to treatments and services that have not shown to be effective enough. For example, a patient opting for an elective surgery may end up bearing more of the cost than they might with a more traditional insurance plan. It should also be noted that value-based insurance designs will often change what treatments are considered effective given an individual patient's health status, meaning treatments deemed ineffective for one patient may be deemed differently for another.

In order for a healthcare provider to participate in the VBP program offered by CMS, there are four different performance domains for which they must meet **quality of care metrics**. These domains are clinical outcomes, person and community engagement, safety, and efficiency and cost reduction. Within each of these domains, CMS has defined different measures in order to further quantify what quality

Business Management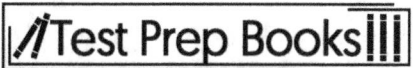

performance in that domain looks like. Within the clinical outcomes domain, for instance, there are measures for post-op complications and the 30-day mortality rate following various common conditions and procedures. The person and community engagement domain measures are taken from the **Hospital Consumer Assessment of Healthcare Providers and Systems (HCAHPS)** survey, a first-of-its-kind survey that collects and reports patients' perspectives of hospital care. The safety domain uses healthcare-associated infection (HAI) measures, which track the occurrences of infection while a patient is in the healthcare facility. Finally, the efficiency and cost reduction domain uses the **Medicare Spending Per Beneficiary (MSBP)** measure, which calculates the cost of services provided by a healthcare provider during the time directly prior to and directly after a Medicare beneficiary's stay in a facility.

It should be noted that VBP reimburses healthcare providers in a variety of ways, reaching beyond the goal of simply meeting the requirements for the four domains. Specifically, there are two assessment scores in each of the domains, referred to as the achievement and improvement scores. **Achievement scores** are awarded by comparing one healthcare provider's measure in a particular domain to all other healthcare providers' measures. In doing so, their measurements are compared against a threshold at the 50th percentile and a benchmark set at the mean of the top decile. **Achievement points** are awarded based on where their score falls in relation to those two numbers. If a healthcare provider scores at or above the benchmark, they will receive the maximum number of achievement points. Meanwhile, if their score is below the threshold, they will receive no achievement points. **Improvement scores,** on the other hand, are awarded by comparing one healthcare provider's measure with their previous recorded measure. Again, maximum improvement points are given for healthcare providers scoring at or above the benchmark, whereas none are given for healthcare providers scoring at or below the threshold. These scores are then compared against each other in each domain, with the highest score determining the score that domain receives.

Financial Compliance Laws

In order to combat fraud and abuse, federal and state agencies have enacted laws that protect consumers from being overcharged for healthcare-related services. Nursing leadership must ensure that these laws and their consequences are comprehended by nursing and ancillary staff. Education should be provided at the time of hire and annually with competencies (such as a quiz) to ensure that staff have knowledge of how these laws protect patients and where to report concerns. Each healthcare organization should have a privacy officer that is adept at understanding and interpreting the regulations and can provide guidance when there is question of whether an action has breached the health consumer's protections.

The Stark Law

The Stark Law, also referred to as the Physician Self-Referral Law, prohibits referrals that are paid by Medicare or Medicaid to be from entities that have a financial interest in the physician or physician's family members. The law includes referrals that cover designated health services such as supplies/equipment, radiology imaging service, radiation therapy services, parenteral or enteral nutrients, home health services, outpatient prescription drugs, outpatient therapies (e.g., physical therapy, occupational therapy, or speech therapy), and clinical laboratory services. This is just a sample of the services that are protected by the Stark Law; a more comprehensive list may be found at the Center for Medicare Services website.

The Stark Law is considered a strict liability statute, which indicates that there is no burden to prove that there was specific intent to break the law. Physicians found guilty of breaking this law are subject to fines and lose their ability to participate in federal healthcare programs such as Medicaid and Medicare.

Anti-Kickback

The Anti-Kickback statute makes it illegal to receive any type of incentive, pay, solicitation, or remuneration in exchange for any service covered by a federal healthcare program. Anything of value may be considered remuneration under this law, including benefits, money, gifts, services, or offers.

False Claims Act

Any individual who knowingly submits a fraudulent or false claim to a federal healthcare program has violated the False Claims Act. These violations may be either civil or criminal. A civil violation falls under the rules of a strict liability statute and does not require proof of specific intent of fraudulent activity. These acts may be due to reckless disregard of the truth, falsification of information, or deliberate ignorance. Organizations or individuals that turn a blind eye to concerns may be liable for claims that are not accurate or truthful. These violations may result in fines and penalties of up to three times the original claim in addition to a fine for each false claim that is filed.

No Suprises Act

The United States government has enacted a No Surprises Act, which provide patients with access to information about the cost of care and treatments. Health consumers are granted access to the amounts a provider or facility can bill insurance companies for healthcare services, including inpatient stays, procedures, surgeries, and medications. This information enables consumers to make informed decisions.

Skills

Financial Management

Budgeting

As might be expected, the systematic change that has occurred in healthcare reimbursement since the CMS began the VBP program has greatly changed how healthcare providers consider and manage their finances. Prior to the start of the program and its expansion under the **Affordable Care Act** (**ACA**), the common reimbursement method for healthcare providers was what can be generally categorized as FFS. Under FFS, there were not as many financial constraints for healthcare providers to consider. Specifically, there was nothing in place to incentivize healthcare providers to reduce costs for their patients, making it very easy for healthcare providers to turn a profit. However, with VBP linking reimbursement to a healthcare provider's cost reduction efficiency, there is now much more of an incentive for healthcare providers to find ways to reduce costs for their patients. Therefore, it has become much more important for healthcare providers, as well as those in management, to understand the basics of healthcare budgeting.

As with any budget, a **healthcare budget** (also called a hospital budget) is an attempt to estimate revenue and expenses over a specific period of time. When budgeting for a healthcare provider specifically, there are a few categorizations or types of budgets that may be helpful to explore further. One basic distinction that is key to most healthcare budgets is the difference between an operational budget and a capital budget. An **operational budget** is used to project costs associated with facility operation and personnel, whereas a **capital budget** is used to estimate costs associated with durable goods, such as patient beds, advanced equipment, or a new hospital wing. Knowledge of these two types of budgets, including the different methodologies that typically underpin them, is essential for understanding many of the factors that impact the expenses a healthcare provider incurs.

One way to understand the difference between an operational budget and a capital budget is to consider the ultimate goals of each. With an operational budget, the goal is most often to balance expenses with income while maintaining the day-to-day operations of the healthcare facility. However, a capital budget often has a more strategic goal than the practical goal of an operational budget. By investing in new equipment and facilities, a healthcare provider is not simply looking to balance the day-to-day expenses associated with running a healthcare facility. Instead, they are looking to improve the quality of care they can deliver, whether through the purchasing of new diagnostic equipment or the acquisition of new business partners or entities. The capital budget can therefore be seen as having more of an incentive toward profit than the operating budget. By investing in improvements to equipment and other durable goods, a healthcare provider can increase their own profitability and invest capital in ways designed to provide them the maximum return on their investment.

Despite the clear distinction in the ultimate aims of the operational and capital budgets, the two budgets are by no means considered or created separately from one another. In fact, it is necessary for healthcare managers to consider operational costs when considering potential capital investments and vice versa. If a healthcare provider is seeking to add an annex to their facility, one of the first discussions must be whether the operating budget itself will allow for the divestment of capital into such a project. On the flip side, capital budget investments, once completed, will impact the state of the operational budget. In this scenario, the new annex will require additional staff to run the facility and naturally increase the daily operating expenses of the facility, in terms of electricity, water, and other sources of power. Due to the natural and unavoidable interconnectedness of the operational and capital budgets, it is best practice for healthcare providers and managers to discuss and create such budgets in tandem with one another.

Another factor to consider when discussing and developing any form of healthcare budget is the length of time for which that budget is designed. As with most other businesses, it has long been standard for many healthcare providers to create **annual budgets**, typically before the beginning of the new financial year. Such budgets are often required by financial lenders and are therefore a necessity for many larger healthcare facilities. However, the fast and ever-changing world of the healthcare industry in general, as well as the particular opportunities and challenges faced by an individual healthcare provider, often gives rise to situations in which an annual budget is too impractical or no longer advisable to use. The **coronavirus disease 2019 (COVID-19)** pandemic provides a tragic real-world example of this paradigm—a healthcare provider attempting to use an operating budget created in December of 2019 would find themselves woefully unprepared and critically ill-equipped in April of 2020. Even under less unprecedented circumstances, there are many healthcare providers who have found their annual budget too prescriptive and/or constrictive to adequately meet the needs of their staff and their patients. A significant reason for this common dilemma is that annual budgets, by their very nature, are attempting to forecast and plan for conditions that may arise far in the future. If those predictions are inaccurate, either because they accounted for something that did not occur or neglected to consider the possibility of something that did, such budgets may quickly become a problem rather than a solution. Therefore, it is becoming increasingly common for healthcare providers to use some form of rolling forecasting in their budgeting plans.

A **rolling forecast** is any type of financial report that uses past data to continuously calculate future financial conditions. The key improvement that rolling forecasts provide over more traditional forms of budgeting is a continuous nature. Although most annual budgets use past trends in data to predict future outcomes, they only make such predictions once, before any current data is generated. By making constant predictions, a rolling forecast allows healthcare providers and managers to see in real time the effectiveness of their financial management and strategies. Furthermore, rolling forecasts allow those responsible for healthcare budgeting to change and adapt to current conditions that are different from those predicted in the annual budget, utilizing accurate and up-to-date data. It should be noted that this strategy can benefit individuals at every level in healthcare, not just those managing the finances of the organization. Those working directly with patients may not always be aware of the exact specifications of a healthcare budget, but rolling forecasts result in less dissonance between the practical realities of caring for and managing patients' health and the financial considerations that exist for any organization that wishes to be financially healthy. Even healthcare executives can greatly benefit from the adoption of a rolling forecast; it is predicted that the average executive at a healthcare provider will spend more than a quarter of their time in a work year preparing for and creating an annual budget. With a rolling forecast, much of that time is freed up for other managerial considerations.

Although much of a healthcare provider's capital budget may be outside the purview of all but the most senior executive members of that organization, the specifics and guidelines of the operational budget should be understood by all those concerned with healthcare management. Many of the strategies that can be implemented to meet and/or surpass the expectations and goals of an operational budget can be categorized as a form of resource utilization practice. **Resource utilization**, in its most general form, refers to the accurate understanding and application of medical resources with the goal of reducing waste and/or redundancy. Medical resources can refer to specific supplies, medical equipment, or medical personnel. In this way, efforts to properly store and care for medical equipment and efforts to educate staff on best medical practices can both be seen as resource utilization efforts. Resource utilization can also be used when referring to specific medical procedures or interventions. Efforts to identify the best combination of medications for a particular illness can therefore also be considered resource utilization efforts.

Cost-Benefit Analysis

Cost-benefit analysis is a tool that can be employed by nurse executives to guide decision making. When weighing the cost of an intervention or initiative, a cost-benefit analysis can compare and contrast the financial and operational impacts. Using a systematic method to compare the anticipated costs and expected benefits of a program or policy allows nurse executives to make informed decisions that align with organizational sustainability and patient care goals.

Cost-benefit analyses may be used to assess nurse-staffing ratios, the offering of a new clinical service line, or a change in care delivery. An example would be a nurse practitioner residency, which would incur an upfront cost for the additional staffing to encompass mentorship, orientation, and ongoing training. However, an analysis may reveal that the longer-term benefits of lowering attrition rates, improving patient outcomes, and decreasing the cost of further recruitment would offset the initial expense.

Cost-benefit analysis can also foster transparency in leadership. Nursing executives face the challenge of improving quality while staying fiscally responsible. They must possess the skill to present hard numbers with proof that the enhancement is highly likely to lead to an improvement in quality, monetary benefit,

Business Management

or operational efficiency. A cost-benefit analysis provides a structured process to support decisions, present definitive evidence to stakeholders, and increase the likelihood of buy-in from the executive leadership team.

Resource Utilization

For a more ground-level view of **resource utilization** practices, it can be helpful to consider how such efforts may play out on the scale of a single patient. When it comes to the care of an individual patient, the cornerstone of their treatment plan should always be the efficacy of the interventions selected. The cost of such interventions should not be a deciding factor, and cost should only be taken into consideration as it pertains to delivering the highest quality of care to the patient. As an example, consider a medical condition that has two common courses of treatment with similar levels of efficacy, but one treatment costs significantly less than the other. With such a condition, providing the highest quality care goes hand in hand with reducing costs—choosing the more expensive course of treatment would cost both the healthcare provider and the patient more. In addition, it would generate medical waste while exposing the patient to unnecessary treatments with potentially harmful side effects. Often, the most important way for healthcare professionals to practice proper resource utilization is to ensure that all individuals involved in a patient's treatment plan are fully aware of the exact specifications of that plan and their role in it. Whether a surgical team is reviewing the exact objectives and specifications of a patient's procedure, a nurse is ensuring that a particular medication is properly administered, or a doctor is providing a patient the appropriate outpatient service, any action taken to provide the most effective and efficient treatment options is a form of resource utilization.

The increasing cost of healthcare for both patients and providers has given rise to more in-depth discussion among providers and management about to how to accurately measure the effectiveness and efficiency of the treatment received by their patients. From an operational standpoint, one of the most commonly used metrics to assess efficiency of care is **hours per patient day (HPPD)**. As opposed to many of the metrics used to assess quality of care in healthcare, HPPD is an incredibly easy value to calculate and utilize. In order to calculate HPPD, only two pieces of data need to be gathered. First, one must know the total number of hours that have been worked by the care provider of interest in a 24-hour period. Second, one must know the number of patients at the medical facility of interest for the same 24-hour period. By dividing the number of hours worked by the number of patients, the HPPD value for that healthcare provider is found. As an example, a hospital that has 250 hours of work completed by their nursing staff and 100 patients under their care would have an HPPD value of 2.5.

A practical way to conceptualize HPPD is that it represents how many hours of care, on average, each patient received that day. On its own, an HPPD value can provide a healthcare provider with an image of both the effectiveness and efficiency of its care. Yet, it's important to note that there is no perfect or best HPPD value for a provider to have, and what that value means may be very different across providers. For example, the burn ward of a hospital may consider an HPPD value of 8 to be desirable because they have relatively few patients who require around-the-clock care. However, the emergency room at that same hospital may find it difficult and impractical to aim for an HPPD value of even 1 because they may see thousands of patients in a day. Although it is clearly preferable in most circumstances to have each patient attended to as much as possible, HPPD serves as a reminder of the cost of that care—both the cost to healthcare companies and to their patients. HPPD can therefore be understood as a metric that informs and reminds healthcare providers of this balance between quality of care and cost of the resources, rather than as a grade with a good or bad score.

Staffing Fundamentals

Staffing in nursing can be a complicated process. Staffing refers to the people within an organization and the specific roles that each individual is hired to fulfill. The first thing to consider is the organizational structure of authority with regard to the management of both people and tasks. Someone must be in charge of identifying the tasks that must be done, determining who is available to do those tasks, and delegating authority to the correct individuals. A clear organizational structure is key in ensuring everyone knows who is responsible for each job or task. An organizational chart can be used to clarify who oversees each task and/or individual, which can help avoid any potential misunderstandings.

Authority

Authority refers to who oversees each task and individual person in an organization. There are three basic types of authority: line authority, staff authority, and team authority. **Line authority** refers to the direct line of supervision from supervisors to staff. Line authority usually involves a chain of command, with staff reporting concerns to their immediate supervisor and information continuing up the "chain" as needed until it reaches the person who has the ability and authority to resolve the issue. For example, a question about how to complete a task can likely be resolved by the employee's immediate supervisor, but a request for a raise in pay would likely need to be moved up the "chain" to someone with a higher authority who can make that determination. By establishing a clear chain of command, resolution of potential problems becomes a clear and straightforward process.

Staff authority refers to a management system based on experience, where supervisors have authority over their area of expertise. Employees report to the appropriate supervisor, depending on what type of issue or concern they are having. For example, if an employee has a concern about a patient, they would see the person designated as the nursing supervisor. If the concern is a janitorial issue, the employee would need to talk to the supervisor of the janitorial department. While this type of authority organization can lead to more immediate resolutions to issues, it can become confusing if the staff is not entirely clear about who is actually in charge of a given situation.

The third type of authority structure is **team authority**. This can be a temporary organizational structure established to manage specific tasks, committees, or work groups. Someone may be designated as the supervisor for their particular team or work group, though they may not hold any authority or supervisory duties outside of that group.

Staffing Models

Once the structure of authority is established, the nurse executive needs to determine the staffing needs of the unit or facility. Staffing involves having a sufficient number of qualified people to handle the necessary tasks that must be completed in any given shift. A staffing plan is used to determine the needs of the unit in addition to the personnel required to meet those needs. Staffing plans can be devised to address daily requirements as well as longer-term needs, such as annual staffing requirements.

Business Management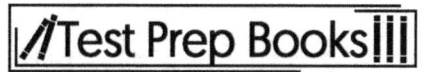

There are three key elements to an effective staffing plan. First, the unit or organization needs a clear statement of philosophy, or the specific values and beliefs that the program seeks to uphold. Next, each department should have clear, specific objectives. Finally, a clearly defined job description for each staffing position must be established, including an understanding of the type of nursing care required for each patient and who is responsible for that care.

One process to consider is the nursing delivery model used by the facility, such as primary nursing, team nursing, modular nursing, or functional nursing. **Primary nursing** involves having the same nurse care for a patient for the duration of the patient's hospital stay. **Team nursing** establishes a collaborative team of different nurses (LPNs, RNs, nursing assistants, etc.) that work together to care for the team's assigned patients. This is also used in **modular nursing**, where the team is assigned to a group of patients within a certain proximity, such as in a given hallway. **Functional nursing** assigns one nurse to handle a specific task for a group of patients. For example, one nurse might be assigned to take vital readings for all of the patients in the unit. Another nurse may be responsible for patient hygiene, while the other oversees administering patient medications. The model used by the facility is key in determining the necessary skills of the nurses and the staffing requirements.

There are three primary nursing staffing models: budget-based, nurse-patient ratio, and patient acuity. No single method is going to be sufficient for any unit or facility. In fact, most use some combination of methods, depending on the needs of the patients, unit, and organization.

Budget-based staffing involves using the number of nursing hours per patient day (HPPD) or another calculation method to determine staffing needs. For example, the number of hours worked in total by all nurses on a unit is equivalent to the nursing hours. The average number of patients in a 24-hour period equals the total patient days. Dividing the nursing hours by the total patient days gives an idea of the needs for any given day and shift. This method does not, however, account for the ebb and flow of needs within a shift or day.

Another common staffing model is the **nurse-patient ratio**, which refers to the number of patients that each nurse is responsible for. There are some state regulations that limit the number of patients under a nurse's care to ensure that they can adequately care for each assigned patient. The more patients a nurse oversees, the less time they can spend with each one. If not managed effectively, this can result in a decrease in the level of care provided.

The nurse-patient ratio model has another drawback, as well. For example, it does not take into consideration the level of care required by any given patient, often referred to as acuity. A nurse who has several high-needs patients will be doing more work than a nurse who is assigned patients needing minimal care. Additionally, if the unit reaches its maximum nurse-patient ratio, it will be unable to accept any new patients. This can result in patients being left in the emergency department for long periods of time while they wait for space to become available on a unit before they can be admitted.

The **patient acuity staffing** model takes into consideration the level of care required by each patient. Under this model, nurses are assigned patients based on the needs of the patient. This model helps to ensure that each nurse has a manageable mix of high-needs patients and lower-needs patients.

No one staffing method works in every given situation, unit, or facility. The mix of skill levels among the staff, referred to as the staffing mix, and the requirements of the patients must be considered. Any changes in these factors may result in the need to change the staffing method, either temporarily or

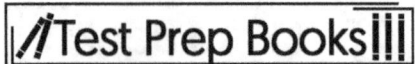

Business Management

permanently. Each nursing executive must work to determine which staffing model, or combination of models, is most appropriate to meet their needs.

Staffing Methods

There are three primary methods of staffing a unit or department. The **fixed staffing** method involves determining the maximum workload and staffing for that load. A **variable staffing** method involves staffing the unit below the maximum and then adjusting the staffing as needed during higher capacity times. The third method, the **semiflexible method**, maintains a 10-15% fixed staff, and the rest are adjusted on an as-needed basis.

Several key factors must be taken into consideration when developing a staffing plan. Daily tasks include consideration of how many patients are in the unit and the level of care they will require; the skill level, qualifications, and availability of the nursing staff; and the level of supervision that will be required. On an ongoing basis, the nurse executive must not only be familiar with the department's current needs, but also anticipate any future requirements to staff the unit efficiently and effectively.

Scheduling

Once the staffing needs are addressed, the nurse executive must determine how to best schedule the staff to meet the needs of the patients via a scheduling plan. There are four primary types of scheduling systems in health care: centralized scheduling, decentralized scheduling, mixed scheduling, and self-scheduling.

Centralized scheduling is done by higher-level management for staff in all departments. The benefit of this type of scheduling is that it is usually impartial and fair to all employees. It is also an effective way to manage resources because management can see the bigger picture for the whole facility. It also tends to be computerized, making it more cost-effective, and relieves managers of the burden of scheduling for their units or departments. The primary complaint about this type of scheduling system, however, is its lack of personalization. Employees who have unique scheduling requests or needs sometimes find it difficult to get these requests handled quickly and reliably.

Decentralized scheduling puts the schedules in the hands of each manager, who then becomes responsible for staffing their own department. This is a simplified and more personal system of scheduling since each manager can address the individual needs of their department and staff members. This method also helps managers more readily see and correct staffing problems within their departments. One of the disadvantages of this system is that it is more susceptible to favoritism and unfair staffing practices. In addition, managers must use their time scheduling rather than seeing to other duties, which is a less effective and more costly use of personnel resources.

Mixed scheduling is a combination of centralized and decentralized scheduling. Managers handle the scheduling of their individual units or departments, but any problems that arise, such as open shifts that the manager is unable to fill, are handled by upper management.

The fourth method of scheduling is **self-scheduling**. This method involves the nursing staff signing up for work shifts of their preference. This method can save the managers the time involved in scheduling while also meeting their individual needs of their nursing staff. Advantages of self-scheduling include increased team camaraderie, feelings of autonomy, job satisfaction, and morale. This system also drastically reduces absenteeism. The primary disadvantage to this method is that the staff may not create an adequate mix of skill levels for each shift on their own and/or they may not adequately cover

Business Management

each shift. It still remains the manager's responsibility to ensure that the unit is fully and appropriately staffed for each shift.

Work Shifts

Part of determining the scheduling for a department or unit is deciding what types of shifts the staff will work. Shifts can vary by the number of hours per shift, days per week, and times of day. Shifts are usually eight, ten, or twelve hours and five, four, or three days per week, respectively.

Once the hourly shift is determined, the days must also be assigned. A rotating, or alternating, pattern follows a predetermined schedule, such as rotating weekends or rotating day and night shifts. These types of shifts are usually done in blocks, such as rotating from day to night shift every three weeks.

A fixed, or permanent, shift schedule means that each person works set shifts, such as having a staff on day shift and a staff on night shift. There are several advantages to permanent shift scheduling. The staff knows exactly what shifts they are working each week and can plan accordingly, resulting in more reliable time off and fewer absences. This type of scheduling can have some disadvantages, however, such as creating a sense of "us" versus "them" between those working different shifts, which can divide the unit and create a negative working environment.

Scheduling can also be done in a cyclical or block pattern. This type of schedule is fixed in that the same schedule is repeated, usually every six weeks. This type of schedule allows staff to plan other aspects of their life ahead of time because they know their schedule far in advance, which reduces absenteeism.

Sometimes staffing schedules need to be varied to meet the changing needs of the patients and the workload of the unit. Staff can be moved from one department to another temporarily to meet increased needs. However, this can disrupt the work the staff is doing in their regular department, create feelings of insecurity, and lead to job dissatisfaction. Another option is to create a system where two units, floors, or departments work together and assist one another as needs vary. Floating nurses can also help to fill in as the need arises. However, floating nurses must be well educated on many different types of care and patient needs in order to be effective, and they can sometimes dislike the instability of such variable work assignments. Full-time regular staff can sometimes be called upon to work extra shifts as the need arises, but this often results in overtime costs and exhaustion for the nurse. Other options to meet changing staffing needs include part-time nurses or temporary staff.

Practice Quiz

1. In reading through annual performance reviews, a leader at a healthcare provider notices that many employees report feeling dissatisfied with their job and unmotivated by the work they do on a regular basis. What style of leadership might the leader find most helpful in amending such an issue?
    a. Democratic leadership style
    b. Laissez-faire leadership style
    c. Situational leadership style
    d. Transformational leadership style

2. A nurse follows up with a patient after their treatment has finished, ensuring that the patient is familiar with low-cost outpatient treatment options. Which of the following principles of proper healthcare management is that nurse using?
    a. Idealized influence
    b. Resource utilization
    c. Overprovision
    d. Permanent care maintenance

3. Which of the following types of budgets usually takes the most resources and time to make?
    a. Operational budget
    b. Capital budget
    c. Annual budget
    d. Rolling forecast budget

4. Which of the following types of budgets would undergo the largest change during a nurses' strike?
    a. Operational budget
    b. Capital budget
    c. Annual budget
    d. Rolling forecast budget

5. Which of the following budgetary concerns would NOT fall under the purview of the capital budget?
    a. The cost of hospital beds for a new ward
    b. The cost of state-of-the-art MRI technology for a new ward
    c. The cost of labor for staffing a new ward
    d. The cost of the building materials needed for a new ward

See answers on the next page.

Answer Explanations

1. D: The style of leadership most often associated with motivating team members and improving their work satisfaction is transformational leadership style. Unlike other styles of leadership, transformational leadership style has as its central concept the idea that team members work best and hardest when they feel the internal motivation to do so. Therefore, the correct answer is Choice *D*. The other answer choices refer to styles of leadership that are not known to be particularly effective at motivating team members or helping them find satisfaction in their work.

2. B: By following up with a patient after their treatment has ended and suggesting further outpatient treatment options, the nurse is ensuring that that patient is offered the most effective and cost-efficient care available. Such efforts are an example of proper resource utilization. Consequently, the correct answer is Choice *B*. Choice *A* is incorrect because such a method can only be practiced between a leader and their team member, not between patient and provider. Choice *C* is incorrect because by offering the patient low-cost treatments, the nurse is in no way contributing to the phenomenon of overprovision. Choice *D* is incorrect because it is not a widely used or known term in the healthcare industry.

3. C: Annual budgets, as the name implies, are budgets made by healthcare providers at the beginning of each financial year. Such budgets are usually designed to serve as predictions for the financial health of the organization over the next year as well as recommended guidelines to reach certain goals. As a result, annual budgets are usually incredibly resource- and time-intensive to make, requiring hundreds of hours of work on average to complete. Therefore, the correct answer is Choice *C*. Although the other answer choices refer to different types of budgets that would also certainly require lots of resources and time, none of them are as resource- or time-intensive as an annual budget.

4. A: Operational budgets are used to calculate and manage the day-to-day expenditures that are a part of any healthcare provider. One of the largest types of these expenditures is the costs associated with properly paying and rewarding employees. During a nurses' strike, the drop in the number of nurses working would result in much less money spent on staffing. Therefore, the correct answer is Choice *A*. Although the other answer choices refer to budgets that would undergo changes during a nurses' strike, none of them are so significantly tied up in the cost of labor as the operational budget.

5. C: Capital budgets are used to assess cost and potential return on investment for durable goods, such as patient beds, pieces of equipment, and new hospital wings. Capital budgets are not used to assess costs associated with staffing; that would fall under the purview of an operational budget. Therefore, the correct answer is Choice *C*. All of the other answer choices refer to budgetary concerns that would fall under the purview of the capital budget.

Health Care Delivery

Knowledge

ANA Code of Ethics

Advocacy

The American Nurses Association (ANA) provides this definition of nursing practice:

> "The protection, promotion, and optimization of health and abilities; prevention of illness and injury; facilitation of healing; alleviation of suffering through the diagnosis and treatment of human response; and advocacy in the care of individuals, families, communities, and populations."

The ANA also addresses the importance of advocacy in its Code of Ethics, specifically in Provision 3:

> "The nurse promotes, advocates for, and protects the rights, health, and safety of the patient."

The ANA Code of Ethics further states that nurses must advocate

> "with compassion and respect for the inherent dignity, worth, and uniqueness of every individual, unrestricted by considerations of social or economic status, personal attributes, or the nature of health problems. "

Advocacy is a key component of nursing practice. An **advocate** is one who pleads the cause of another; a nurse is an advocate for patient rights. Preserving human dignity, patient equality, and freedom from suffering are the basis of nursing advocacy. Nurses hold a significant role that gives them the opportunity to care for patients in every way: meeting their needs, addressing concerns, and working to achieve positive outcomes. Additionally, they aid in communicating with physicians and serve as a guide through the complexities of the medical system. Nurses educate the patient about tests and procedures, while maintaining awareness of how culture and ethnicity affect the patient's experience. Throughout the process, nurses strictly adhere to all privacy laws.

Advocacy is the promotion of the common good, especially as it applies to at-risk populations. It involves speaking out in support of policies and decisions that affect the lives of individuals who do not otherwise have a voice. Nurses meet this standard of practice by actively participating in the politics of healthcare accessibility and delivery. They are educationally and professionally prepared to evaluate and comment on the needs of patients at the local, state, and national level. This participation requires an understanding of the legislative process, the ability to negotiate with public officials, and a willingness to provide expert testimony in support of policy decisions. The advocacy role of nurses has the potential to address the needs of the individual patient, society, and members of the nursing profession.

In clinical practice, nurses represent the patient's interests through active participation in the development of the plan of care and subsequent care decisions. Advocacy, in this sense, is related to patient autonomy and the patient's right to informed consent and self-determination. Nurses provide the appropriate information, assess the patient's comprehension of the implications of the care decisions, and act as patient advocates by supporting the patient's decisions. In the critical care environment, patient advocacy requires the nurse to represent the patient's decisions even though those decisions may be opposed to those of the healthcare providers and family members.

Professionally, nurses advocate for policies that support and promote the practice of all nurses regarding access to education, role identity, workplace conditions, and compensation. The responsibility for **professional advocacy** requires nurses to provide leadership in the development of the professional nursing role in all practice settings that may include acute care facilities, colleges and universities, or community agencies. Leadership roles in acute care settings involve participation in professional practice and shared governance committees, providing support for basic nursing education by facilitating clinical and preceptorship experiences, and mentoring novice graduate nurses to the professional nursing role. In the academic setting, nurses work to ensure the diversity of the student population by participating in the governance structure of the institution, conducting and publishing research that supports the positive impact of professional nursing care on patient outcomes, and serving as an advocate to individual nursing students to promote their academic success. In the community, nurses may collaborate with government officials to meet the needs that are specific to that location.

The nurse must function as a moral agent. This means that the nurse must be morally accountable and responsible for personal judgment and actions. Nurses who practice with moral integrity possess a strong sense of themselves and act in ways consistent with what they understand is the right thing to do. **Moral agency** is defined as the ability to identify right and wrong actions based on widely accepted moral criteria. The performance of nurses as moral agents is dependent on life experiences, advanced education, and clinical experience in healthcare agencies. Moral agency can often be difficult to decipher when managing complex patient situations. When ethical dilemmas arise, such as handling end-of-life and refusal of treatment cases, the care team must work together to make the best care decisions possible with the patient in mind.

The role of moral agent requires nurses to have a strong sense of self and a clear understanding of the definition of right and wrong; however, nurses must also be aware that these perceptions of right and wrong will be challenged every day. The nurse can expect to encounter difficult situations where the moral action related to the patient's right to self-determination is opposed to the moral action with respect to competent patient care.

ANA Nursing Administration Scope and Standards of Practice

There are six standards of Nursing Administration Practice outlined by the American Nurses Association: assessment; identifying issues, problems, or trends; outcomes identification; planning; implementation; and evaluation. These standards are a **framework** for nurse administrators to successfully perform their roles and responsibilities. They help guide nurse administrators to deliver high-quality, safe, patient-centered care, while simultaneously maintaining organizational compliance and success.

Below is an outline of each step in the process.

- *Assessment:* The nurse administrator must gather extensive data pertaining to an issue or situation and consider all aspects available to them to identify areas of improvement. This includes reviewing existing policies and procedures related to the issue as well as surveillance data. Any data collected will be called baseline data.

- *Identifies issues, problems, or trends*: Once the nurse administrator gathers information regarding the issue or situation, this data needs to be analyzed. Critical analysis of the data allows for the identification of problems, issues, or trends that are occurring within the healthcare organization. Methods of data analysis may include root cause analysis, statistical analysis, qualitative analysis, comparative analysis, or data visualization through graphs and charts. Nurse administrators may also seek input from primary and secondary stakeholders.

- *Outcomes identification:* After the issues and trends have been identified through careful analysis, the nurse administrator should determine the desired outcomes that would be anticipated following the implementation of a plan. The nurse administrator should consider creating a SMART goal (Specific, Measurable, Achievable, Relevant, and Time-bound) at this stage. Working in partnership with stakeholders—including frontline staff, organization leaders, and patients—is also helpful in identifying desired outcomes.

- *Planning:* At this point, the nurse administrator designs a plan that outlines strategies and interventions to achieve the expected outcomes. The planning stage involves developing a comprehensive and strategic plan that identifies the strategies, interventions, and resources necessary to achieve the desired outcomes. During this stage, the nurse administrator determines the timeline, allocates resources, sets priorities, and engages stakeholders. Successful planning allows for the optimization of resource utilization, fosters collaboration, and promotes organizational efficiency.

- *Implementation*: This is the stage where the nurse administrator implements the plan that has been identified, which occurs in several stages. This includes coordination of care; health promotion, health teaching, and education; and consultation. In the first step of the process, the nurse administrator is responsible for exercising leadership in facilitating the coordination of multidisciplinary healthcare resources. In the second step, the nurse administrator utilizes strategies to promote health through teaching and the allocation of additional educational services or resources. The final step of the implementation process is consultation. In this stage, the nurse administrator is responsible for offering consultation to shape the identified plan, strengthen the capabilities of others, and drive meaningful change.

- *Evaluation*: Once the plan has been implemented, the nurse administrator will assess the progress made in achieving the desired and expected outcomes. This includes data analysis, comparison with baseline data, receiving stakeholder feedback, identifying barriers and success factors, and initiating continuous improvement.

Below is an example of the process in practice.

- *Assessment:* The nurse administrator is running an assessment of the healthcare facility's infection control practices. First, the nurse administrator reviews the organization's policies and procedures on infection control practices. Next, the nurse administrator reviews surveillance data and environmental observations related to healthcare-associated infections. Additional items to review include staff or patient interviews and surveys.

- *Identifying issues, problems, or trends:* During the assessment, the nurse administrator identifies an alarming trend of increasing healthcare-associated infections. Specifically, data analysis reveals an increase in central line-associated bloodstream infections (CLABSIs) within the facility. At this point, the nurse administrator determines that infection prevention and control measures need to be improved.

- *Outcomes identification:* The nurse administrator identifies the expected and desired outcome. In this case, after collaboration with the interdisciplinary healthcare team, the nurse administrator identifies a specific and measurable goal: to reduce the incidence of CLABSIs by 50% within six months by implementing evidence-based infection control practices.

- *Planning:* The nurse administrator now develops a plan to address the issue at hand. This includes improving hand hygiene compliance rates, conducting staff education on infection prevention and control, and enhancing surveillance and reporting systems. A hand hygiene campaign is created to raise awareness and highlight the importance of proper hand hygiene among staff. Implementing random and regular observations of hand hygiene practices and providing feedback to healthcare workers allows for increased compliance rates. The nurse administrator also designs and implements a comprehensive education program on infection prevention and control, highlighting CLABSI prevention. This includes providing training sessions, workshops, and online modules to facilitate staff learning.

- *Implementation:* The nurse administrator will oversee the implementation of the plan. In terms of coordination of care, the nurse administrator is responsible for the effective coordination between various departments within the healthcare facility and their implementation of infection control strategies. These various departments can include nursing, infection control, and quality improvement. When it comes to health promotion, health teaching, and education, the nurse administrator will conduct training sessions for healthcare personnel to increase their knowledge and skills in infection control practices and prevention. The nurse administrator will also develop and disperse educational resources and materials for patients and families. This will encourage compliance with infection control measures by increasing understanding of the importance of this initiative. The final step in the implementation process is consultation. Here, the nurse administrator provides consultation and guidance to interdisciplinary teams and leaders on best practices for preventing CLABSIs. The nurse administrator will also address any concerns that arise and offer recommendations for improvement.

- *Evaluation:* At this stage, the nurse administrator will evaluate the effectiveness of the implemented plan and measure the progress toward reducing CLABSIs. The nurse administrator will evaluate the effectiveness by analyzing data on infection rates and other relevant metrics to determine if they have achieved the desired outcome of reducing CLABSIs by 50% within the designated time frame of six months. The nurse administrator may refine the plan and interventions as needed to further improve outcomes or continue with the plan depending on the evaluation findings.

Regulatory and Compliance Standards

Nurse administrators have an important role when it comes to the implementation and delivery of safe, high-quality care and maintaining **regulatory compliance** within their organizations. In order to achieve these responsibilities, nurse administrators must have a thorough understanding of the regulatory and compliance standards that govern healthcare practices. These standards are in place to protect patients and staff as well as maintain the integrity of an organization. Nurse administrators must abide by these standards as they navigate the complex landscape of healthcare administration. Regulatory and compliance standards include licensing and accreditation, federal regulations, quality and patient safety standards, ethical guidelines, infection control, professional practice standards, and medication safety and management.

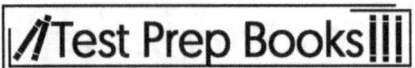

Licensing and Accreditation

One crucial area that nurse administrators must focus on is **licensing** and **accreditation**. Healthcare organizations are required to obtain and maintain appropriate licenses and accreditations to function. It is the responsibility of nurse administrators to ensure that their facilities are meeting the requirements set forth by regulatory bodies, including state health departments. Some of these requirements include adherence to professional practice guidelines, staffing ratios, and safety standards within the facility. Since requirements are ever-changing, nurse administrators must stay up-to-date on such requirements to maintain organizational and corporate compliance.

Federal Regulations

Nurse administrators are responsible for staying informed and updated on federal regulations that control healthcare practices. One example of this is the Health Insurance Portability and Accountability Act (HIPAA). This is a federal law that provides standards for the protection and privacy of patient health information. The primary goal of HIPAA is to ensure patient confidentiality and avoid unauthorized access or misuse of health data. Under HIPAA, a patient's information is required to be protected and kept confidential regardless of the form. Nurse administrators should enforce and maintain institutional compliance with HIPAA laws.

Nurse administrators are also responsible for complying with federal regulations and regulations set forth by federal agencies, such as the Occupational Safety and Health Administration (OSHA). OSHA is a federal agency that ensures safe and healthy working environments for employees via workplace regulations. The main goal of OSHA is to prevent work-related illnesses or injuries. In summary, the nurse administrator serves as the bridge between patient care and legal regulations.

Quality and Patient Safety Standards

Nurse administrators must maintain the highest quality standards for patient safety within their healthcare organization, including implementation of **quality improvement** practices. They should also follow quality standards that are set forth by organizations, such as the **National Committee for Quality Assurance (NCQA)**. Standards outlined by this organization include patient-centered care, evidence-based practice, and patient safety. When nurse administrators have robust quality improvement programs in place, data can be analyzed to identify areas of improvement or concern. Overall, these actions help meet quality and safety goals or standards.

Emergency Medical Treatment and Labor Act

The Emergency Medical Treatment and Labor Act is a federal law that was enacted in 1986 to provide the American public with the assurance that emergency services would be provided regardless of the ability to pay. It is also referred to as the "anti-dumping" law and was enacted due to a trend of hospitals refusing to treat patients who either did not have full insurance coverage or were not insured. Under this law, hospitals are barred from refusing to treat patients with emergent conditions or from transferring the patient to another healthcare facility without first stabilizing them.

Any hospital that participates in Medicare or operates an emergency department is legally bound to offer a medical screening exemption to any individual who presents to an emergency department and requests treatment. The screening is mandated whether there is an evident emergency medical condition or not. When an emergency medical condition is identified, the hospital is obligated to provide stabilizing treatment if possible or to transfer the patient to another facility that does offer the required medical treatment. There are strict rules and regulations surrounding the conditions and requirements for a safe transfer.

Health Care Delivery

This law also has a provision for pregnant women in active labor. The medical facility must provide the care necessary until either a safe transfer is available or the baby is delivered. Infractions of this law can result in costly fines, removal from participating in Medicaid and Medicare programs, and loss of accreditation or licensing for both the medical facility and the healthcare providers involved.

Ethical Guidelines

Ethics play an important role in decision-making in the healthcare field. Nurse administrators bear the responsibility of complying with ethical principles and guidelines that have been established by organizations, such as the American Nurses Association (ANA). The ANA has written the Code of Ethics, highlighting principles and standards to guide nursing practices that nurse administrators should follow. The Code of Ethics ensures patient advocacy, rights, and dignity. Nurse administrators are the leaders in demonstrating and maintaining **ethical decision-making**. When ethical dilemmas arise, they must handle such dilemmas promptly and appropriately, referring to ethical laws. They must also educate their staff on ethical principles and maintain their implementation in nursing practice.

Infection Control

Infection control is arguably one of the most important concepts in healthcare. Nurse administrators are obligated to ensure compliance with infection control standards within their organizations. They can do so by staying up-to-date with guidelines and procedures set forth by health organizations, such as the **Centers for Disease Control (CDC)** and World Health Organization (WHO). They must also enforce guidelines and procedures outlined by these organizations in their facilities. Another responsibility of the nurse administrator includes infection prevention, which can be accomplished through staff education via online modules or professional development days. The nurse administrator can also utilize surveillance methods to monitor healthcare-associated infections within the organization. Additionally, nurse managers may utilize random monitoring of staff infection control methods, such as hand hygiene practices.

Professional Practice Standards

Maintaining professional practice standards is another important role of the nurse administrator. They must follow standards that have been set forth by professional nursing bodies, such as the ANA. One way that nurse administrators can achieve this goal is through participating in **professional development** opportunities alongside their staff. They can also maintain professional practice standards by providing skill competency sessions and continuing education opportunities. Each of these components promote and facilitate quality nursing care delivery.

Medication Safety and Management

Patient well-being is closely aligned with nurse executive safe medication practices. Nurse administrators are responsible for facilitating **medication safety** within their respective healthcare organizations. To do so, they must abide by medication management standards. Examples of such standards include proper medication storage and handling, appropriate reconciliation processes, education on safe administration practices, and correct medication administration. Another component nurse managers are accountable for is monitoring and addressing medication-related incidents and enacting strategies to prevent and reduce medication errors.

Health Care Delivery

Emergency Preparedness

In the event of a **medical emergency**, there are specific steps to take depending on the situation. There will be written policies for these types of emergencies in the workplace that are used for patients, staff, and/or visitors. Below are some examples of medical emergencies:

- Choking
- Unresponsive or unconscious person
- Excessive bleeding
- Head injury
- Broken bones
- Severe burns
- Seizures
- Chest pain
- Difficulty breathing
- Allergic reactions that cause swelling and/or breathing difficulties
- Inhalation or swallowing of a toxic substance
- Accidental poisoning

Choking

If someone is **choking**, the victim will most likely grab at their throat, or they may have a cough that eventually stops, indicating blockage of the airway. If the airway is blocked, they will need the Heimlich maneuver to be performed immediately. Oftentimes people cough and may leave the room to get a drink or to avoid disrupting others. It is best to follow that person to ensure they are not choking.

When someone is choking and conscious, the responder, or person at the scene who witnesses and intervenes, should:

- Ask the victim if they are choking and tell them help is here.
- Assist the victim to a standing position.
- Stand behind the victim and wrap the arms around the victim's waist.
- Make a fist with one hand and place the thumb against the victim's stomach just above their belly button.
- Place the other hand on top of the fisted hand.
- Thrust quick, hard, and upward on the victim's stomach.
- Continue this until the food or object comes out of the victim's mouth.
- Do not swipe the victim's mouth with one finger, as this could push the blockage further down the airway.

Health Care Delivery

If the victim is still choking and goes unconscious:

- Lower the victim to the floor, shout for help, and have someone call 911.
- Begin cardiopulmonary resuscitation (CPR) by following the basic life support steps until emergency medical services (EMS) arrives.

Unconsciousness or Unresponsiveness

If someone is **unconscious**, first try to arouse the person by shaking or tapping them. If they are indeed unresponsive, call for help, have someone call 911, and proceed to:

- Make sure the patient is lying flat and place a backboard under them for CPR.
- Follow basic life support (BLS) protocol.
- Look and listen for breathing by watching for chest rise.
- Check for a pulse in the radial artery, which is located on the volar surface of the wrist.
- If there is a pulse but no breathing, begin rescue breaths. Give one breath every 5 or 6 seconds. Check pulse every 2 minutes.
- If no pulse, begin CPR and continue until EMS arrives. Direct someone else to get the automated external defibrillator (AED) as CPR is continued.
    - CPR: 30 chest compressions then 2 breaths, repeat for 2-minute cycles.
    - Chest compressions should be firm and deep at a rate of about 100 to 120 beats per minute for an adult. This ensures adequate perfusion of organs since the heart is not pumping on its own.
- When the AED arrives, turn it on and follow the prompts for use.

If the patient recovers, turn them onto their left side and continue to monitor them until EMS arrives. Healthcare workers will be trained and certified in BLS, including AED use.

Excessive Bleeding

For **excessive bleeding**, call for help and call 911. Then:

- Have the patient sit down or lie down.
- Use a towel or shirt to hold continuous pressure on the bleeding area.
- Elevate the area above their heart. For example, if the leg is bleeding, have the patient lie down and put their leg on a chair.
- Talk to the patient and monitor their responsiveness.
- Stay with them until EMS arrives.

Head Injury

Concussions, contusions, and skull fractures are all common types of traumatic brain injuries. **Concussions** occur when the brain is jarred against the skull, usually during sports, hard contact with another person, or hitting the head on the ground. Concussions can cause mental confusion and lead to disruptions in normal brain functioning. The effects of a concussion can show up immediately, or they

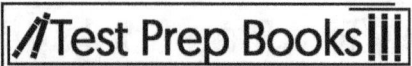

may not show up for hours or days. Although uncommon, concussions can cause a loss of consciousness; in this case, it is important to note the length of time this occurs along with other associated symptoms of the event.

Another type of traumatic brain injury is a **contusion**, which is a bruise on the brain. This bruise can swell in the brain and cause a **hematoma**, or bleeding in the brain. A skull fracture is a break in the skull bone and can occur with or without brain damage.

The following list includes symptoms of traumatic brain injuries:

- Confusion
- Depression
- Dizziness or balance problems
- Foggy feeling
- Double vision or changes in vision
- Tiredness
- Headache
- Memory loss
- Nausea
- Sensitivity to light
- Trouble remembering and concentrating

If a patient has a known head injury, or they stated that they hit their head, stay with the patient and call for a supervisor. Monitor the patient for mild symptoms from the list above. Even if the symptoms are not initially concerning, the patient may require a visit from the physician. If the patient is elderly or has other serious health issues, hospitalization may be required to rule out more serious consequences from the head injury.

Health Care Delivery

The pie chart below depicts the leading causes of traumatic brain injury, with falls being the most common.

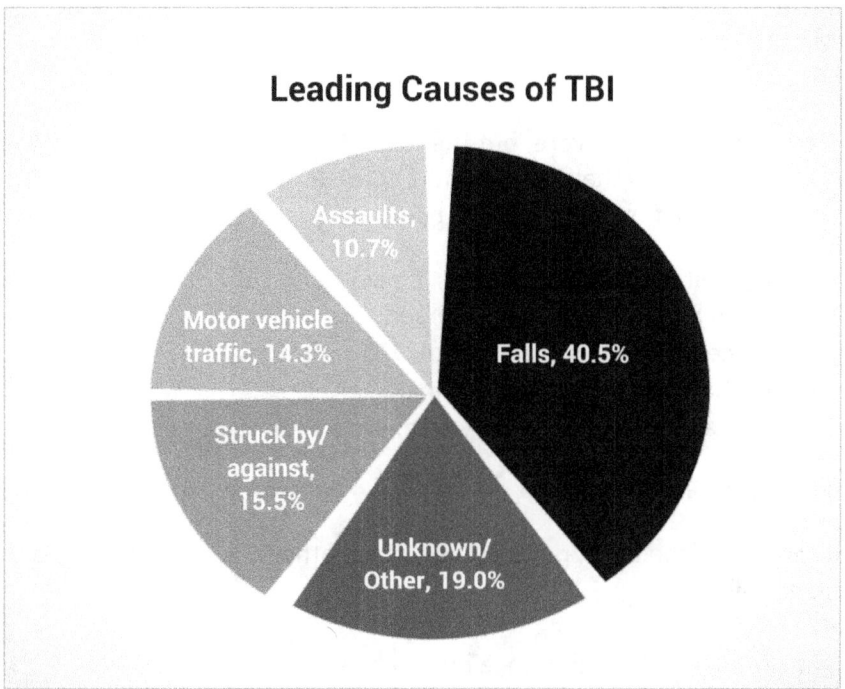

Symptoms of a head injury that are more serious and require immediate emergency treatment include:

- Unequal pupils
- Convulsions
- Fracture of the skull or face
- Inability to move legs or arms
- Clear or bloody fluid coming from the ears, nose, or mouth
- Loss of consciousness
- Persistent vomiting
- Severe headache
- Slurred speech and distorted vision
- Restlessness and irritability

If any of the above symptoms appear after a head injury, call for help and call 911.

Broken Bones (Compound Fractures)

A **compound fracture** is a fracture in which the bone is protruding through the skin. Other symptoms include pain, swelling, deformity in the fractured area, and bruising. This is the most serious type of fracture and requires immediate attention. The following comprises first aid for fractures:

- Call for help and call 911, especially if a fracture in the head, back, or neck is suspected.
- Don't move the patient unless they are in danger of further injury.
- Keep the injured area still and stay with the patient.
- Treat any bleeding by holding pressure with a towel or gauze.

- Look for signs of shock in the patient, such as shallow, fast breathing or feeling faint. Lay them down with their feet elevated.
- Wrap ice packs in a towel and ice the injured area.
- Wait for EMS to arrive.

Burns

Burn injuries can range from mild to severe, but the initial treatment for all burns is the same. First-degree burns affect the top layer of the skin, second-degree burns affect two layers, and third-degree burns affect all three layers. Call for an emergency response if:

- The burn is through all the skin layers.
- The burn is severe in an infant or elderly person.
- The hands, feet, face, or genitals are burned.
- The burn is larger than two inches or is oozing.
- The burn is charred and leathery, or has white, brown, or black patches.

Initial treatment for all burns includes:

- Remove the source of the burn: put out the fire, smother the burning area, or have the person stop, drop, and roll.
- Remove any hot or burned clothing.
- Remove tight clothing and jewelry since burns can swell very quickly.
- Hold the burned area under cool, running water for 20 minutes.
    - Use two cold cloths if running water is not available. Alternate holding them on the area every 2 minutes.
- Do not put ice on the burn.
- Keep the patient warm by covering the rest of the body.
- Wrap or cover the burn loosely with gauze, or a use a sheet for large areas.
- If EMS has been called, stay with the patient and keep them warm until help arrives.

Seizures

Seizures are categorized according to type, presenting symptoms, and severity. Some symptoms include jerking motions, shaking, unconsciousness, stiffness, and blank staring. If someone is having a violent seizure, follow these steps:

- Protect the victim's head by moving hard objects out of the way and placing a blanket under their head.

- Loosen clothing around their neck.

- Do not try to hold them down or put anything in their mouth.

- Get help to control bystanders so that the victim has some space.

- When the seizure is over, have the victim lie on their side and make sure their airway is open.

Health Care Delivery

- Call 911 if the seizure lasts more than five minutes, if the victim has other medical conditions, or if the person has never had a seizure before.

- People with known epilepsy may have seizures that are short and frequent, so calling 911 may not be necessary.

Chest Pain

Chest pain can be a symptom of a heart attack or other serious heart or lung condition. Prompt attention is necessary so that the person can be treated before serious heart damage or death occurs. Chest pain can also be a result of a lung infection, excessive coughing, broken ribs from an injury, anxiety, indigestion, or muscular injury. If the patient has not fallen or does not have any outward physical signs of injury to the chest area, assume that the chest pain is cardiac related.

When someone complains of chest pain, do the following:

- Have the person sit down and ask them where the pain is located.

- Assess if they have any injuries on or near their chest.

- Call for help and call 911 if the pain lasts more than a few minutes or they have the following symptoms:
    - Pain in the arms, shoulders, back and chest
    - Difficulty breathing
    - Fatigue
    - Nausea
    - Sweating
    - Dizziness

- If there is oxygen available, a respiratory therapist or nurse will place a nasal cannula in their nose and give between two and four liters of oxygen.

- If available and the person is not allergic or taking any blood thinner medication, the nurse will have the person chew a regular-strength aspirin. Aspirin helps the blood flow to the heart and chewing the medication allows it to get into the bloodstream faster.

- Stay with the person until EMS arrives.

- If the person becomes unconscious, follow BLS guidelines and initiate CPR.

Difficulty Breathing

Breathing difficulties or **shortness of breath** can be caused by many factors, such as asthma, bronchitis, pneumonia, heart conditions, pulmonary embolism, anxiety, or exercise. People may occasionally have shortness of breath because of an underlying condition that is being monitored by a physician. They may take medication for this symptom and be able to continue to live relatively normal lives. However, if a person has sudden difficulty catching their breath, and it is not relieved with rest, change of position, or their inhaler medication, immediate attention is required.

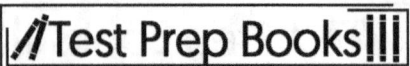

Health Care Delivery

Do the following if a person begins to struggle with breathing:

- Call for help and have the person sit up in their chair or in their bed.
- Instruct the person to try to take slow breaths, inhaling though their nose and exhaling out of their mouth.
- Continue to talk to them reassuringly and soothingly. Anxiety can make breathing even more difficult.
- If their breathing becomes easier and they seem to calm down, have a physician see them as soon as possible, especially if this is something new for this person.
- If breathing continues to be difficult, call for help and call 911.
- Place oxygen on the patient with a mask or nasal cannula, if available.
- Stay with the patient until help arrives and monitor their level of consciousness and breathing rate.

Allergic Reactions

Allergies can cause many symptoms and range in severity from mild to severe. Some examples of mild symptoms might include itching, erythema, hives, sneezing, runny nose, and itchy eyes. Wheezing may occur and may be treated with a prescribed inhaler. Life-threatening allergic reactions include swelling of the tongue or throat, difficulty breathing, and anaphylaxis, which is a systemic reaction. **Anaphylaxis** is rare but can lead to death if it is not recognized and treated quickly. Allergies to foods, medications, latex, and insect bites can cause anaphylaxis. Individuals with serious allergic reactions should always carry an epinephrine pen, or "epi-pen," to be administered in case of a reaction. Call for help and call 911 if the following symptoms associated with anaphylaxis are observed:

- Difficulty breathing
- Swollen tongue or throat tightness
- Wheezing
- Nausea and vomiting
- Fainting or dizziness
- Low blood pressure
- Rapid heart rate
- Feeling strange or sense of impending doom
- Chest pain

Call 911 even if an epi-pen has been administered for the allergic reaction. Reaction symptoms can continue to occur or can reoccur later.

Poisoning

Poisoning can occur due to something eaten, inhaled, or absorbed in excess, as well as exposure to toxic substances. This type of emergency can happen to patients and employees. If there is an accidental poisoning and the person is awake and alert, call the Poison Control hotline at 1-800-222-1222. Stay on the phone with poison control and stay with the victim. Try to have the following information available for the responders:

Health Care Delivery

- Weight and age of the victim
- The label or bottle of the substance taken
- The time of exposure to the substance and time elapsed since
- The address of where the victim is located

If the person goes unconscious or is not breathing, call 911.

Many chemical labels, such as cleaning supplies, have warning labels and instructions for dealing with toxic exposure. The eyes may need to be flushed with water, for example. Read labels, consult available resources, and call for help when needed. In healthcare facilities, protocols for chemical spills or exposures exist so that clean up and injury can be handled quickly. Always follow the policy provided by the facility or workplace.

Unexpected Response to Therapies

There are a vast multitude of unexpected responses that may occur during a patient's therapy. With every desired effect, there are many undesired effects that may develop. The nurse works with the healthcare team to prevent, watch for, and treat unexpected patient responses right away.

One of the most dangerous complications for a woman who has just given birth is a **postpartum hemorrhage**. This occurs when the uterus continues to bleed excessively, losing more than 500 milliliters of blood after the baby has been delivered. An accompanying signal of postpartum hemorrhage is a drop in the hematocrit by more than ten percentage points. A postpartum hemorrhage may be primary, occurring shortly after childbirth, or secondary, occurring between twenty-four hours to twelve weeks postpartum. Postpartum hemorrhage arises from many different causes, including abnormal uterine contractility, placental complications, injury due to caesarean section or uterine rupture, or congenital coagulation disorders.

The nurse assesses the mother for potential postpartum hemorrhage by taking vital signs, massaging the uterine fundus, and preventing bladder distention by encouraging the mother to empty her bladder regularly. Heart rate and blood pressure readings provide measures of hemodynamic stability. Massage of the uterine fundus encourages continued uterine contractions and prevents bleeding associated with a boggy fundus. Boggy means that the uterus is soft, as opposed to the firmness of a contracted muscle. Bladder distention can cause a displacement of the woman's uterus, which can interfere with proper contractions and increase the risk for hemorrhage.

A patient receiving total parenteral nutrition (TPN) is at risk for the unexpected development of a **pneumothorax**. When the physician is inserting the catheter that will deliver the TPN, there is a potential for the catheter to enter the pleural space, causing air, fluids, or blood to leak into the pleural cavity. The potential development of pneumothorax, hemothorax, and hydrothorax is one of many reasons why checking the placement of lines in patients is a crucial first step to take before using them.

Maintaining **sterile technique** when placing central lines, dialysis catheters, and other invasive devices into patients is critical. The nurse, as part of the healthcare team, works to prevent patient infection by ensuring that proper sterile technique is observed during sterile procedures. The nurse also supervises the process of disposing sharps, such as needles, into the proper receptacle in each patient's room. **Needlesticks** from contaminated syringes can spread bloodborne infections such as HIV/AIDS, hepatitis B, and hepatitis C.

Emergency Response Plans

In the case of an emergency, a nurse must be prepared to recommend certain clients for an immediate discharge, activate the **emergency response plan**, and participate in disaster drills. Each facility must have plans for emergency situations, and the nurse executive may be part of such planning.

Disasters can be internal or external. Examples of **internal disasters** include fires; violence in the workplace; failure of utilities, such as water or electricity; and electrical outage or flooding caused by weather disasters such as tornadoes, hurricanes, or earthquakes. An **external disaster** can include a serious community event in which a population sustains many injuries. Such events can include mass shootings, train wrecks, and airplane crashes. Acts of terrorism or bioterrorism can affect a facility both internally and externally. Likewise, weather events can affect a healthcare facility both internally and externally, depending on the extent of damage that occurs.

An example of an act of terrorism that caused a massive influx of patients to local hospitals was the Route 91 shooting in Las Vegas. This was an external event that caused the activation of certain emergency response plans to deal with the influx of incoming patients. Such events must be discussed as a potential occurrence in each facility. Healthcare facilities must put plans in place to deal with such catastrophes in a smooth, coordinated manner to effectively care for the maximum number of patients.

The hurricanes Irma and Harvey that struck the Gulf states in 2017 are an example of an external weather situation that directly affected those communities with electrical power losses, flooding, destruction of property, and injuries and illness related to the flooding and high winds. The healthcare system must be ready for these situations with an effective emergency response plan.

One of the first steps when activating an emergency response plan is to discharge patients who are medically stable enough to clear beds for incoming patients. Facilities only have a set number of beds available for patients. When the influx of patients is greater than the number of beds available, a crisis arises. When a **catastrophic event** occurs, nurses are part of a triaging process that determines whether certain patients can be relocated to open beds for incoming patients. Unstable clients will stay put; they are at the top of the rung of patients to stay. Stable patients may be discharged only if it is likely they will remain stable without ongoing nursing and medical care. On the bottom rung, below unstable and stable clients, are ambulatory and self-care clients. These are patients who are walking around and able to independently care for themselves outside of a hospital facility. Ambulatory and self-care patients will be discharged to clear beds for incoming disaster patients.

The nurse executive plays a key role in disaster preparedness and designation of roles to team members, which is necessary for successful execution of each emergency response plan. During a fire, for example, the nurse must competently implement all four elements of the **RACE** acronym, as follows:

- **R**: Rescue all those in danger, including patients, visitors, and staff.
- **A**: Activate the alarm after those in danger have been cleared.
- **C**: Contain the fire in the smallest possible area. This is accomplished by closing all windows and doors, preventing the fire from spreading.
- **E**: Extinguish the fire if it is small enough and the nurse can do so safely.

Concurrent with knowledge of the RACE acronym during a fire is knowledge of how to use a **fire extinguisher**. There are five main types of fire extinguishers: Type A, Type B, Type C, Type AB, and Type ABC. Type A extinguishers are used for common solids, such as paper, mattresses, and clothing. Type B extinguishers target oil, gasoline, and grease fires, common in kitchens. Type C extinguishers fight electrical fires. Type AB extinguishers combines the roles of Type A and Type B, while Type ABC extinguishers combines all three. Type ABC is most common due to its ability to extinguish all types of fire sources. This is likely the type of extinguisher located within a hospital facility for that reason.

When attempting to use a fire extinguisher, the nurse must remember the acronym **PASS**, which describes the following steps for effective use:

- **P**: Pull the pin to begin using the fire extinguisher.
- **A**: Aim directly at the bottom of the fire.
- **S**: Squeeze the trigger to release the spray.
- **S**: Sweep, moving from side to side across the base of the fire. This will effectively extinguish the fire.

Along with knowing their role when fire threatens the safety of patients, the nurse must also know what to do when the hospital's utilities fail. Electricity powers many life support machines for patients, such as oxygen delivery systems and mechanical ventilation machines. Most hospitals have back-up **generators** to keep these machines going when the power goes down. The nurse must alert maintenance and management immediately if the power goes off. Many hospitals have special red outlets into which important patient machinery should be plugged for just that reason.

There are times in the workplace when the nurse may encounter violence, harassment, or aggression. The source of these behavioral conflicts may be a visitor, fellow staff member, or patient. Causes of **workplace violence** may include delirium and disorientation, especially in hospitalized patients with illness and medication side effects in play. Visitors and family members may become disruptive for any number of reasons, including misunderstandings about care during high-stress and emotionally charged healthcare situations involving a loved one. Whatever the cause, the nurse must work to deescalate the situation verbally, enlisting help from team members and hospital security staff when needed.

Each healthcare facility will have explicit guidelines that must be followed in the case of a **weather emergency**, such as a hurricane, tornado, or earthquake. Closing windows, doors, and curtains, as well as moving patients to the appropriate predetermined safe place, are all part of the nurse's role during these situations.

For each of these emergencies, a chain of command needs to be established long before a catastrophic event occurs. A **chain of command** clearly defines who is in charge during the disaster, how information will be communicated, and the roles of each team member. **Emergency drills** are an excellent chance to rehearse each role and ensure that things run smoothly and efficiently in the event of a disaster.

Social Determinants of Health and Health Equity

Nurse executives play a crucial role in addressing social determinants of health and advancing health equity within healthcare organizations and the broader community. As leaders responsible for strategic planning, resource allocation, and clinical outcomes, they must be acutely aware of how social, economic, and environmental factors influence the health and well-being of patients and populations.

Housing stability, education, income, nutrition, transportation, and safety directly affect health outcomes and access to care. Nurse executives must ensure that these factors are considered in both clinical practice and organizational policy. This includes supporting community health assessments,

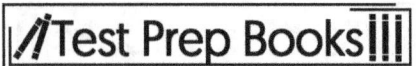

advocating for future interventions, and incorporating screening tools into patient assessments to identify risks related to levels of vulnerability.

Health equity is the principle that all patients should have the opportunity to attain their full health potential. Nurse executives must champion policies that address disparities in healthcare access, outcomes, and experiences—particularly for historically marginalized and vulnerable populations. Nurse executives also lead efforts to break down barriers to care, improve access to care, and reduce disparities, ensuring that every patient receives equitable treatment. Through strategic planning, training programs, performance improvement initiatives, and strong relationships with patients and families, they drive lasting change. This can include promoting culturally competent care, diversifying the nursing workforce, and ensuring equitable access to resources and services across all patient populations.

Within the organization, nurse leaders can promote inclusivity by integrating equity metrics into quality improvement initiatives, offering training on implicit bias, and ensuring that leadership structures reflect the diversity of the communities served. Externally, they should collaborate with public health agencies, social service organizations, and community stakeholders to design programs that target root causes of health inequities.

Data-driven strategies are essential to effective community initiatives. Nurse executives must analyze outcomes by race, ethnicity, income, and geography to identify disparities and monitor trends. This information should be widely shared in order to guide strategic priorities, budgetary decisions, and performance metrics.

Nurse executives have the power and voice to advocate at the policy level for healthcare reform that supports equity (e.g., expanding access to care, increasing funding for public health, and addressing systemic racism within the healthcare system). They have the unique opportunity to advocate for patient care, influence legislation, and drive organizational change.

Embedding the principles of social determinants and health equity into the backbone of an organization's healthcare delivery is also vital to promoting healthcare access. By using their leadership platforms to promote structural change, nurse executives have opportunities to improve individual patient outcomes and contribute to a just and effective healthcare system. Supporting health equity is a responsibility of nursing leadership as well as a strategic imperative for organizations committed to delivering high-quality, person-centered care in today's diverse and complex clinical care environment.

Skills

Person-Centered Care

Person-centered care is a foundation of today's healthcare continuum; it emphasizes a patient's individualized preferences, values, and needs. Nurse executives must ensure that person-centered care is supported and embedded in the culture of care delivery. This leadership responsibility is a strategic necessity in order to prioritize the patient experience, improve outcomes, and enhance patient satisfactions. All of these factors must be supported through initiatives, policies, and employee engagement.

A key strategy that can support person-centered care throughout the organization is leader rounding, which involves leadership being visible to patients, family, and frontline staff. This is a proactive

Health Care Delivery

approach to ensure that care is personally observed, feedback is provided and received in the moment, and there are opportunities to identify and address areas of improvement. Leader rounding has been found to identify patient safety concerns while also recognizing areas or staff that are excelling at providing care. Trust and psychological safety amongst staff are established through transparent and consistent relationship building and communication.

Patient engagement must be continually assessed for optimal participation in person-centered care delivery. Nurse executives must encourage patients to be active participants in their own care; this can involve discussing treatment choices, explaining medical terms clearly, and providing access to tools like online health records and care management programs. Patients who feel heard and informed are more likely to own their healthcare journey, fully participate in care plans, be an active member of the multidisciplinary care team, and have improved patient outcomes.

When something goes wrong or a patient has a bad experience, service recovery may be employed to mitigate concerns and dissatisfaction. Nurse leaders should develop strategies for staff to know how to respond quickly and kindly to concerns or adverse events. This could include apologizing, fixing a voiced problem or concern, and following up to ensure patient satisfaction with the result. Policies and tools to reduce the patient's disappointment or dissatisfaction will build stronger relationships with patients, families, and the community.

Nurse executives must also pay close attention to patient feedback such as surveys and satisfaction scores. These provide valuable information on what is functioning properly and meeting patient expectations while revealing areas that require improvement. This information may be used to enact effective change to improve the overall patient experience.

Patient Experience

Patient experience is a concept that reflects the goal of healthcare systems to provide patient-centered care. **Patient experience** encompasses the entire scope of the patient's interaction with those that provide their inpatient, outpatient, and at-home care. It includes fundamental healthcare behaviors, such as communication, information sharing, coordination, cultural awareness, and support for self-management. Understanding patient experience requires healthcare staff and leaders to see things from the patient's point of view.

The focus on patient satisfaction has received criticism in recent years. While patient experience differs represents a neutral view of a patient's interaction with the healthcare system, **patient satisfaction** focuses on whether the patient's expectations for the interaction were met.

The **Consumer Assessment of Healthcare Providers and Systems (CAHPS)** arm of the Agency for Healthcare Research and Quality (AHRQ) provides patient experience surveys tailored to a wide variety of different service lines and care delivery systems. The CAHPS patient experience survey assesses patient experience with questions that address if and how often specific actions occurred. For example, a patient will be asked if they experienced emotional difficulties related to their illness and, if so, whether their healthcare team gave them advice or assistance with coping mechanisms.

Experience of care is one of three points in the **Institute for Healthcare Improvement's (IHI)** Triple Aims for improving the U.S. healthcare system, along with population health and reducing per-capita cost. Patient experience comprises the six domains of healthcare quality: safety, effectiveness, patient-centeredness, timeliness, efficiency, and equity. Research supports the link between positive patient experience and improved healthcare outcomes.

Patient experience data should be approached as an **indicator**, not an outcome. This data can be used to identify areas for improvement and target system-level process improvements, such as shortening wait times in outpatient clinics or improving response time to call bells in the inpatient setting.

Patient experience facilitation is a collaborative process that involves understanding patient goals and desires and setting patient expectations. Some healthcare systems employ designated patient facilitators who work as multidisciplinary coordinators and advocates to individualize interventions and improve patient experience. Patient experience facilitators are sometimes called patient experience managers, liaisons, or directors. While these roles are fairly new, many existing roles in the hospital contribute directly to facilitating patient experience, such as bedside nurses, social workers, care coordinators, and discharge coordinators.

All members of the healthcare team and support staff contribute to patient experience, even those who are not directly involved in patient care. For example, an understaffed pharmacy team can impact patient experience if there are delays in the delivery of needed medications, even if the patient never meets the pharmacy staff.

The patient's physical environment plays a large role in their experience. Pay attention to accessibility needs, comfort, and ease of use for the patient and family. Dietary and environmental service teams have a direct impact on patient experience and should not be overlooked.

Facilitating patient experience requires flexibility and creative thinking. Many strategies and tools are available to healthcare staff and leaders as part of the process.

In the inpatient setting, it is important to ask open-ended questions on admission to give the patient a voice in their plan of care and to understand what unique issues and priorities the patient has for their stay. These may include dietary needs, communication needs, or cultural concerns related to their care.

The nurse's **bedside shift report** involves the patient and family in the handoff of care between nurses. This allows the patient and family to meet their new caregivers face-to-face, communicate their goals and desires for their care, update their caregivers on their status, and prevent incorrect information from being passed on.

Multidisciplinary rounding contributes to a positive patient experience by improving communication between the patient and different disciplines, such as physicians, nurses, and pharmacists. As a result, the negative effects of lapses and breakdown in communication are avoided.

Dry-erase boards with updated information on the patient's care team, goals, and plans for the shift help patients and families understand what to expect. Providing a notepad and pen to write down questions and concerns to share during rounds also helps patients and families communicate with their healthcare team.

Discharge is an exciting but vulnerable time for patients. Family and/or care partners should be included in the **discharge process**. Using strategies such as **teach-back**, where the nurse teaches the learner, then has the learner demonstrate or "teach" the skill back to the nurse, helps patients and families feel more confident in managing their care at home. Including home-health liaisons and social workers in the discharge process helps promote a seamless transition from hospital to home. Even the trip from bedside to car can have an outstanding impact on patient experience.

Health Care Delivery

In the outpatient setting, the friendliness and efficiency of front desk staff contributes to the beginning of a positive patient experience. Consider the cleanliness and comfort of the waiting area as well.

A great deal of outpatient care is managed by phone and, increasingly, by **secure messaging** on online portals. Methods for communicating with the care team from home should be easy to understand and access, and responses from the care team should be timely.

The more data that healthcare leaders have regarding the actual events of the patient experience, the better they can target improvements. Surveys should be provided frequently and should be easy to complete and return.

Patient experience is a primary driver of where patients go for their medical care. Ongoing positive patient experiences will not only improve safety and health-related outcomes, but they will also improve the reputation of the healthcare provider or system in the community.

Care Delivery Evaluation

Evaluating the delivery of patient care is an essential part of nursing practice. By evaluating the care that is being implemented, nurse administrators can identify areas of improvement, guarantee quality patient care, and help strengthen overall healthcare outcomes for patients.

Importance of Care Delivery Evaluation

Care delivery evaluation is important because it helps enhance patient outcomes. When nurse administrators identify and fix gaps in patient care, this leads to fewer adverse events and higher patient satisfaction. Evaluating care delivery helps identify areas for improvement. This allows for delivery processes to be enhanced, specifically with the incorporation of evidence-based guidelines and best practices in nursing care. Moreover, evaluation allows for quality improvement initiatives to be created and implemented. When quality improvement initiatives are implemented, they improve the overall safety, success, and productivity of the healthcare services provided.

Key Concepts

There are four **core measures** in care delivery evaluation: performance measurement, outcome evaluation, process evaluation, and structure evaluation. **Performance measurement** involves evaluating the quality and effectiveness of healthcare delivery through a variety of performance metrics. Such metrics include patient outcomes, adherence to protocols, and resource utilization. **Outcome evaluation** is when the impact of care delivery is assessed based on several indicators, including, but not limited to, morbidity, mortality, and patient satisfaction. **Process evaluation** occurs when the individual processes involved in care delivery are assessed. Some examples include clinical guideline adherence, interdisciplinary collaboration, and the efficiency of workflow on a daily basis. Finally, **structure evaluation** is the assessment of the overall organizational structure and the available resources to help facilitate care delivery. Some factors that are assessed include staffing levels, equipment, and infrastructure of facilities.

Methodologies

Nurse administrators can use several methods, including qualitative, quantitative, mixed-methods, and benchmarking, to obtain data that can be analyzed. **Qualitative methods** involve the use of interviews, focus groups, or observations to collect descriptive data regarding the care delivery process, patient experiences, and the workflow of nurses. **Quantitative methods** incorporate data collection tools, conduct surveys, and utilize statistical analyses to measure specific variables to assess care delivery

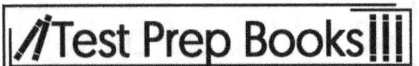

outcomes. Factors in the healthcare setting that can be measured using quantitative methods include infection rates, medication errors, and patient satisfaction scores. A **mixed-method approach** incorporates both qualitative and quantitative data collection methods. This allows for a more comprehensive understanding of care delivery and provides validation of data. Lastly, **benchmarking** is a method that utilizes the comparison of delivery performance metrics with established standards to help determine areas of improvement. This allows for goal setting and quality improvement overall.

Quality Indicators

There are several indicators that nurse administrators should assess during care delivery evaluation. These include structure, process, outcome, safety, and nurse indicators. When looking at **structure indicators**, the nurse administrator focuses on assessing the organizational resources, policies, staffing levels, education, and training opportunities. This is a non-exhaustive list, however. Some of the process indicators that nurse administrators assess to ensure that they are adhering to evidence-based practices can include interdisciplinary communication, documentation practices, and the use of standardized protocols. In terms of outcome indicators, nurse administrators evaluate mortality rates, readmission rates, infection rates, and patient satisfaction ratings. **Safety indicators** that nurse administrators utilize in the evaluation process include medication errors, falls, hospital-acquired infections, adverse events, and similar measures.

Nurse-sensitive indicators are indicators that reflect the quality and effectiveness of nursing care. Nurse administrators should consider the following common nurse-sensitive indicators: patient satisfaction, patient falls, pressure ulcers, hospital-acquired infections, medication errors, nursing staffing levels, patient readmissions, nurse turnover, and job satisfaction.

Care Coordination

Care coordination is a critical responsibility for nurse executives because it directly impacts patient outcomes, safety, and satisfaction. It involves organizing patient care activities and sharing information among all members of the healthcare team to ensure that patients receive timely, appropriate, and efficient care. Nurse executives play a key role in designing, implementing, and overseeing systems that support effective care coordination across the continuum of care. Policies and procedures must clearly delineate the activities that will support care coordination within the multidisciplinary care team.

One primary responsibility of a nurse executive is to create a structure that promotes collaboration among different departments, disciplines, and care settings—including hospitals, outpatient clinics, rehabilitation facilities, home health agencies, and community-based services. Nurse executives work to eliminate silos and promote seamless communication, ensuring that patients experience a smooth transition from one level of care to another. This may be within a facility or through the transfer of a patient to a different facility or level of care. Disjointed or difficult coordination can lead to hospital re-admissions, medication errors, and gaps in follow-up care.

Nurse executives are responsible for aligning care coordination efforts with organizational goals (e.g., reducing length of stay, improving patient satisfaction scores, and meeting value-based care metrics). They are responsible for ensuring that care teams have the tools, training, and support needed to manage complex patient needs, especially for those with chronic conditions or social challenges.

Certain patient populations require more intensive and carefully coordinated care due to their complex health needs. Nurse executives must ensure that systems are in place to support critical care patients, who often face life-threatening conditions and require fast, expert interventions from highly skilled multidisciplinary teams. Similarly, elderly patients often have multiple chronic conditions, cognitive

Health Care Delivery

impairments, and mobility challenges, making their care particularly sensitive to issues like medication management and discharge planning. Vulnerable populations (e.g., those experiencing homelessness, mental illness, language barriers, or lack of insurance) need tailored care coordination that addresses both medical and social determinants of health. Nurse executives must champion programs that provide ongoing support, community partnerships, and equitable access to services for these at-risk groups.

Nurse executives oversee the use of care coordination technologies such as electronic health records (EHRs), patient portals, and communication platforms that streamline information sharing. They also advocate for adequate staffing, strong case management programs, and interdisciplinary team collaboration.

Below is an example of the care delivery evaluation process in action:

Sarah is the nurse administrator in a busy surgical unit. She understands the significance of medication safety in achieving positive patient outcomes, having fewer adverse events, and increasing patient satisfaction. She has a goal to improve the medication administration process on her unit—specifically reducing medication errors related to high-alert medications. She knows that if medication administration practices are improved on her unit, overall patient safety and surgical unit productivity will be improved.

The first action Sarah takes is to determine the objectives for the care delivery evaluation plan. The main objective she decides to address is to decrease medication errors related to high-alert medications by 50% within six months. This is a SMART goal—one that is specific, measurable, achievable, relevant, and time-bound.

Next, Sarah collects baseline data on medication errors with high-alert medications over the past fiscal year using both quantitative and qualitative methods. She looks at documented medication errors, reviews staff surveys, and observes daily medication administration. Once data is collected, she analyzes the data to identify what types of errors are occurring, any contributing factors, and any patterns. The purpose of this baseline data is to allow for comparison of future outcomes. Sarah determines that errors are mainly occurring with drugs that have similar names.

After data collection, Sarah looks inward to the facility and unit itself, focusing on its infrastructure, available resources, and compliance with evidence-based practices and guidelines regarding medication safety. Some of the important concepts she identifies are effective communication, double-checking procedures, barcode scanning, clear labeling, and staff education and training. These concepts will help her develop an interventional plan. Sarah notices that the two main issues found were nurses not double-checking medications and the fact that labels from the pharmacy were very similar, making it difficult to differentiate certain medications. There were also a few incidences of mislabeling from the pharmacy, which the barcode cannot detect.

To develop an intervention plan, Sarah works closely with the interdisciplinary team. This includes her nursing staff, hospital pharmacists, physicians, and other relevant stakeholders. Together, they come up with a plan to implement several strategies. First, they will implement a new standardized medication administration process. Next, they will improve communication channels, highlighting the importance of closed-loop communication. They will also conduct regular and unannounced competency assessments. Ongoing education and training for staff will be implemented. Sarah and her team find it important to implement a **double-checking system** with another nurse when administering high-alert medications.

Sarah implements the intervention plan with the help of her nursing staff and the rest of the interdisciplinary team. They ensure clear protocols and guidelines are developed for medication administration, monitor the distribution of appropriate supplies and resources (such as labeling and barcode systems), and facilitate educational workshops for staff.

To monitor the interventional plan and evaluate its effectiveness, Sarah creates a **reporting system** for medication errors. Nurses are instructed to report incidents in a prompt and thorough manner. Periodic medication safety audits and observations are also conducted to identify any gaps or areas for improvement.

Sarah will retrieve all collected data that has been reported through the new reporting system, safety audits, and observations to provide a thorough analysis. She compares this data to the baseline data that was obtained prior to the implementation of the interventional plan. Data is analyzed to identify medication errors, contributing factors, and recurring patterns and issues. This will allow her to identify gaps in the interventional plan that require further improvement or alteration. After the six months is over, Sarah determines that errors have decreased by 40%—not the 50% that she was hoping for.

Sarah decides to meet with the interdisciplinary team to create additional changes and implement them accordingly. They decide to revisit the **"look-alike drug" policy** by coordinating with the pharmacy and **electronic medication administration record (eMAR)** systems to utilize capitalization in several look-alike drug names. This will help reduce errors with mislabeling. They also decide to provide training modules, including mock scenarios and situations for the staff to practice, to determine areas that still need improvement. To ensure that high-alert medications being administered are accurately confirmed before administration, a mandatory double-check system with the charge nurse is implemented on the unit.

Since care delivery evaluation is an ongoing process, Sarah ensures that she maintains an environment of monitoring and evaluation within the surgical unit. She continues to have randomized and unannounced observations, audits, and staff discussions, so she can monitor medication safety practices. This allows her to identify any shortfalls with adherence to established protocols and guidelines, which she addresses immediately.

Care delivery evaluation is not a one-time process. It is an ongoing and lengthy process that needs to be thorough. Even if new interventional practices are implemented that meet set SMART goals, there are always additional factors that may arise and cause issues within the system. An example of this would be new staff members joining the nursing or pharmacy team. Although additional safety measures have been put in place, new staff members have the potential to make medication errors due to inexperience or lack of knowledge. This factor could be something that the nurse administrator can create an interventional plan for—to help onboard new hires through extensive training programs in this area.

Technology Evaluation and Integration

With the ever-changing and improving world of technology, it is more crucial than ever to evaluate and integrate technology within the healthcare industry. **Technology** allows healthcare organizations to enhance patient care, improve operations, and create better outcomes. Some common areas that nurse administrators need to consider include telehealth, predictive analysis, and remote monitoring since these can affect technology evaluation and integration. **Telehealth** can affect technology evaluation and integration because administrators must assess the available technology, evaluate workflows, train staff, optimize infrastructure, and ensure compliance with regulatory requirements to successfully implement

Health Care Delivery

telehealth in their healthcare organization. **Remote monitoring** is a form of telehealth that allows healthcare providers to monitor patient data outside of healthcare settings, such as their homes. Nurse administrators must assess these technologies and their integration with electronic health records to successfully utilize remote monitoring in patient care. **Predictive analysis** allows nurse administrators to make data-driven decisions regarding technology evaluation and integration. By utilizing predictive analysis, nurse administrators can make informed choices that will improve patient care measures and operational efficiency.

Technology Evaluation

In simple terms, **technology evaluation** is the systematic assessment of technological solutions being utilized by an organization to determine their effectiveness and suitability for the needs of an organization. The purpose of evaluating technology is to confirm that the investment is worthwhile, align with organizational goals, and delivers the promised benefits.

Steps in Technology Evaluation

The first step in evaluation of technology is for the nurse administrator to identify the needs of the organization. The goal is to identify areas where technology can remedy organizational challenges or enhance processes.

The next step in the process is to establish criteria. For the technology evaluation to be effective, the nurse administrator must define specific measurements of focus. For example, they may choose to focus on cost, functionality, or security.

Once criteria are established, the nurse administrator must research the technology and develop a shortlist of preferred options. This can help identify potential technological solutions that fall within the chosen criteria.

When the shortlist is generated, it is time to assess the options available by interviewing vendors, participating in site visits, and having demonstrations of such technology.

The nurse administrator must decide which to choose by comparing the strengths and weaknesses of each option. They should choose the option that is the most appropriate for their organization and its needs.

Once the technology option has been chosen, it is important to test such technology in a controlled environment to determine its functionality and feasibility to the needs of the organization. This is called **pilot testing**.

A plan needs to be implemented to run pilot testing. The nurse administrator will create a detailed plan to implement the technology, which can include training modalities, stakeholder roles and support, and requirements of the organizational infrastructure.

Once pilot testing is implemented, there should be continuous evaluation. This includes monitoring the technology's performance and gathering feedback from those using the technology to determine areas for improvement.

Health Care Delivery

Best Practices in Technology Evaluation

There are several best practices that nurse administrators should follow when it comes to technology evaluation. They need to engage stakeholders, involving them in the evaluation process. **Stakeholders** can include nurses, IT staff, and other administrators.

Another important consideration for best practice is **interoperability**. The nurse administrator should ensure that chosen technology can integrate seamlessly with existing systems that are in place; furthermore, the communication between these technological platforms must be viable.

Evaluating the long-term costs of technology improvements is another important factor in the decision-making process. It is the responsibility of the nurse administrator to consider the financial burden of implementation, maintenance, and upgrades of the implemented technology.

Since medical information is protected by laws such as HIPAA, assessment of security measures is a vital component of best practice. It is important to evaluate the technology's security features and how they comply with regulations set forth by not only the hospital, but also national laws and regulations.

Finally, the nurse administrator should ensure that the technology aligns with the goals of the organization. This includes the organization's overall vision and strategic objectives.

Technology Integration

It is important to ensure that **technology integration** in healthcare is seamless with the current workflows and processes of an organization. When effective technology integration occurs, there is enhanced communication, increased efficiency, and improved patient outcomes.

Strategies for Technology Integration

There are several strategies that a nurse administrator can utilize to help integrate technology into their organization. The first thing step is to assess how implementing technology will impact current workflows and determine what adjustments are needed. The nurse administrator should also consider offering training programs and additional support to help staff members become familiar and comfortable with newly implemented technology. When it comes to choosing technology to utilize in an organization, it is important to consider usability. In other words, choosing user-friendly technology that is easy to navigate will help make the transition easier for staff. The use of "**super-users**", or staff members with advanced training in the new technology, can be a great resource to aid those with questions during the implementation process. Another strategy the nurse administrator can utilize is to facilitate collaboration between hospital IT staff and healthcare providers to identify areas where technology can be integrated or improved. Finally, the nurse administrator should continuously monitor the integration of technology, gather feedback, and determine areas that need improvement.

The following is a real-world example of a nurse administrator who is planning to integrate technology in his hospital after evaluating existing methods.

Mark is a nurse administrator working for a hospital that is looking to implement a new **electronic health record (EHR)** system to improve patient care and make documentation easier and more efficient. Currently, nurses are using manual charting methods and keeping paper records. Mark's role is to evaluate the technology and oversee its integration throughout the hospital.

The first thing Mark will do is participate in a technology evaluation.

Mark begins to identify the current issues and challenges in documentation at the hospital. He determines that there are issues in manual charting and insufficient communication between nursing staff and healthcare providers. These are the main areas that the EHR system can help fix.

Next, Mark identifies specific criteria on how to evaluate the EHR systems available. He chooses to focus on ease of use, data security, interoperability, and functionality. Mark works closely with the nurses, physicians, and hospital IT staff to obtain input and ensure that the selected criteria align with the goals of the hospital organization.

Once criteria are established, Mark conducts research on current EHR systems available and generates a shortlist of preferred options. Some important factors that he evaluates include user reviews and overall features. He decides on three potential vendors that meet the established criteria.

Now Mark is tasked with evaluating the options. He does so by arranging vendor demonstrations and site visits for EHR system to understand their functionality and capabilities. He pays close attention to overall user experience, ease of navigation, and interoperability capabilities.

Once all vendor demonstrations and site visits are complete, Mark composes lists of strengths and weaknesses of each EHR system. He considers the cost, user feedback, implementation timeline, and reputation of the vendors. After consulting with the executive leadership of the hospital and the IT department, they come to an informed decision and select the most suitable EHR system for their organization that helps them meet their strategic goals.

Finally, it is time for pilot testing. Mark chooses to implement the new EHR system within the neurology department. He works closely with IT and nursing staff to help customize the system according to the needs of their workflow. Mark closely monitors the performance of the system, its usability, and its impact on patient care and overall documentation processes. He regularly obtains feedback from the nursing staff and IT via surveys and interviews to identify areas of improvement before implementing the system in the entire hospital.

Once the evaluation piece has been completed, Mark decides to integrate the new EHR system within the rest of the hospital.

Mark assesses how the EHR system can impact **workflows**. He collaborates with frontline staff and nursing managers on each unit, adjusting workflows to align more closely with the capabilities of the new EHR system. This allows for an easier, more seamless integration.

Mark develops a comprehensive training program with the help of the IT department, vendor, and nursing managers to ensure that healthcare providers are proficient in using the new EHR system. Initial training is provided for all staff, but there is ongoing support through the vendor and IT department. Super-users are assigned in each unit who can help provide guidance and support to their coworkers.

Mark wants to ensure that the system is **user-friendly**. He works closely with nurses, physicians, and other healthcare providers to obtain input on the layout of screens and the organization of patient information. This allows him to work with IT and the vendor to customize the system, preventing duplicate data entry and ultimately optimizing data retrieval.

Mark also utilizes change management strategies that can help address any resistance from staff members regarding the new EHR system and facilitate the transition. He communicates the benefits of the new system to the staff and helps address their concerns. Highlighting the fact that there will be continuous support and communication throughout the implementation process will help provide successful integration overall.

Finally, Mark continuously monitors the integration process. He obtains feedback from all end-users to help determine staff satisfaction. He also assesses data to determine the impact on patient care, its efficiency, and documentation accuracy. By reviewing key performance indicators regularly, Mark can determine the success of the EHR system and work with IT to adjust if warranted.

Information Technology

Information technology (IT) is a field of nursing that continues to evolve with the rest of healthcare. Nurses must not only understand the science that is associated with nursing, but they must also be able to navigate various forms of technology. While there are nurses still in the workplace who can recall what it was like to physically fill out forms and track vitals on paper, there are also nurses who have no concept of having documented their activities in these systems. All nurses must be able to function within today's technologically advanced world.

IT is important for many reasons including:

- Cost savings
- Decreased medication errors
- Improved documentation efficiency by removing paper charting
- Enhanced accessibility to quality health care

Medical technology needs to be fully integrated in a larger system within an institution to support the continuum of patient care. This connection provides information sharing throughout each stage of the treatment period and eventually allows for the collection of statistical data in the future.

Next, medical technology must support the user's ability to navigate without difficulty. The goal here is not to slow down the pace of the medical environment, but to increase efficiency so that technology is seamless. These qualities then allow for real-time data and real-time decision-making capabilities, while reducing the risk of errors or redundancy.

There are a few gaps that remain on the IT front of the medical environment that have their roots in the computerized physician order entry (CPOE) arena. In some instances, CPOE software is not able to meet the needs of various interdisciplinary roles, such as in the OR. The reason for this is that it tends to favor the inpatient setting.

Health Care Information Technology

Health care IT (HIT) has characteristics that are steeped in supporting broad processes or functions. HIT is software that can perform operations associated with:

- Admissions
- Scheduling
- Clinical documentation
- Pharmacy
- Laboratory
- Clinical Information Technology

Clinical IT (CIT) concentrates on a particular set of clinical tasks, instruments, equipment, and imaging.

Health Care Delivery

Radio Frequency Identification
Radio frequency identification (RFID) provides support for real-time surgery scheduling. This technology has been shown to drastically enhance the structure and functions within medical software. RFID functions on wireless networks, helps to "tag" items, and tracks their movement as they remain on or leave a particular unit. This may be especially important when tracking equipment or supplies that are used to care for the patient or during a surgical procedure.

Nurses will need to stay current with IT trends and engage in ongoing education and exposure to technology. Continuing education and training can be accomplished through independent reading, e-learning, and live classroom instruction.

Finally, nurses may encounter a broad range of technologies including:

- Robots
- Medication delivery devices
- Instruments
- Biotechnology and nanotechnology
- Digital tracking
- Mobile and wireless devices
- Nurse Informatics

Nurses may assist in the development of standards for EHR (electronic health records) or other clinically based IT systems that nurses utilize for their sphere of health care. In today's landscape, many nursing applications fall into a variety of categories including:

- Internet-based patient education systems
- EHR
- Telemedicine and telenursing

These systems have the capacity to exchange information and enable the decision-making process to progress along the continuum.

Some nurses possess a master's degree in **informatics** and work in a variety of roles to assist with development of clinical systems designed to support nurse activities including:

- Business or clinical analyst
- Project management
- Software developer

These systems are designed to accommodate patient education resources, nursing procedures, and critical pathways, to name a few.

Nurses may also serve in the role of perioperative **robotics nurse specialist**. As robotic surgery utilization continues to evolve into standard practice, the robotics nurse specialist supports a variety of tasks, ranging from scheduling maintenance to assisting during surgery.

Virtual Nursing
As healthcare delivery evolves, nurse executives play a central role in the expansion of virtual nursing programs that can meet the diverse and specialized needs of today's patients. Their leadership ensures

that virtual care has a wide reach, is efficient, and maintains the integrity and personalization of nursing practice—particularly in specialty healthcare services.

One major responsibility of nursing executives is to align virtual nursing with specialty care delivery. This includes developing remote nursing services for high-need areas such as oncology, cardiology, diabetes management, behavioral health, and post-surgical recovery. Patients with chronic or complex conditions often require frequent monitoring, detailed education, and multidisciplinary coordination. Services that incorporate virtual nursing can efficiently meet patients' needs when structured correctly. Nurse executives must collaborate with specialty providers to create protocols and training to ensure that virtual nurses are fully prepared to support these unique clinical needs.

Additionally, nurse executives must address barriers to care and digital equity. This means ensuring that patients in rural or low-income communities can access virtual services. Strategies may include providing internet connectivity, mobile device compatibility, multilingual interfaces, and caregiver involvement for patients with cognitive or physical limitations. Nurse executives may also advocate for organizational investment in telehealth infrastructure and funding for digital literacy programs.

Another core responsibility is developing personalized care models within virtual nursing. Not every patient benefits from the same approach, so nurse executives must guide teams in tailoring virtual interactions based on age, cultural background, language preference, and health literacy. This person-centered strategy is core to maintaining engagement and trust in virtual settings.

Nurse executives must conduct continuous quality improvement and evaluation. By analyzing data on patient outcomes, satisfaction, and access trends, they can refine virtual nursing models to deliver safe, equitable, and high-quality care, regardless of the patient's location or condition.

Practice Quiz

1. The nurse executive is reviewing several surveys to assess patient experience. The nurse executive expects a patient experience survey to focus mainly on which type of questions?
    a. Questions that measure the patient's satisfaction and if their expectations were met for their care on a scale of one to ten.
    b. Questions that ask which behaviors and events occurred during the patient's stay, usually in a yes/no format.
    c. Short-answer questions that ask the patient to reflect on what went well or didn't go well with their care.
    d. Questions related to demographic and health history information.

2. Which action is the cornerstone of providing a positive patient experience?
    a. Maintaining a clean and comfortable physical environment
    b. Preventing errors
    c. Talking with the patient about their own goals, fears, concerns, and priorities
    d. Using plain language to discuss medical care so that the patient and family can understand

3. Regarding ethical practice, nurses are responsible for which document?
    a. The policy and protocol of their hospital
    b. Their State Board of Nursing list of prohibited activities
    c. The AHRQ six domains for healthcare improvement
    d. The American Nurses Association Code of Ethics

4. Which of the following is NOT an example of a nurse-sensitive indicator on an inpatient obstetric unit?
    a. Catheter-associated urinary tract infection (CAUTI) rates
    b. Patient falls
    c. Primary C-section rate
    d. Patient satisfaction scores

5. The nurse executive understands that HIPAA protects the confidentiality of a patient's medical information. However, she wants to know how her friend who was admitted for surgery in the morning is doing. What is the best action for the nurse executive to take?
    a. Look up her friend's chart.
    b. Call her colleague in surgical admissions and ask for an update.
    c. Post on social media that her friend is in surgery and ask if anyone knows how she's doing.
    d. Wait until her friend can answer the phone and tell her how it went.

See answers on the next page.

Answer Explanations

1: B. Patient experience refers to what did or did not happen in the patient's course of care. Patient satisfaction is distinct from patient experience in that it gauges whether their expectations were met, which makes Choice A incorrect. Choice C is incorrect because patient experience data does not focus on the patient's opinion about what happened. Choice D is incorrect because demographic and health history information is not a primary focus of patient experience.

2: C. While Choices A, B, and D are all contributors, placing the patient at the center of conversation, listening to their concerns, and making them feel included and respected is the fundamental basis of a positive patient experience.

3. C. Guides for ethical decision-making for nurses include The American Nurses Association Code of Ethics, the regulations set forth by the individual's State Board of Nursing, and hospital policies and protocols, making Choices A, B, and D all correct. Choice C is incorrect because the AHRQ six domains relate to healthcare quality, not ethical decision-making.

4: C. C-section rates are not a nurse-sensitive indicator because they reflect physician decision-making, not the quality and effectiveness of nursing care. Choice A, CAUTI rates, are a nurse-sensitive indicator because they are directly related to activities such as catheter placement and care, which nurses perform. Choice B, patient falls, are a nurse-sensitive indicator because they are directly related to nursing activities during patient transfer and ambulation. Choice D, patient satisfaction scores, are a nurse-sensitive indicator because they reflect the nurse's interactions with the patient.

5: D. In speaking directly with the friend, the nurse allows her friend to control their medical information. Choices A and B are HIPAA violations because the nurse does not have a treatment-related need to access the information. Choice C is incorrect because the fact that the patient is undergoing surgery is privileged medical information. The nurse's post on social media reveals that information to the public in violation of HIPAA.

Practice Test #1

1. Which of the following choices is consistent with the Value-Based Purchasing (VBP) care model in terms of reimbursement?
    a. Provider groups accept all financial risk.
    b. Providers are reimbursed for the quality rather than the number of patient-care encounters.
    c. Hospitals are rewarded for timely discharge of preterm infants covered by Medicaid.
    d. Hospitals can opt out of the program.

2. Which of the following is NOT one of the basic care responsibilities the nurse must practice when caring for patients?
    a. Discouraging a patient's independence
    b. Ensuring patient safety
    c. Minimizing pain and harm
    d. Decreasing medical errors

3. Which of the following laws prohibits the discrimination against any individuals who are over the age of forty related to hiring, firing, promotions, changes in wages or benefits, or other employment-related decisions?
    a. Age Discrimination in Employment Act of 1967
    b. Fair Labor Standards Act
    c. Title VII of the Civil Rights Act of 1964
    d. Equal Employment Opportunity Commission

4. Which of the following is a tool from the Six Sigma approach?
    a. Value stream mapping
    b. HRIS
    c. SMART
    d. Flow state diagram

5. Which of the following statements most accurately describes the difference between how achievement scores and improvement scores are calculated?
    a. Achievement scores are calculated by determining how effective a patient's particular treatment course was, whereas improvement scores are calculated by determining how cost-efficient a patient's particular treatment course was.
    b. Achievement scores are calculated by comparing a healthcare provider's performance to that of other healthcare providers, whereas improvement scores are calculated by comparing a healthcare provider's current performance to their previously calculated performances.
    c. Achievement scores are calculated by assessing the effectiveness and efficiency of healthcare leaders, whereas improvement scores are used to calculate and assess care effectiveness and efficiency for all healthcare employees.
    d. Achievement scores are used to calculate quality of performance for healthcare providers already considered to be in the top 50% for patient outcomes and experiences, whereas improvement scores are used to calculate quality of performance for healthcare providers ranked in the bottom 50% for patient outcomes and experiences.

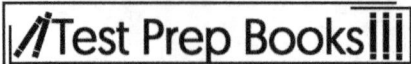

Practice Test #1

6. Value-based care models are associated with varying degrees of financial risk. Which of the following choices is consistent with the definitions of upside risk and downside risk?
    a. Upside risk is associated with penalties for failure to meet metrics.
    b. CMS can limit participation in downside risk models.
    c. Plans that assume downside risk must be well coordinated to be successful.
    d. Downside risk models are not penalized for failure to meet CMS benchmarks.

7. What type of data does a rolling forecast financial report use to calculate financial conditions?
    a. Data from similar healthcare facilities
    b. Current data
    c. Data provided by CMS
    d. Past data

8. The nurse is caring for a patient admitted with diabetic ketoacidosis (DKA) who requests to have orange juice with their breakfast. The nurse denies this request, stating that the orange juice could raise their blood sugar to a dangerous level, and offers to get water or black coffee for the patient instead. This is an example of which ethical principle?
    a. Beneficence
    b. Autonomy
    c. Nonmaleficence
    d. Unethical practice

9. Which of the following is NOT a performance domain designated by CMS for participation in a VBP program?
    a. Clinical outcomes
    b. Patient volume
    c. Safety
    d. Efficiency and cost reduction

10. Which accompanying documentation ensures appropriate patient care in any environment?
    a. List of symptoms, CDC registered diagnosis to inform PPE use, all prescription medications, and the appropriate referral
    b. Complete health history, detailed symptoms, testing performed, diagnosis, and treatment/medications
    c. A driver's license or state ID, an insurance card, a doctor's referral for services, and a list of prescriptions
    d. Patient name on wristband, unique identifier in the medical records system, and a referral by the patient's insurance company

11. An individual enrolls in a private insurance program that employs value-based insurance design. Their insurance would be LEAST likely to offer coverage for which of the following programs?
    a. A program offering education on diabetes prevention and treatment
    b. A program encouraging physical activity and engagement among seniors
    c. A program offering cosmetic plastic surgery
    d. A program offering education on drug addiction and treatment

12. The following are the federally protected classes of the Equal Employment Opportunity Commission EXCEPT?
    a. Pregnancy status
    b. Genetic information
    c. Disability
    d. Employees/applicants between eighteen and twenty-six years old

13. With patients who have Medicare or Medicaid coverage, who is considered to be the payor for the cost of that patient's care?
    a. A private health insurance company
    b. The government
    c. The patient's employer
    d. The patient

14. Which of the following is an example of a short-term strategy to develop workforce competencies?
    a. Increase the academic and professional qualifications in job postings.
    b. Enroll targeted employees in a high-potential development program.
    c. Reassign underperforming employees to positions that better fit their skills.
    d. Organize a week-long training class focused on development of the desired skill.

15. Which Lean Six Sigma format targets current processes?
    a. Define, measure, analyze, improve, and control
    b. Define, maintain, analyze, improve, and control
    c. Define, measure, analyze, design, and verify
    d. Define, measure, analyze, investigate, and contain

16. The nurse is caring for a 75-year-old patient with end-stage terminal pancreatic cancer. A family member expresses concern to the nurse that the patient has not been eating enough and wants them to receive increased supplemental nutrition. Should the nurse ethically encourage this increased nutritional intake?
    a. Yes, the patient should be started on tube feeding if they cannot take in enough nutrients orally.
    b. No, increased nutrition could accelerate tumor growth and lead to nausea and vomiting.
    c. No, increasing their nutritional intake could lead to weight gain.
    d. Yes, the increased nutrition could help extend the patient's life.

17. Which of the following is true of competitive benchmarking?
    a. It is not advised by TJC.
    b. It can be done by reviewing a competitor's public summary.
    c. It helps improve internal quality processes.
    d. It involves comparison of functions within an organization to each other.

18. A blood vial is dropped on the floor of a medical facility and breaks. What method of cleaning should be followed to reduce the risk of transmitting potential bloodborne pathogens to others?
    a. A disinfectant solution approved by the Environmental Protection Agency (EPA) and prepared according to manufacturer's instructions is required.
    b. A solution of ordinary soap without antibacterial properties and water is all that is required.
    c. An enzymatic cleaner and water solution approved by the FDA should be used in this case.
    d. A third-party vendor must be hired to contain the area and decontaminate it with an approved sterilizing solution.

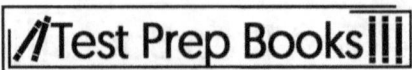

19. In performance management, what is a principal function of rating?
    a. Rating allows management to identify their most productive workers and provide them incentives to retain them.
    b. Because of its narrow statistical application, rating is generally an infrequent practice by management.
    c. Rating provides a way for management to designate their most favored employees.
    d. By having employees rate management, they can more accurately decide for whom and under which conditions they wish to work.

20. Which of the following statements regarding the Family Medical Leave Act is accurate?
    a. Employers are required to maintain employees' group health insurance coverage while they are out on FMLA leave.
    b. Spouses who work for the same employer each receive twelve weeks of FMLA time for the birth of their child.
    c. Employers cannot require employees to take their paid leave, such as vacation or sick leave, when using FMLA.
    d. FMLA only covers leave for the birth or adoption of a child or a serious health condition of the employee or child.

21. Which part of Medicare is medical insurance that covers health care expenses such as outpatient care and physician's care, considered optional, and provided for a monthly fee for those enrolled?
    a. Medicare Part A
    b. Medicare Part B
    c. Medicare Part C
    d. Medicare Part D

22. Which piece of legislation requires employers to pay employees for preliminary and postliminary tasks, such as job-related travel time that is outside of an employee's regular work commute and time spent in job-related training?
    a. Equal Pay Act
    b. Portal-to-Portal Act
    c. Fair Labor Standards Act (FLSA)
    d. Davis Bacon Act

23. What are the two regulatory categories applied to environmental policies and procedures directed at reducing incidence of healthcare-associated infections?
    a. Standard care of patients in outpatient settings and precautions for inpatient environments
    b. Short-term patient care and long-term, residential patient care
    c. Care of patients in private office settings and institutional settings
    d. Standard patient care and precautions taken in instances of known or suspected infection risk

24. Which of the following statements accurately reflects how the adoption of rolling forecast budgeting would affect members of a healthcare organization?
   a. It would only benefit healthcare executives because the added scrutiny would negatively affect doctors and nurses.
   b. It would primarily benefit healthcare executives but will also save healthcare managers on the organization time.
   c. It would primarily benefit doctors and nurses, as it would take up more resources and time from healthcare executives and managers.
   d. It would benefit all members of a healthcare organization because it would save executives and managers time and resources while providing doctors and nurses with the proper funding.

25. Which of the following employees could qualify to be exempt under the Fair Labor Standards Act (FLSA)?
   a. An employee earns over $80,000 a year, but makes routine decisions.
   b. The employee earns less than $23,000 a year, but makes non-routine decisions.
   c. The employee is regularly supervising two or more employees and has management as their main job duty.
   d. The FLSA lets employers decide who is and isn't exempt.

26. A quality improvement tool is being used to determine the most frequently occurring factors related to increased respiratory infection rates in a healthcare facility. The tool uses a bar graph to determine the frequency of occurrence. This quality improvement tool is known as a:
   a. Fishbone diagram
   b. Pareto chart
   c. Flow chart
   d. Gap analysis

27. Which of the following agencies ensures safe working conditions for employees by establishing process safety management standards?
   a. ADA
   b. OSHA
   c. HIPAA
   d. SOX

28. What type of programs are used to promote organizational culture by identifying and rewarding individual employees for the work done?
   a. Special event programs
   b. Recognition programs
   c. Inclusion programs
   d. Incentive programs

29. Which of the following is the correct meaning for the abbreviation MSPB?
   a. Medicare Supplement Per Bed
   b. Medical Situations Pre-Bereavement
   c. Medical Saves Per Body
   d. Medicare Spending Per Beneficiary

30. Which of the following would be the most effective way to present information about workplace misconduct to employees?
    a. Give employees a checklist of workplace DON'Ts based on EEOC guidance.
    b. Show news stories of the recent high-profile cases, along with commentary from legal experts about corporate liability and other worst-case scenarios concerning violations of workplace conduct policies.
    c. Set up a self-paced, remote training session to allow for greater flexibility so the information can reach as many employees as possible.
    d. Schedule mandatory in-person training with employee involvement, such as skits, role plays, and mock juries, to encourage engagement and focus on real-world implications.

31. Any deviation from the standard process typically results in higher risk, according to which methodology?
    a. 5 S Methodology
    b. Six Sigma
    c. Lean
    d. National Safety Standards

32. Hospital-wide decisions and committees involving client rights in a healthcare setting should include which of the following groups?
    a. Administrative heads of the hospital
    b. Doctors and nurses
    c. Medical staff, administration, patients, and family members
    d. Administration and doctors

33. Which of the following would be the quickest way to correct a lapse in the practice of wearing gloves while working with patients who may be carriers of infectious disease?
    a. Schedule several training seminars throughout the month so each worker has a chance to attend and learn about the importance of wearing gloves.
    b. Retrain the entire staff on the procedures of caring for patients with a possible infectious disease.
    c. Create a notice that reminds and educates workers on the importance of wearing gloves while working, and post the notice around the hospital in areas where it can be clearly read.
    d. Develop a system where workers can provide feedback regarding why they sometimes do not wear gloves.

34. Which key factors determine the type of PPE used to reduce risk of infection in patient care providers?
    a. Type of exposure, appropriateness for task, proper fit
    b. Manufacturer, type of material, size
    c. Size, level of training, personal preference
    d. Durability of material, manufacturer, and proper fit

35. A new healthcare employee lacking an updated immunization for whooping cough joins the staff of a hospital. The employee is given ten business days to update this immunization. On day three, an outbreak of whooping cough is documented at the facility. What happens to this employee?
    a. The employee is immediately dismissed for noncompliance.
    b. The employee is excluded from caring for patients suspected of having whooping cough.
    c. The employee is charged with direct patient care, and everyone hopes for the best.
    d. The employee is sent on work time to get the immunization the same day.

36. An outpatient facility has appointed a committee to conduct an audit of its infection prevention program. Although three of the members have done an audit previously, the audits involved acute care facilities and a hemodialysis facility. What should the committee do first?
    a. Review facility policies and procedures to create a checklist
    b. Collaborate on past experience to create audit tools and timelines
    c. Visit the CDC website for facility-specific checklists and resources
    d. Conduct a gap analysis of existing data to prepare a checklist

37. Which of the following is true of telemedicine?
    a. It is a form of medical care provided remotely by credentialed and licensed healthcare professionals.
    b. It is prohibited by the Health Insurance Portability and Accountability Act of 1996.
    c. It is the primary role of the CPHQ professional.
    d. It is required by the Health Insurance Portability and Accountability Act of 1996.

38. Which of the following sources would contain the most credible information related to sexually transmitted infections (STIs) in college students?
    a. Student publications
    b. Personal anecdotes of those who have been tested for an STI
    c. A hospital report about the types of STIs that are prevalent in an area
    d. A campus survey

39. The nurse is caring for a patient who has just received a terminal diagnosis and was told they likely have less than a year to live. Which of the following is an appropriate response for the nurse to make?
    a. "Everything will turn out okay."
    b. "What do you think you could have done differently to prevent this?"
    c. "This must be difficult for you; I am here to answer any questions."
    d. "I think you should start looking at local hospice care facilities."

40. Evelyn is a nurse executive who is having trouble with supervisors not submitting their employee evaluations on time. What should Evelyn immediately do to engage the management and supervisory staff in the performance management process?
    a. Provide training, forms, required timeline (including due dates), and coaching on delivering employee evaluations.
    b. Implement a new policy that requires evaluations be conducted by the annual due date or disciplinary actions will be taken.
    c. Discuss the situation with the HR director and CEO and request their immediate attention to the issue.
    d. Continue to send out emails and communications requesting the documents within the time frame needed.

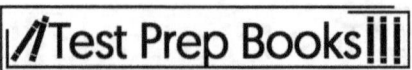

41. Considering they have met all of the necessary requirements, which of the following individuals is eligible to take unpaid, protected leave from work under the Family Medical Leave Act (FMLA)?
    a. An employee who is non-weight bearing, recovering from ankle surgery, and who will have multiple follow-up appointments with his surgeon and physical therapy visits to attend
    b. An employee who is out of the office for three days sick with the flu
    c. An employee who wants to take care of her aunt who is suffering from end-stage lung cancer
    d. An employee who wishes to travel to China to support her sister who is in the process of adopting a child in that country

42. Which of the following accurately represents the population of patients that can have an advance directive?
    a. Patients with a terminal illness
    b. All patients
    c. Patients 65 years and older
    d. Patients with cancer

43. Which of the following policies encourages openness and transparency with employees?
    a. Communications policy
    b. Social media policy
    c. Open-door policy
    d. Code of conduct policy

44. Susan is preparing her team's department objectives that will be used to create individual goals and accomplishments for her employees' performance reviews. What should Susan ensure that each of these objectives includes?
    a. Well-written, clear, concise, and specific language to ensure understanding
    b. Specific, measurable, achievable, relevant, and time-bound aspects
    c. Professional growth, development, training, and learning opportunities
    d. Recognition and appreciation for previous performance and accomplishments

45. How long should medical instruments be soaked in solution for complete disinfection?
    a. 24 hours
    b. 20 to 30 minutes
    c. 1 hour
    d. 10 minutes

46. What does the HCAHPS survey purport to do?
    a. Calculate and publicize data on the likelihood of various medical complications at different healthcare providers
    b. Estimate how much a healthcare provider spends on each of its patients
    c. Calculate and show medical team leaders the unique strengths and weaknesses of each of their team members
    d. Collect and publicize patients' perspectives on healthcare providers and the quality of care they received

Practice Test #1

47. Which statement best describes the Lean Six Sigma approach to process improvement?
   a. The continual and collaborative discipline of measuring and comparing the results of key work processes
   b. A plan to eliminate or lower the likelihood of an error, or to make the occurrence of an error so obvious that any possibility of that error impacting the consumer is practically impossible
   c. To produce more effective processes, policies, and procedures that reduce variation and significantly lower the chances of negative outcomes
   d. A specific methodology that calculates the true costs of a potential solution compared to the actual benefits

48. Which of the following terms refers to the formal process used to settle a dispute?
   a. Deauthorization
   b. Arbitration
   c. Mediation
   d. Confrontation

49. Which of the following nursing models refers to the patient-focused care that centers around the integration of patient characteristics and nurse competencies within the healthcare environment?
   a. Nursing Leadership Model
   b. Professional Practice Model
   c. Synergy Model
   d. Modular Nursing Model

50. A healthcare provider scores in the 75th percentile for their achievement score for a certain VBP performance domain and in the 97th percentile for their improvement score in the same domain. How many points will they receive, and for what score?
   a. They will receive the maximum number of points due to their achievement score.
   b. They will receive the maximum number of points due to their improvement score.
   c. They will receive less than the maximum number of points due to their achievement score.
   d. They will receive less than the maximum number of points due to their improvement score.

51. A nurse who is completely engaged in client care and can help anticipate the needs of the patient and family members is said to be at which level of caring practice?
   a. Level 1
   b. Level 3
   c. Level 4
   d. Level 5

52. Which of the following is NOT one of the eight indicators of nursing competencies?
   a. Systems thinking
   b. Facilitation of learning
   c. Clinical inquiry
   d. Adherence to discharge plans

53. Which of the following solutions should NOT be used for high-level disinfection?
   a. Boiling water
   b. Chlorine solution
   c. Hydrogen peroxide solution
   d. Ethyl alcohol

141

54. In the AACN Synergy Model of nursing practice, which of the following is one of the eight types of client characteristics?
    a. Medical knowledge
    b. Predictability
    c. Insurance coverage
    d. Positivity

55. Which part of Medicare is prescription drug coverage, considered optional, and provided for a monthly fee to those enrolled?
    a. Medicare Part A
    b. Medicare Part B
    c. Medicare Part C
    d. Medicare Part D

56. The National Labor Relations Act (NLRA) protects the following EXCEPT:
    a. Allowing employees to talk about their wages
    b. Requiring employers to pay employees during the formation of a union
    c. Allowing employees to form or join a union
    d. Striking and picketing

57. A healthcare provider, while laying out tools and equipment for heart pacemaker surgery, including the pacemaker in a sterile package, remembers hearing about a Category II recall of a pacemaker but cannot remember the details. What is the appropriate next step?
    a. Recognize that the employee who sent the pacemaker device to the operating room followed regulatory compliance procedures to verify the recall status of the pacemaker.
    b. Inform the surgeon in charge that the surgery may have to be delayed or postponed until a replacement pacemaker can be found.
    c. Make a note of the serial number of the device and then go to an office with a computer to search the FDA database to determine the recall status of the pacemaker.
    d. Follow regulatory compliance procedures to notify the designated individual that confirmation of the recall status of the pacemaker must be ascertained prior to surgery.

58. Which of the following refers to money awarded to an individual in a workplace discrimination case, generally equal to lost earnings?
    a. Retroactive pay
    b. Front pay
    c. Back pay
    d. Specialty pay

59. What are the two most common workplace safety risks?
    a. Bloodborne pathogens and tripping hazards
    b. Lockout/tagout and confined space hazards
    c. Noise exposure and bloodborne pathogens
    d. Lockout/tagout and tripping hazards

60. Which of the following benefits is associated with a diverse workplace?
    a. Higher employee retention
    b. Higher employee complaints
    c. Increased training needs
    d. Higher employee turnover

61. Innovation in healthcare can best be described as which of the following?
    a. Spreading of a new process in a passive manner or unplanned fashion
    b. A form of predictive technology that will enhance physicians' ability to provide medical care
    c. Developing a new process, policy, or standard that improves upon the quality outcomes of previous processes
    d. Providing a format to create uniformity of practice across other departments within the organization

62. Which of the following statements most accurately describes the difference between an operational budget and a capital budget?
    a. An operational budget is used by healthcare providers, whereas a capital budget is used by health insurance companies.
    b. An operational budget is used to calculate costs associated with the day-to-day operation of a healthcare facility, whereas a capital budget is used to calculate costs associated with durable goods.
    c. An operational budget is almost always constructed with a rolling forecast budget in mind, whereas a capital budget is almost always constructed with an annual budget.
    d. An operational budget is used exclusively for surgical centers, whereas all other forms of healthcare providers use capital budgets.

63. Which process administers, manages, and supports significant transitions related to resource allocation, operations, business processes, and other large-scale changes?
    a. Risk management
    b. Strategic planning
    c. Critical evaluation
    d. Change management

64. Loyalty in adversity and an outcome-focused approach are two of the five factors of which of the following?
    a. Human Factor Engineering
    b. Standard Operating Procedures
    c. Lean/Six Sigma
    d. A high reliability organization

65. What is the ultimate goal of an assessment or audit of an infection prevention program?
    a. Collect data about compliance
    b. Evaluate and improve the program
    c. Track infection control training
    d. Perform gap assessment

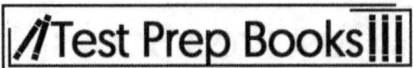

66. What is a Lean way of communicating HR programs, policies, and practices, including real-time updates?
    a. An employee handbook that is reprinted and redistributed with each new version
    b. In-person conferences that regularly review protocols
    c. An online employee handbook that is accessible to every employee and is updated online
    d. Social media

67. The following are considered paid time according to Fair Labor Standards Act (FLSA) EXCEPT:
    a. Short rest periods during the workday
    b. Travel time during a workday commuting from job site to job site
    c. A voluntary lecture the employee attends that is outside normal working hours and is not job related
    d. Travel time to a special one-day location, much further than the normal job site, for the employee

68. What would NOT be included when preparing educational content for nurses on new hospital cleaning, sterilization, and disinfection procedures?
    a. The cost of all educational content for training
    b. Which areas to clean when a patient leaves the hospital
    c. How to check if a room is disinfected enough for another patient to occupy
    d. The average number of times a surface is cleaned in a hospital daily

69. Two nurses get into an argument during their shift about restocking the supply room and go to the charge nurse to intervene. What is the first step of conflict resolution the charge nurse should instruct them to take?
    a. Present their sides of the argument
    b. Come to a compromise
    c. Discuss options for resolution in detail
    d. Dismiss their argument as non-productive

70. To participate in the value-based payment program by CMS, healthcare providers must meet quality of care metrics in the following four areas: clinical outcomes, person and community engagement, safety, and:
    a. Efficiency and cost reduction
    b. Research and scientific advancement
    c. Medical and pharmaceutical knowledge
    d. Insurance and patient responsibilities

71. The nurse is caring for a patient who is one day post-op from a lung resection and chest tube placement. The patient has been receiving acetaminophen (Ofirmev) 1000mg every 6hrs and requests to have something additional for pain management. The nurse understands that recovering from this surgery with a chest tube can be extremely painful and contacts the surgeon to request an additional PRN medication for pain. This nurse is exhibiting which level of advocacy and moral agency?
    a. Level 1
    b. Level 2
    c. Level 3
    d. Level 5

Practice Test #1

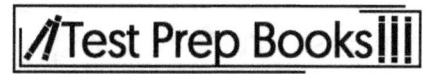

72. A healthcare facility maintains a database that tracks immunization and health screening details required for employees that reduce their risk of healthcare-associated infections. It is designed to flag those individuals in need of updates. The individual responsible for this data notes that five employees show flags for an update on TB screening. What is the next step?
    a. A group email is sent to these five individuals with locations where the screening may be conducted.
    b. At the next staff meeting, the five individuals are asked to stay behind and are verbally informed of this requirement as a small group.
    c. Each individual is sent a memo making them aware of this situation and a deadline by which the screening should be completed.
    d. Nothing is done; it is assumed that the individuals know what to do and when to do it.

73. When is an employer allowed to deny Consolidated Omnibus Budget Reconciliation Act (COBRA) to an employee?
    a. If the employee stopped showing up to work without putting in a resignation.
    b. If the employee passed away.
    c. If the employee went from full-time benefit eligible status to a part-time benefit ineligible status.
    d. If an employee was fired for gross misconduct.

74. Which of the following is NOT a type of leave covered by the FMLA?
    a. Qualifying exigency
    b. Professional sabbatical
    c. Foster-care placement
    d. Military caregiver

75. Which of the following is the correct meaning of the abbreviation HPPD?
    a. Hours per physician day
    b. Harm potential per disease
    c. Honorary practice physician degree
    d. Hours per patient day

76. What is an employer with more than fifty employees required to do for a nursing mother employee under the Fair Labor Standards Act (FLSA)?
    a. Provide a private bathroom for a mother when it is their normal break time.
    b. Provide a private non-bathroom space for the mother during their normal break time.
    c. Provide a private non-bathroom space for the mother as frequently as needed.
    d. There is no space requirement for accommodation if the mother has a car in the parking lot and breaks are provided when necessary.

77. The Americans with Disabilities Act applies to which of the following?
    a. An employer with fifty or more employees
    b. All employers regardless of their size
    c. Employers who have at least $50,000 in federal contracts
    d. An employer with fifteen or more employees

78. The nurse is caring for a post-op patient with a history of prescription drug abuse who is having difficulty managing their pain. Which of the following actions will help the nurse manage this patient's pain appropriately?
    a. Assess pain at least twice in a 12-hour shift
    b. Provide care in the least invasive ways possible
    c. Refuse pain management due to history of drug abuse
    d. Offer pain medication after dressing changes and when patient has finished ambulating

79. Which of the following is true regarding informed consent forms?
    a. They must be completed at admission.
    b. They must be signed, dated, and witnessed.
    c. They must be maintained under lock and key.
    d. All of the above

80. Which of the following information is NOT included in a literature review?
    a. Opinions about the usefulness of each source
    b. An analysis of the credibility of each source
    c. A summary of each source
    d. Test data performed by the researcher

81. What is the suggested preparatory schedule for accreditation?
    a. Six months of current-process analysis in advance of survey
    b. One year of current-process analysis prior to survey
    c. At least one year of current-process analysis, followed by status updates every three months
    d. One should begin preparing for the next survey immediately after the current one ends.

82. Which of the following terms is described as the process of removing a union's security clause and authority to negotiate?
    a. Deauthorization
    b. Arbitration
    c. Mediation
    d. Confrontation

83. Which of the following federal laws established employee classification and regulated minimum wage, overtime pay, on-call pay, recordkeeping, and child labor?
    a. Family Medical Leave Act
    b. Fair Labor Standards Act
    c. Davis Bacon Act
    d. Walsh-Healy Act

84. Systems thinking uses which of the following?
    a. A centrist approach
    b. Cognitive mapping
    c. Scorecards
    d. Technology to drive ideas

85. Which of the following best represents the purpose of Six Sigma?
    a. To eliminate ineffective and wasteful techniques that diminish productivity
    b. To organize management and employee councils
    c. To gain valuable feedback from employees to determine the most ineffective use of company resources
    d. To increase productive capacities by recruiting employees with the most experience

86. A unit team leader is providing guidance on the use of a new central line dressing kit. The team leader is implementing which educational concept?
    a. Competency
    b. Knowledge
    c. Training
    d. Evaluation

87. Which of the following is NOT an outcome of the performance management process?
    a. Salary increases and promotions
    b. Growth and development opportunities
    c. Employee satisfaction and morale rate
    d. Disciplinary actions and training needs

88. HR wants to organize a training program on cultural differences in the workplace. Whom should this training target?
    a. Managers and other employees in leadership positions, so they can communicate key practices to their subordinates
    b. Employees who have had problems with cultural misunderstandings in the past
    c. New employees because they are more likely to come from diverse backgrounds
    d. Employees from all levels of the organization

89. Which of the following laws is also known as Obamacare, named after President Barack Obama?
    a. Americans with Disabilities Act
    b. Patient Protection and Affordable Care Act
    c. Mental Health Parity Act
    d. Family Medical Leave Act

90. Two employees who perform well individually have been placed on a project team together. However, in a team setting, they often clash due to very different work styles and attitudes. How can an HR staff member help resolve this issue?
    a. Separate the two team members and put them on different projects.
    b. Put them on a probationary warning.
    c. Provide coaching to the employees to find common ground.
    d. Allow them to resolve it autonomously, as this is more empowering.

91. Which strategy assumes individuals are rational and will naturally follow a path that benefits their self-interest?
    a. The power-coercive strategy
    b. The empirical-rational strategy
    c. The technology-innovation strategy
    d. The normative-reductive strategy

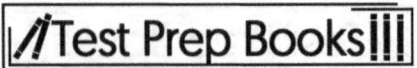

92. Which part of Medicare is hospital insurance, considered mandatory, and generally at no cost to qualifying individuals?
    a. Medicare Part A
    b. Medicare Part B
    c. Medicare Part C
    d. Medicare Part D

93. "The protection, promotion, and optimization of health and abilities, prevention of illness and injury, alleviation of suffering through the diagnosis and treatment of human response, and advocacy in the care of individuals, families, communities, and populations." This statement is best described as which of the following?
    a. The ANA Code of Ethics
    b. The AACN definition of clinical care
    c. The ANA definition of nursing practice
    d. The five assumptions of the Synergy Model

94. Which of the following would be the best source of information related to the way patients were treated to handle the symptoms of hepatitis B in the past?
    a. Medical libraries
    b. Web browsing
    c. Old television hospital dramas
    d. Recent medical journals

95. Which of the following statements accurately describes the difference between value-based payment models and value-based insurance design?
    a. Value-based payment models directly link reimbursement to patient outcomes, whereas value-based insurance design offers discounted rates for treatments shown to be effective.
    b. Value-based payment models are determined using a healthcare provider's achievement score, whereas value-based insurance design models are determined using a healthcare provider's improvement score.
    c. Value-based payment models have been shown to be effective in reducing costs for both patients and healthcare providers, whereas value-based insurance design has only been shown to be effective in reducing costs for healthcare providers.
    d. Value-based payment models have been promoted and popularized by CMS and other governmental organizations, whereas value-based insurance design models have been pioneered by commercial health insurance companies.

96. The nurse is working with a certified nursing assistant (CNA) to help provide care for a 55-year-old patient who is morbidly obese. Which of the following tasks would be appropriate to delegate to the CNA to perform independently?
    a. Giving an oral pain medication that has already been scanned
    b. Inserting a new peripheral IV
    c. Repositioning the patient in bed
    d. Recording output from a foley catheter

97. Which of the following situation(s) would be considered compensable time according to the Fair Labor Standards Act (FLSA)?
    a. An employee who is on-call but is given a long lead time before they need to come back to work and is allowed to use the time as they want
    b. An employee who is on-call but is required to remain on campus and be ready to work
    c. The commute time from the employees' home to the normal work location
    d. Both A and B

98. A venous catheter is required for a patient in a reputable and highly rated research hospital. The technician picks up the packaged venous catheter and notices a small tear in the sterile packaging. What is the appropriate next step for the technician?
    a. Assume that the small tear just occurred and use the venous catheter.
    b. Locate a new venous catheter with an intact sterile package and use it.
    c. Use a sterile swab to clean the outside of the venous catheter.
    d. Return the venous catheter in the torn package to the supply department for replacement.

99. Which of the following positions falls under the Fair Labor Standards Act (FLSA) regulations?
    a. Non-exempt positions
    b. Exempt positions
    c. Professional positions
    d. Administrative positions

100. What does the abbreviation POS mean in the context of private health insurance companies?
    a. Part of system
    b. Partly open service
    c. Point-of service
    d. Position of system

101. Which of the following terms refers to a planned and practiced protocol used during an emergency?
    a. Strategic plan
    b. Emergency response
    c. Evacuation plan
    d. Hazard communication

102. Which of the following statements most accurately describes the difference between an HMO and a PPO?
    a. Both are examples of commercial insurance plans, with HMOs typically being less expensive but offering patients fewer choices for where and how they may seek out coverage.
    b. HMOs are examples of private health insurance plans, whereas PPOs are examples of government-provided health insurance plans.
    c. HMOs follow an FFS model, whereas PPOs follow a VBP model.
    d. HMOs and PPOs are synonymous terms for the same type of health insurance plan, and there is no functional difference between the two.

103. Which of the following statements most accurately describes the current state of FFS payment models in the healthcare insurance marketplace?
    a. FFS models are as prevalent as they have ever been because many customers and those in the healthcare industry become increasingly dissatisfied with VBP models.
    b. FFS models, although once unpopular, have now been reformed and refined to the point where they are comparable and almost preferable to VBP models.
    c. Because FFS models have become increasingly associated with practices such as overprovision, they have largely been replaced by models involving some form of VBP.
    d. Since the passing of the ACA, FFS models are now illegal to practice in the United States.

104. In discussions on healthcare reimbursement methods, what does the term overprovision refer to?
    a. The idea that hospitals that receive patients from higher socioeconomic backgrounds are usually perceived to be higher-performing facilities
    b. When healthcare providers attempt to treat all of a patient's perceived medical problems, not just the one for which they were initially seeking treatment
    c. Stockpiling medical supplies at a particular healthcare provider, usually to the financial detriment of that organization and others in its area
    d. When healthcare providers prescribe a patient more services than may otherwise be necessary or advisable in order to increase the amount they can bill the payor

105. How does a healthcare facility know who is restricted, who is excluded, and for how long these periods last?
    a. The details of these restrictions and exclusions must be documented in a database program.
    b. The nursing supervisor keeps a complete list of all department restricted or excluded personnel.
    c. The pass keys of restricted and excluded personnel are deactivated until they can return to work.
    d. A daily report of restricted and excluded employees is printed and distributed to area supervisors.

106. Which of the following statements about strategic plans is NOT correct?
    a. Strategic plans involve objectives, analysis, looking at strengths and weaknesses, and implementation.
    b. Strategic plans are executed by employees and HR professionals to ensure these employees have the necessary skills to accomplish the identified goals.
    c. Strategic plans are a one-time activity that should always guide the organization toward the overall goals and objectives.
    d. Strategic plans should maximize the organization's strengths, take advantage of industry opportunities, and regularly be improved.

107. Which of the following nursing interventions is most consistent with the competencies of caring practices, advocacy, and moral agency?
    a. Developing cultural awareness of care team members
    b. Mentoring novice nurses in the use of research findings
    c. Facilitating the patient's transition from one level of care to another on the health continuum
    d. Refining educational programs for patients and families

108. What percent of eligible employees are required to sign authorization cards by the National Labor Relations Board before it will order an election where employees can vote on whether to be represented by a union?
   a. At least 30%
   b. At least 40%
   c. At least 45%
   d. A majority of the employees who are eligible to vote

109. A leader who discusses ideas with their group but then seldom incorporates the group's suggestions into their presented changes is said to be which kind of leader?
   a. Democratic leader
   b. Consultative leader
   c. Participatory leader
   d. Delegative leader

110. In the cognitive domain of Bloom's Taxonomy, which of the following is the highest level of cognitive complexity?
   a. Understanding
   b. Analyzing
   c. Applying
   d. Evaluating

111. In what circumstance can an employer NOT pay overtime to an employee who works over forty hours a week?
   a. The employee works two different jobs for the same employer. In each job, they only work thirty hours a week.
   b. The employee works sixty hours one work week, but only twenty hours the next work week.
   c. The employee waives the right to overtime by signing a form.
   d. The employee is considered exempt.

112. When working with adult learners, it is important for the nurse to incorporate which concept into their lesson plan and teachings?
   a. Relate teachings to real-life experiences
   b. Assume the patient has no prior knowledge of the topic
   c. Maintain authority and control of the patient during education
   d. Keep objectives fluid and subjective

113. According to the 1961 text, *The Planning of Change*, which of the following is NOT a strategy for managing change?
   a. The normative-reductive strategy
   b. The power-coercive strategy
   c. The technology-innovation strategy
   d. The empirical-rational strategy

114. Which of the following accurately represents the Fishbone Diagram?
   a. It focuses on the analysis of management and does not consult the entire organization.
   b. It identifies the strengths and weaknesses of an organization.
   c. It investigates the causes of problems.
   d. It provides a visual representation of a distribution of data.

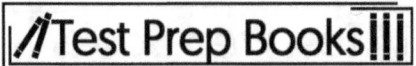

115. The nurse is receiving new medication orders from the patient's medical team during rounds. Which action can help reduce medication errors?
    a. Request a verbal order
    b. Use standard medical abbreviations when possible
    c. Read back and verify new orders received
    d. Rely on paper charting to double-check for error

116. Which of the following is NOT a required component in informed consent?
    a. Medical team members involved in treatment or procedure
    b. Risks and benefits of alternative options
    c. Reason for the treatment or procedure
    d. Alternative treatment options

117. A healthcare provider decides to do away entirely with having an annual budget, opting instead to only do a rolling forecast. In which of the following areas would that healthcare provider most likely experience difficulties?
    a. In negotiations with financial lenders
    b. In making future budget predictions
    c. In assessing the viability of the current budget
    d. In gathering information about past budgets and finances

118. Which of the following is NOT one of the components of effective assertive communication?
    a. Look for areas of compromise
    b. Have a defined and clear message
    c. Use "you" statements
    d. Control delivery of information

119. An individual believes that being a good leader is an innate trait and cannot be taught to others. This individual most likely subscribes to which of the following theories of leadership?
    a. Autocratic Leadership Theory
    b. Laissez-faire Leadership Theory
    c. The Great Man Theory of Leadership
    d. Democratic Leadership Theory

120. Who would be the best featured speaker(s) for a training on workplace misconduct?
    a. A panel of employees who have made workplace misconduct complaints in the past
    b. Someone from the C-suite (e.g., CEO, CFO, or COO)
    c. A Department of Justice representative
    d. The HR professionals who organized the training

121. Which of the following tools would NOT be used to determine why goals were not achieved or why there was a discrepancy between expected outcomes and actual outcomes?
    a. Six Sigma
    b. Gap analysis
    c. Root cause analysis
    d. Cause-and-effect diagram

122. Risk managers are trained to evaluate which of the following?
    a. Potential for harm
    b. Outcomes of events
    c. Patient safety
    d. All of the above

123. Who is the employer required to cover under the Consolidated Omnibus Budget Reconciliation Act (COBRA)?
    a. An employee who left a week before they reached their eligibility date for insurance
    b. A former employee AND that employee's spouse who were on the company's insurance
    c. An employee who declined benefits at work, but now wants COBRA coverage
    d. A current employee is who eligible for benefits

124. When using the empirical-rational strategy to initiate change, what is the best way to accomplish the change successfully?
    a. Provide an employee lunch when communicating the change
    b. Educate employees with new information on the change
    c. Incentivize the change to relay the benefit employees will experience
    d. Have the leader of the organization communicate the change

125. When meetings have dysfunctions, they impact which of the following?
    a. The quality agenda
    b. The cost and team confidence
    c. The cost, schedule, quality, and project manager's credibility
    d. The schedule and cost

126. The Family and Medical Leave Act (FMLA) is a federal law that provides for leave due to medical reasons. Which of the following is NOT a provision of the law?
    a. Available for new fathers
    b. Continued pay while on leave
    c. Continued medical insurance while on leave
    d. Maintaining equal position within the company

127. What type of budget is used to plan for future FTE needs as well as costs of routine functions and activities of the organization?
    a. Functional
    b. Operational
    c. Organizational
    d. Capital

128. A nurse executive is evaluating potential education options for teaching in the community about healthy food choices and preventative diabetes care. What type of role would this advocacy fall under?
    a. Public health
    b. Legal
    c. Home health
    d. Patient rights

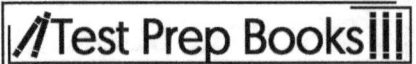

129. What does the Fair Labor Standards Act (FLSA) NOT provide for?
    a. Overtime pay
    b. Minimum wage
    c. Breaks or mealtimes
    d. Recording of hours worked

130. The nurse executive is reviewing areas for improvement with an interdisciplinary team that includes nurses, doctors, pharmacists, and other care providers. Which of the following would the nurse executive understand to be *most* directly influenced by nursing practice?
    a. Incidence of patient falls
    b. Proper patient consent before procedures
    c. Sterile preparation of blood products
    d. Rate of handwashing among healthcare professionals

131. The Americans with Disabilities Act (ADA) provides for the elimination of discrimination in the workplace and hiring practices. Which of the following is NOT a strategy for the nurse executive to employ to maintain compliance with the ADA?
    a. Providing a handicapped-accessible environment
    b. Creating reasonable accommodations for the job or work environment
    c. Making broad descriptions of job duties
    d. Determining mandatory job functions

132. The executive team is briefed on a patient advocacy concern in which the care that family at the bedside is demanding does not align with the incapacitated patient's stated wishes in their durable power of attorney for healthcare (DPOAH). What is the next best step to protect the patient's rights?
    a. Continue providing care according to the patient's DPOAH.
    b. Call security and have the family removed.
    c. Refer the case to the ethics committee for review and recommendation.
    d. Have the provider explain to the family that they are wrong.

133. The nurse executive is gathering a team to conduct a root cause analysis after a sentinel event. Which statement should the executive use to best describe the overall goal of the team?
    a. "We will be looking to identify the person most responsible for the sentinel event so that we can take appropriate action to either remediate or discipline their behavior."
    b. "We will try to identify the greatest risks to our organization created by this sentinel event and mitigate them."
    c. "We will be looking for the system, human, and cultural failings in the organization that led most directly to this sentinel event so that we can change them."
    d. "We will be conducting a literature search on the best ways to prevent this kind of event from happening in the future."

134. What is the primary purpose of the National Labor Relations Act (NLRA), also known as the Wagner Act?
    a. Protection of workers from unfair labor practices
    b. Creation of unions in the workplace
    c. Prevention of strikes and picketing
    d. Coverage of independent contractors

135. The nurse executive is creating a progressive budget proposal for the board. The previous fiscal year's performance was analyzed to predict change and adaptability of the organization. What is this type of budget called?
    a. Fiscal year analysis
    b. Performance-based budget
    c. Resource allocation
    d. Rolling forecast

136. What is the first step of the framework that the nurse executive will use to address an employee-related patient safety concern that has been voiced through a reporting system aimed at supporting a just culture?
    a. Talk to the nurse manager about the employee's disciplinary record.
    b. Ask the affected patient if they were harmed by the staff member.
    c. Assess the situation and investigate the concern.
    d. Implement a new protocol that fixes the problem.

137. Which of the following is a key principle in communication for the nurse executive?
    a. Active listening
    b. Ambiguity
    c. Speaking quickly
    d. Multitasking

138. A nurse executive is reviewing patient satisfaction data over the last quarter from an acute care unit. The scores have decreased significantly compared to the previous two quarters. What quality metric may be used to evaluate quality and delivery of care?
    a. Bed occupancy rate
    b. Average hospital stay
    c. Insurance reimbursement claims
    d. Hours per patient day

139. Which of the following describes reflective communication?
    a. Actively involving the audience through enthusiasm, imagery, or humor
    b. One person communicates a message, and the recipient confirms with a response
    c. Questioning, listening, and speaking
    d. Actively listening and restating the message in one's own words

140. A team has been assembled to complete a root cause analysis and recommend a solution for a safety issue. In reference to goal development, what term is NOT part of a SMART goal?
    a. Standard
    b. Achievable
    c. Measurable
    d. Time-bound

141. At which interval does the Joint Commission conduct its unannounced surveys of nursing units?
    a. 24-48 months
    b. Exactly two years
    c. Every year
    d. 18-36 months

142. Which of the following is an example of the assessment stage of Nursing Administration Practice outlined by the American Nurses Association?
    a. A newly written policy is reviewed to ensure that it aligns with current accreditation standards.
    b. After the cause of several falls is identified, patient rounds are increased to every 15 minutes for high-risk patients.
    c. A root cause analysis is completed on a unit that demonstrates chronically late medication administration times.
    d. After implementation of an intervention, data is gathered on the metrics related to new wounds acquired on a palliative care unit.

143. Which of the following is NOT a type of managerial communication?
    a. Upward communication
    b. Backward communication
    c. Downward communication
    d. Lateral communication

144. Which of the following is NOT one of the measures involved in regulatory compliance to maintain accreditation?
    a. Patient satisfaction
    b. Infection control
    c. Staff qualifications
    d. Emergency preparedness

145. Which of the following statements about the value-based purchasing model of reimbursement is NOT correct?
    a. Utilizes evidence-based practice to drive care decisions
    b. Reduces the number of adverse events related to patient harm
    c. Reimbursement is directly linked to meeting performance-based goals
    d. Funding and oversight is provided by the Joint Commission (TJC)

146. The nurse executive is working with nurse scientists to create a research project on nosocomial infection. The executive understands that the PICOT question format refers to which elements?
    a. Population, introduction, cost, outcome, test group
    b. Practice, intervention, change, options, time
    c. Participation, inquiry, cooperation, organization, teaching
    d. Population, intervention, control, outcome, time

147. The six key processes in communication are thinking, encoding, transmitting the signal, decoding, understanding, and which of the following?
    a. Writing
    b. Calculating
    c. Listening
    d. Perceiving

148. The nurse executive is seeking information to improve quality practices related to electronic health record safety. Which organization is most likely to provide information specific to this query?
    a. Centers for Disease Control and Prevention (CDC)
    b. National Committee for Quality Assurance (NCQA)
    c. Centers for Medicare and Medicaid Services (CMS)
    d. World Health Organization (WHO)

149. Which of the following best describes the first step in Rogers' Five-Stage Change Theory?
    a. Implement change and ensure that staff are adhering to the new practice.
    b. Initiate a trial of the new practices indicated after gathering data.
    c. Announce the change that will be taking place, when it will start, and how it will be measured.
    d. Communicate the reason for the change, what will happen, and who will be most affected.

150. Which of the following best describes the process of informed consent?
    a. Ensuring the patient is competent to make a decision
    b. A signed, witnessed form
    c. Convincing the patient to submit to a provider's suggested care
    d. A comprehensive patient education regarding benefits, risks, and alternatives for an intervention or procedure

Answer Explanations #1

1. B: Even though the United States spends more than twice as much money on healthcare as other developed nations, healthcare outcome measures are worse and life expectancy is shorter. CMS is moving to a value-based reimbursement plan to address rising costs and declining quality of care. Providers are advised to identify and measure the effectiveness of KPIs such as hospital readmission rates, patient satisfaction, and ER visits as evidence of the quality of care. The financial risk assumed by the provider varies with the design of the value-based care model used by the practice. There are three basic models—the accountable care organizations, bundled payment plans, and patient-centered medical home model—and each model assumes some but not all of the financial risks; therefore, Choice A is incorrect. Value-based modifiers address provider care, not hospital care, which means that Choices C and D are incorrect.

2. A: Since it is important to help promote a patient's independence to assist them with recovery, discouragement of this goal would be counter to the basic care responsibilities of the nurse. Choices B, C, and D are incorrect because these are the basic care responsibilities the nurse must provide. The nurse should provide safe care, minimize harm and pain, and reduce or eliminate any occurrence of medical errors.

3. A: The Age Discrimination in Employment Act of 1967 prohibits discrimination against anyone forty years of age or older regarding hiring, promotions, wages, benefits, termination, and other actions. The EEOC administers and oversees this law along with Title VII of the Civil Rights Act of 1964.

4. A: Value stream mapping is a tool from the Six Sigma approach that shows the value added by each step within a process. HRIS (Choice B) refers to information systems. SMART (Choice C) is an acronym to guide goal setting. Flow state diagrams (Choice D) are not a business tool.

5. B: Achievement and improvement scores are both used to assess a healthcare provider's performance in a specific performance domain and their compliance with the guidelines of CMS's VBP program. As the names imply, achievement scores are designed to quantify a hospital's overall quality of care, whereas improvement scores depict how a particular healthcare provider's quality of care has changed compared to previous years. Achievement scores are calculated by comparing an individual healthcare provider's score to other similar healthcare providers' scores, whereas improvement scores are calculated by comparing an individual healthcare provider's score with their previous scores. Therefore, the correct answer is Choice B. Choice A is incorrect because both achievement and improvement scores are measures determining effectiveness and efficiency of treatment. Choice C is incorrect because achievement and improvement scores are assessed for an entire healthcare provider and cannot be used to quantify an individual's performance. Choice D is incorrect because achievement and improvement scores are calculated for all healthcare providers, regardless of the percentile of their performance.

6. C: Value-based care models are associated with financial risk for the provider. Generally speaking, upside risk means that if the provider meets the patient-care goals set by CMS or a private payer, the provider shares the savings with the payer, and downside risk means that the provider is penalized for failing to meet the patient-care goals. Although there are greater rewards for quality patient care by providers in models with downside risk, many providers, especially groups that include hospitals, are not joining these models.

Answer Explanations #1

7. D: A rolling forecast uses past data to calculate future financial conditions of a healthcare facility. It does not use current data, data provided by CMS, or data from other healthcare facilities.

8. C: A patient with diabetic ketoacidosis (DKA) requesting drink or food that may dangerously raise their blood glucose level and increase mortality and morbidity should be denied; this is defined within the ethical principle of nonmaleficence, which means to cause no harm to a patient. Choice A is incorrect because beneficence is the ethical principle to promote welfare and actively help the patient. Choice B is incorrect because autonomy refers to the ethical principle and right for patients to make informed, independent decisions about their care. The patient in this scenario is not being denied their autonomy; instead, they are being redirected to make a safer decision. Choice D is incorrect because this is not unethical practice. The nurse made a decision in the best interest of the health of the patient and offered them appropriate alternative choices.

9. B: In order for a healthcare provider to be allowed to participate in a VBP program, there are four distinct performance domains for which they need to demonstrate quality of care. These domains are clinical outcomes, person and community engagement, safety, and efficiency and cost reduction. Therefore, the correct answer is Choice B because no considerations are made depending on the overall number of patients a healthcare provider sees and treats. All of the other answer choices accurately reflect the various performance domains designated by CMS for participation in a VBP program.

10. B: Medical records that reflect complete health history, detailed symptoms, testing performed, diagnosis, treatment, and medications are required to ensure continuity of care. Electronic medical records enable ease of sharing among departments and facilities, but all documentation must be accurate and up to date to best benefit patients and best inform caregivers. Choice A is incorrect. Although symptoms and medications are part of the documentation, not all diagnoses need to be registered with the CDC. Choice C is incorrect because although a driver's license/state ID, insurance card, and a referral for services are often requested for the admission process, they do not contain all the essential information that determines continuity of care. Choice D is also incorrect because although matching the patient's name to documentation prevents errors in care, if electronic or paper medical records are incomplete, there may be an interruption in care that puts the patient at risk.

11. C: Value-based insurance design is a form of VBP that aims to improve both patient outcomes and lower overall costs by incentivizing customers to choose effective and cost-efficient treatments. An individual with a value-based insurance plan can typically expect to pay less for treatments that are shown to be cheap and broadly effective, whereas they may pay more for treatments or programs that either haven't been deemed effective or necessary. Therefore, the correct answer is Choice C. All of the other answers describe programs that are provided at a relatively low cost and have been shown to be effective, so it is likely that such programs would be incentivized with coverage and reduced rates.

12. D: While you should not discriminate for any reason, the EEOC guideline on ageism protects those above the age of forty. Pregnancy status, genetic information, and disability are all protected under the Equal Employment Opportunity Commission, making Choices A, B, and C incorrect.

13. B: Medicare and Medicaid both refer to government insurance programs and are aimed at providing insurance to specific groups that may be more likely to lack the necessary health coverage. Medicare is a federal insurance program that covers individuals who are older than 65 years of age (as well as some select conditions), whereas Medicaid is a joint federal and state program that provides coverage to individuals with limited income and/or resources. In both cases, the government is the payor rather than a private health insurance company, the patient's employer, or the patient. Therefore, Choice B is

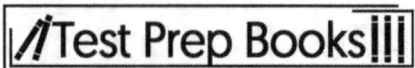

Answer Explanations #1

correct. The other answer choices do not accurately reflect the correct payor for patients with Medicare or Medicaid coverage.

14. D: Organizing a week-long training class focused on desired skill development, Choice *D*, is the best strategy. Although building the skills, knowledge, and competencies of the workforce is an ongoing responsibility of the HR department, sometimes there are short-term skills gaps that need to be closed. In this case, organizing a class or workshop to directly target the missing skill is a practical and effective approach. For example, if many employees are struggling with adopting new workplace software, a few training courses can help them get up to speed. Choice *A* is not the best choice because interviewing and onboarding new employees is very time-consuming and not the best short-term strategy. Choice *B* is also not the best choice because a high-potential development program should carry employees throughout the time at an organization until they are positioned to become leaders; again, this is a long-term rather than short-term development strategy. Finally, Choice *C* is not the best choice because, while internal reassignment can help employees to find positions that best fit their competencies, this choice does not solve the problem because it removes underperforming employees without replacing them or building the skills of remaining workers.

15. A: The Lean Six Sigma format that targets current processes is DMAIC, which stands for define, measure, analyze, improve, and control.

16. B: A patient who is terminally ill may not physiologically need as much nutritional intake due to the dying process. The nurse should understand ethically that even though this nutrition may extend life for the patient, it can cause a great deal of discomfort, increase nausea and vomiting, and even cause increased tumor growth, making Choice *B* correct. The nurse should always explain their reasoning to the patient and family members and encourage open discussion. Choice *A* is incorrect because starting supplemental tube feeding can cause the aforementioned side effects and may not be within the wishes of the patient. Choice *C* is incorrect because weight gain is not a strong concern during the dying process and does not present an ethical dilemma for the nurse. Choice *D* is incorrect because although nutrition can extend life, it can result in a lower quality of life that the patient may not wish to endure.

17. B: Competitive benchmarking can help reveal how comparable organizations solved defects similar to what a given healthcare organization is facing. The comparative analysis can also illuminate how the current processes are outpacing the competitors, which encourages the integration of what works with what does not work well enough. This approach will help the leadership team deliver on the promise of providing exceptional care. All hospitals are required to post their quality information on their websites for public view, which can be utilized for competitive benchmarking, as in Choice *B*. Choice *A* is incorrect since the Joint Commission does not discourage this practice. Choices *C* and *D* are incorrect since they refer to internal benchmarking.

18. A: Disinfecting methods remove most pathogens, particularly those approved for this use by the EPA or the FDA and prepared according to manufacturers' instructions. Choices *B* and *C* are both incorrect because ordinary soap or an enzymatic cleaner are only formulated to remove visible dirt and grime, not necessarily disease-causing pathogens. Choice *D* is incorrect because although methods of sterilization do remove nearly all pathogens, hiring a third-party vendor to attain this level of clean would incur an unnecessary expense.

19. A: There are multiple functions of rating in performance management. The first purpose of rating is to give management the opportunity to identify the best performing employees. Once this is done, these employees can be rewarded in various ways, making Choice *A* correct. Conversely, rating is a technique used by management to distinguish poorly performing employees. Underperforming employees can be dealt with in many ways: they can receive a decrease in pay, be forced to attend additional training programs, or ultimately have their employment terminated. Choices *B*, *C*, and *D* do not accurately reflect functions of rating in performance management, since rating is used frequently and not for the purpose of designating favorites or employees rating management.

20. A: Employers are required to maintain group health insurance coverage for an employee who is out on FMLA leave. The coverage must be the same as prior to the FMLA leave. Spouses who work for the same employer receive a TOTAL of twelve weeks of FMLA time for the birth of their child, making Choice *B* incorrect. Employers can require employees to take their paid leave, such as vacation or sick leave, when using FMLA; additionally, this requirement must be stated in the company policies, making Choice *C* incorrect. FMLA covers leave for the birth or adoption of a child; placement of a foster child; the serious health condition of the employee, spouse, child, or parent; and additional needs related to military servicemembers and caregivers, making Choice *D* incorrect.

21. B: Medicare Part B (Choice *B*) is voluntary medical insurance that covers health care expenses, such as outpatient care and physicians' services. Individuals pay a monthly fee for this coverage.

22. B: The Portal-to-Portal Act deals with the preliminary and postliminary tasks of employees. The act requires employers to pay employees who are covered under the FLSA for time spent traveling to perform job-related tasks, if that travel is outside of the employees' regular work commute. Additionally, employees are to be paid for hours spent in job-related training that is outside of their normal workday.

23. D: Standard patient care and precautions taken in instances of known or suspected infection risk are the two categories under which environmental policies and procedures are regulated. Choices *A* and *C* are incorrect because risk of infection is dependent on specific pathogens regardless of the treatment offered or the type of facility visited. Choice *B* is also incorrect because although duration of care may result in a greater exposure to at-risk infections if policies and procedures are not regulatory compliant, all medical facilities require the same two categories to reduce HAIs.

24. D: Rolling forecast budgeting has been shown to benefit healthcare workers across the board. For frontline healthcare workers, a rolling forecast budget can help lessen the dissonance between an annual budget's predictions and the day-to-day financial realities of the healthcare industry. In addition to clearly saving accountants and those directly responsible for budgeting time, rolling forecast budgeting saves the time of healthcare executives. As it currently stands, healthcare executives spend thousands of hours every year considering and deciding their annual budgets, and adopting rolling forecast budgeting has been shown to decrease the amount of time executives are tied up considering budgetary concerns. Therefore, the correct answer is Choice *D*. All of the other answer choices do not accurately reflect how the adoption of rolling forecast budgeting would affect members of a healthcare organization.

25. C: Employees that supervise other employees and have management as a significant part of their job are considered exempt. To classify as exempt, employees need to make over $23,600 per year and pass the duties test. The duties test needs to include either executive job duties, professional job duties, or exempt administrative job duties. These two requirements eliminate Choices *A* and *B*, as Choice *A* does not meet the duties test and Choice *B* does not meet the salary level test. Choice *D* is incorrect, as an employer must justify why an employee is exempt.

Answer Explanations #1

26. B: Choice *B*, a Pareto chart, is a quality improvement tool that uses a bar graph to determine the frequency of causative factors. Choice *A* is not correct because a fishbone diagram focuses on a main problem statement and identifies causative factors in linear form. Choice *C* is not correct because a flow chart produces a step-by-step diagram of a process or workflow. Choice *D* is not correct because a gap analysis identifies the needs or barriers between a desired goal of an implementation strategy and the actual clinical situation.

27. B: OSHA, the Occupational Safety and Health Administration, is responsible for creating and enforcing workplace safety standards, making choice *B* correct. OSHA sets minimum standards, provides job training in multiple languages to ensure understanding, and protects employees. The other abbreviations, listed in choices *A*, *C*, and *D*, are not relevant to workplace safety standards.

28. B: Recognition programs are programs used to promote a positive organizational culture by recognizing individual employees for the work they have done. Recognition programs can be formal or informal and can have a large impact on employees. Special event programs (Choice *A*) are designed to promote a positive culture; they generally do not reward employees for their work. Inclusion programs (Choice *C*) are incorporated into day-to-day operations to ensure that all employees' voices are heard. Incentive programs (Choice *D*) provide financial rewards to those employees who perform at a higher level than others and have a larger impact on the organization.

29. D: MSPB is a metric used to calculate a healthcare provider's score according to the efficiency and cost reduction performance domain of CMS's VBP program. MSPB specifically seeks to calculate the total cost of services provided by a healthcare facility during a Medicare beneficiary's stay. Therefore, the correct answer is Choice *D*. All of the other answer choices do not provide the correct meaning for the abbreviation MSPB.

30. D: Scheduling mandatory in-person training with employee involvement, such as skits, role plays, and mock juries, encourages engagement and focus on real-world implications, making Choice *D* correct. Workplace conduct is a topic that HR should emphasize for all employees with a high level of engagement. HR has made the right first step in deciding to proactively address workplace harassment and misconduct; however, establishing clear guidance and creating a culture of civility comes from true engagement with employees. For this reason, Choice *C* is not the best choice, because employees will be passive learners. Also, while Choice *A* might be a good supplementary resource, employees also need positive modeling and information about how they *should* behave in the workplace, rather than just negative information about how they *should not* behave. Finally, Choice *B* is not the best choice because abstract legal implications may not have a strong connection to employees. Instead, Choice *D* gives employees a chance to explore situations that affect their everyday workplace interactions.

31. B: According to Six Sigma, any deviation from the standard process typically results in higher risk. Choice *A*, the 5 S method, is incorrect because it is an organization tool used in Lean. Choice *C*, Lean, is incorrect because it focuses specifically on reducing waste, not variety. The National Safety Standards are not a methodology in process improvement, so Choice *D* is incorrect.

32. C: When committees are being constructed to make hospital-wide changes regarding client rights, it is best to involve not only administrative and medical staff, but also patients and their family members, since these matters directly concern them. Additional feedback can be gained from patients and family members through surveys, feedback cards, and follow-up appointments. Choices *A*, *B*, and *D* are incorrect because they do not include all groups of people that should be involved in decisions regarding client rights.

Answer Explanations #1

33. C: Immediate action needs to be taken when lapses in established procedures are observed. Posting a notice could be done to reach the most amount of people without taking up too much time. Retraining the entire staff, Choice *B*, or waiting for more feedback, Choice *D*, are processes that would take too long to organize. Choice *A* would also take too long and cause too much loss of work time for procedures that have already been taught.

34. A: According to OSHA, type of exposure, appropriateness for task, and proper fit are the three factors upon which PPE selection is based. Choices *B* and *D* are incorrect. Although multiple manufacturers produce PPE for a variety of situations, sizes, materials, and quality levels, they are not the three key factors for the selection of required PPE. Neither Choice *B* nor Choice *D* presents all three key factors. Choice *C* is incorrect because personal preference does not extend to the choice of PPE for a specific task.

35. B: The CDC publishes guidelines for work restrictions and exclusions based on the particular disease or pathogen. This is designed to protect the employee lacking an updated immunization for whooping cough from contracting the disease. Work restriction and work exclusion policies are not punitive. Choice *A* is incorrect. The employee cannot be dismissed for noncompliance until ten days have passed and the immunization has not been obtained. The time period of this incident occurred on day three, which was well within the ten-day timeframe given. Choice *C* is incorrect because charging the individual lacking proper immunization with direct patient care is not only a risky policy, but also not in line with regulatory compliance. Choice *D* is incorrect because although sending the individual for immediate immunization on work time will expedite immunity, vaccines take some time to work, so this won't necessarily prevent infection.

36. C: Facility-specific checklists and resources published on the CDC website include all the information required to plan and conduct an effective audit. Choice *A* is incorrect; although reviewing facility policies and procedures is part of an audit, creating a checklist from existing policies may miss a policy that has not been updated to meet a new regulation or requirement. Choice *B* is incorrect because although past experience has value, audit items specific to an outpatient facility might be missed if relying on previous experience alone. Choice *D* is incorrect because data for gap analysis are not available until the audit is completed.

37. A: Telemedicine is a form of medical care provided remotely by credentialed and licensed healthcare professionals. It has reformed healthcare delivery across the country. Providers can now conduct patient assessments, prescribe medications, and collaborate with other medical professionals remotely, via Skype, telephone, email, and secure chatrooms. This type of distance healthcare eliminates the constraints of geography and mobility and allows providers access to increasing numbers of previously underserved populations.

38. C: Observational data that has been recorded and validated (Choice *C*) is always more credible than unpublished accounts, such as personal anecdotes, Choice *B*. Student publications, Choice *A*, or surveys, Choice *D*, might also contain fabrications because the information could be falsified by individuals who are participating, and the data collected from their accounts cannot be validated as accurately as hospital data.

39. C: Nurses should always try to use therapeutic communication, but they should take special care when speaking with patients and family members who have received difficult news. The nurse is letting the patient know in this response that they are available to care for the patient's needs and recognize the stressful situation they are in. This communication helps put the focus on the patient and allows for an open line of communication. Choice A is incorrect because this gives false reassurance to the patient and may make it more difficult for the patient to accept their prognosis. Choice B is incorrect because this question is accusatory and places blame on the patient, which is not comforting or productive. Choice D is incorrect because the nurse is offering advice when it may not be the patient's wish to begin looking at hospice. This also does not put the patient as the focus of the nurse's response and does not allow them time to properly process the new information they received.

40. A: Although of all these actions may be appropriate at times to address the issue, the first thing Evelyn should do is to provide training to the managers and supervisors, making Choice A correct. This training should include information on the process, forms, and timeline, as well as coaching on how to deliver an effective evaluation. Evelyn should respond to questions and provide real-life examples to situations that may arise during the process.

41. A: FMLA only covers unpaid, protected leave for the following reasons: the birth of a child, adoption or foster-care placement; the serious health condition of a spouse, child, or parent; the serious health condition of the employee, which requires inpatient care or continuing treatment by a healthcare provider; qualifying exigency leave; leave to address the most common issues that arise when an employee's spouse, child, or parent is on active duty or call to active duty status (e.g., making financial and legal arrangements and arranging for alternative childcare); military caregiver leave; or leave to care for a covered service member (e.g., employee's spouse, child, parent, or next of kin) with a serious injury or illness. Employees are to be granted up to twenty-six weeks of job-protected, unpaid leave during a twelve-month period to care for a covered service member with a serious injury or illness.

42. B: Advance directives can be made available to any and all patients that are admitted. This allows for the protection of the patient's legal right to self-determination in their care. Advance directives can also include types of do-not-resuscitate (DNR) orders that may be more commonly seen in terminally ill or elderly patients. Choices A, C, and D are incorrect because they do not include the entire patient population that is eligible to receive an advance directive as part of their medical care.

43. C: An open-door policy specifically encourages openness and transparency with employees. Managers and leadership often implement an open-door policy to ensure that employees know they are welcome to provide insights and feedback without fear of recourse. Choice A is incorrect because a communications policy is a broad policy that encompasses all areas of communication, including a social media policy, which is Choice B. Choice D is incorrect because a code of conduct policy is written to ensure employees are aware of and understand ethical and appropriate behaviors in the workplace.

44. B: Susan should ensure that each objective includes the SMART aspects: specific, measurable, achievable, relevant, and time-based. Without these aspects, an objective may not be met, or the status could be unknown. By including the SMART aspects, there can be a clear understanding of performance expectations. Choice A is incorrect because all language should be well written, clear, concise, and specific, but without SMART aspects, there could still be misunderstandings as to what is to be accomplished. Choices C and D are inaccurate because professional development and recognition are items within a performance review that are separate from performance objectives. If a training opportunity is to be an objective for an employee, the item should be written as an objective, containing the SMART aspects.

45. B: Medical instruments only need to remain in a disinfecting solution for 20 to 30 minutes. Too much time could deteriorate the tool, and too little time might not remove all the bacteria present.

46. D: The HCAHPS survey is a revolutionary survey that attempts to collect, synthesize, and publish consumer experiences when seeking and receiving health care. The HCAHPS survey is used to determine a healthcare provider's performance according to the person and community engagement performance domain of CMS's VBP program. Therefore, the correct answer is Choice D. All of the other answer choices refer to other healthcare metrics and do not reflect consumer experience at all.

47. C: The primary goal of Lean Six Sigma is to produce more effective processes, policies, and procedures that reduce variation and significantly lower the chances of negative outcomes.

48. B: Arbitration is a form of mediation but is the more formal process. Arbitration is a way to settle disputes using a third-party mediator without going to court. Deauthorization (Choice A) is the official process to remove a union's negotiating authority, as well as the requirement that employees must join the union. Mediation (Choice C) is generally the precursor to arbitration through a less formal process to resolve concerns and issues. Confrontation (Choice D) is also a form of mediation that is used when a stalemate occurs and neither side is willing to consider resolving the matter.

49. C: The model of nursing that shows the interactions and interconnectivity of a patient's health, the nurses' knowledge and clinical expertise, and the healthcare environment describes the Synergy Model of nursing practice. The Synergy Model encompasses eight client characteristics, eight nursing competencies, and six indicators of quality outcomes in the healthcare environment. Choice A is incorrect because the Nursing Leadership Model describes collaborative nursing environments that encourage teamwork and motivation. Choice B is incorrect because the Professional Practice Model refers to the overarching model of nursing practice that describes general values and beliefs in the nursing profession. Choice D is incorrect because the Modular Nursing Model describes the hierarchy and separate care units involved in patient care.

50. B: Achievement and improvement scores are the two kinds of measurements used to determine a healthcare provider's score for a particular performance domain of the CMS VBP program. Both scores are calculated as a percentile, with achievement scores being compared against other health providers' scores for that particular measurement and improvement scores being compared against the healthcare provider's previously recorded measurements. The number of points a provider ultimately receives is determined by first choosing whichever score is higher and then comparing that score against a threshold and benchmark score, set at the 50th percentile and the mean of the top decile, respectively. If the provider scores at or above the benchmark score, they receive full points for that measurement. Therefore, the correct answer is Choice B. As described, the other answer choices cannot be correct in this scenario.

51. D: There are three levels of caring practice for the nurse: level 1, level 3, and level 5. A nurse who is completely involved in a patient's care and able to anticipate needs to provide safe, dignified, and comfortable care is considered to be at the highest level of caring practice, level 5, Choice D. Choice A is incorrect because level 1 care provides the most basic care of creating a safe environment for a patient. Choice B is incorrect because level 3 care involves kind and compassionate care from a nurse, but the nurse may not be as fully engaged in managing and anticipating a patient's needs. Choice C is incorrect because level 4 is not one of the levels of caring practice for the nurse.

52. D: Adherence to discharge plans is not one of the eight indicators of nursing competencies; however, it is one of the six indicators of quality outcomes in the healthcare setting. Choices A, B, and C are incorrect because they are all indicators of nursing competencies. The other nursing competencies are clinical judgement, advocacy, caring practices, collaboration, and diversity response.

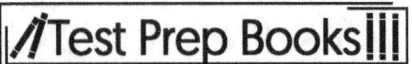

Answer Explanations #1

53. D: Alcohol should not be used for high-level disinfection processes because it does not kill all bacteria spores that might be present on a tool. The remaining choices, when mixed properly, have been proven to be more effective at removing all harmful bacteria from an object—something that is critical to do when conducting high-level disinfection.

54. B: Predictability is one of the eight types of client characteristics in the AACN Synergy Model. The other client characteristics are resiliency, stability, vulnerability, complexity, resource availability, participation in care, and decision-making ability. Choices A, C, and D are incorrect because these are not characteristics or factors that affect the patient aspect of the Synergy Model.

55. D: Medicare Part D (Choice D) is voluntary prescription drug coverage that individuals pay a monthly fee for. Part D is available to those who are eligible for Part A and also enrolled in Part B.

56. B: Employers are not required to provide compensation for the time employees spend forming a union, but must allow formation a union on company property, such as break rooms and parking lots. The NLRA gives employees the right to discuss their wages, making Choice A incorrect. Choices C and D are rights also granted by the NLRA.

57. D: Following regulatory compliance procedures may take a few extra steps; however, this method best reduces risk of potentially reversible harm to this patient if a recall has indeed been issued. Choice A is incorrect because it relies on an assumption that another individual performed the check. Even if checking is part of that individual's job, there is no guarantee this was done, and it is better to verify twice than never verify. Choice B is incorrect. Although delay or postponement of the surgery may be necessary, this is not the first step. Choice C is incorrect because even though searching this database by manufacturer and serial number will confirm the recall status, leaving the pacemaker in the operating room without informing the proper personnel risks use of a defective device and, ultimately, patient safety.

58. B: Front pay, Choice B, is money awarded to an individual that is generally equal to potential lost earnings. It is usually required when a position is not available or an employer has not made any effort to address ongoing issues. Front pay could also be warranted if the employee would be forced to endure a hostile work environment if returned to the original position. Back pay, Choice C, refers to corrected compensation for unpaid work while retroactive pay, Choice A, refers to correction of underpaid work.

59. A: Although all of the hazards listed can occur in a workplace and employers should have a plan to address each, the most common workplace safety risks are bloodborne pathogens and tripping hazards, making Choice A correct.

60. A: Organizations that have a more diverse workplace experience higher rates of employee retention, making Choice A correct. Additionally, employees are generally more satisfied and perform at a higher level than employees in workplaces that lack diversity, making Choices B, C, and D incorrect.

61. C: Innovation involves developing a new process, policy, or standard that improves upon the quality outcomes of previous processes. Choice A refers to diffusion. Choice B refers to patient analytics and medical informatics. Choice D refers to internal benchmarking.

62. B: Operational budgets and capital budgets are both examples of budgets typically created by healthcare providers. The key distinction between the two comes down to the kind of expenses assessed. With an operational budget, the focus is on the daily functioning and financial maintenance of the organization, whether that concerns the cost of basic utilities or the cost of employees' labor. A

Answer Explanations #1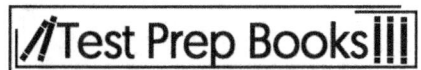

capital budget, on the other hand, is concerned with the cost and risk associated with durable items, ranging from hospital beds to new buildings and facilities. Therefore, the correct answer is Choice *B*. Choice *A* is incorrect because both operational and capital budgets are used by healthcare providers. Choice *C* is incorrect because both operational and capital budgets are just as likely to use an annual and/or rolling forecast budget plan. Choice *D* is incorrect because both operational and capital budgets are used by all forms of healthcare providers.

63. D: Change management is the process that seeks to support significant transitions within an organization and could include large-scale changes, resource allocation, operations changes, and an updated business process. Effective change management can help an organization to be successful during transition periods. Choices *A*, *B*, and *C* relate to management of risk, strategy, and evaluation processes, rather than assisting with change.

64. D: Loyalty in adversity and an outcome-focused approach are two of the five factors in any high-reliability organization, making Choice *D* correct. The other three are reliance on practical experience, an emphasis on operationalized definitions of expected outcomes, and a deeper-dive perspective when unexpected problems arise. Organizations that adopt this method of risk management achieve a high level of excellence because they focus on anticipating the best response to the worst-case scenario. Human Factor Engineering, Standard Operating Procedures, and Lean/Six Sigma, Choices *A*, *B*, and *C*, are not characterized by these factors.

65. B: CDC recommendations about infection prevention and regulatory requirements change as scientific knowledge about pathogens improves, so it is incumbent upon facilities to assess and improve infection prevention and control programs on a regular basis to ensure the best effort at reducing risk of HAIs. Choices *A, C,* and *D* are incorrect. Although collecting data about compliance, tracking infection control training, and performing gap analysis are important parts of an effective program, they do not represent the ultimate goal of the program. Compliance data should cover all requirements for day-to-day compliance to be effective. Education and training about infection prevention strategies geared toward job specificity are found to be most effective. Gap assessment is the difference between what is required and what is practiced and is an important part of the assessment/audit process.

66. C: An online handbook (Choice *C*) is the best option, as it is a paperless method with an immediate notification system that minimizes waste yet keeps all employees informed. Choice *A* and *B* are not as immediate or up-to-date, making them incorrect. Social media, Choice *D*, is not an appropriate place to house policies and practices.

67. C: If a lecture the employee attends is genuinely voluntary, outside of working hours, not job related, and no work activities take place, the employee does not need to be compensated for that time. Choice *A* is compensable since short rest periods, not including meal breaks, are typically paid. The time varies by state, but these are normally shorter than twenty minutes. Choice *B* and Choice *D* are both considered compensable working time, as they are traveling during normal working hours.

68. A: Educational content should include only information that the specific audience can best use. The cost of procedures and education would be unrelated to the nurse's job and would be more useful to stakeholders or mangers who handle the financials of the hospital. In this case, the audience of nurses would need to know as much as possible about the day-to-day procedures of cleaning areas, Choices *B, C,* and *D,* so they can adequately perform their duties.

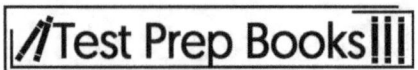

Answer Explanations #1

69. A: The first step of conflict resolution should be for both sides to present their side of the disagreement calmly and professionally. This allows whoever is mediating the conflict to understand the opinions of both sides. Choices B and C are incorrect because these steps come later in conflict resolution. After presenting the sides of the argument, the disagreement should be discussed in detail, eventually coming to a compromise or some negotiation or re-evaluation. Choice D is incorrect because disagreements should not be dismissed. Using conflict resolution can help teams grow and build better communication.

70. A: For healthcare providers to participate in the value-based payment program by CMS, they must meet quality of care metrics in: clinical outcomes, person and community engagement, safety, and efficiency and cost reduction. The other choices are not requirements of CMS.

71. A: The nurse who is easily able to advocate for a patient and agrees morally with the decision the patient is making is exhibiting Level 1 advocacy and moral agency, the most basic level that emphasizes the work of the nurse. There are three levels of nurse advocacy and moral agency: Levels 1, 3, and 5. Choice B is incorrect because Level 2 is not a level of advocacy and moral agency. Choice C is incorrect because Level 3 advocacy and moral agency has the nurse advocate for the patient even if what they are advocating for does not directly align with their own personal values. Choice D is incorrect because Level 5 advocacy and moral agency is when the nurse uses their position and power to empower clients to request the care and resources that are within their best interests, even if it goes against their personal values.

72. C: All medical data are private, even for employees, so private notification of required immunizations and screenings is necessary. A deadline encourages compliance in a reasonable time frame. The memo may also include locations where the screening is available. A friendly reminder of required immunizations or screenings is generally appreciated and highly recommended to protect employees and patients from healthcare-associated infections. Choices A and B are incorrect because both email and small group notification violate Health Insurance Portability and Accountability Act (HIPAA) regulations—they are not private. Choice D is incorrect. Although some employees may keep careful track of their own information, many lose track.

73. D: COBRA has a caveat that if there was willful misconduct by an employee, the employer does not have to offer COBRA. This is the only allowance for an employee who was covered and ended employment where the employer does not need to offer COBRA. Choice A and Choice C are both situations where an employee had coverage and lost it, so they would need to be offered coverage. Choice B is incorrect since that employee could have family members covered. COBRA should still be offered to those family members.

74. B: Professional sabbaticals are not covered by the FMLA. Choice A, qualifying exigency leave, Choice C, leave for foster-care placement, and Choice D, military caregiver leave, are all covered by the FMLA.

75. D: HPPD is a commonly used healthcare metric meaning hours per patient day. In order to calculate HPPD, a healthcare provider must know the total number of patients treated in a 24-hour period as well as the total number of hours that were worked by healthcare personnel. By dividing the first value by the second, the provider has arrived at their HPPD, which offers an image of that provider's effectiveness and efficiency of care. Therefore, the correct answer is Choice D. The other answer choices do not accurately reflect the meaning of the abbreviation HPPD and are therefore incorrect.

Answer Explanations #1

76. C: Under the Patient Protection and Affordable Care Act (PPACA) in the FLSA, employers that have fifty or more employees are required to take extra precautions for their employees. This requirement mandates that employers provide a non-bathroom private location for expressing milk and provide breaks as much as needed. Compensation for breaks occurs the same as it would for other employees, but the breaks must be provided when needed. Choices A, B, and D fail to meet this criterion.

77. D: The Americans with Disabilities Act applies to employers with fifteen or more employees. The number or value of federal contracts an employer has is irrelevant, making Choice C incorrect.

78. B: To help manage and minimize pain, care should be provided in the least invasive and painful ways possible. Choice A is incorrect because pain should be assessed at least every two to four hours, depending on a patient's needs. Choice C is incorrect because all patients have the right to pain management, regardless of histories of drug abuse. Patients with history of drug abuse may need to have their pain management regimen reviewed and more closely monitored, but their pain is still real and must be addressed. Choice D is incorrect because the nurse should identify ambulation and dressing changes as times that may cause increased pain and consider managing pain before these events take place. Additional means to help provide supportive pain management include emotional support, open communication, creating a pain control plan, and working with an interdisciplinary team to address pain concerns.

79. D: All of the choices are accurate statements regarding informed consent. Informed consent forms must be completed at admission. Additionally, they must be signed, dated, and witnessed, as well as maintained under lock and key (in the case of hard copies).

80. D: A literature review does not include test data performed by the researcher. It only reviews work done in the past, and validation of the source is based on the source's credentials and information provided, not on the ability to reproduce its data. It consists of an examination of all the literature compiled for research on a subject, including opinions, Choice A, analyses, Choice B, and summaries, Choice C, of each source.

81. C: The suggested preparatory schedule for accreditation typically involves a year of planning along with close monitoring. The other choices represent incorrect timelines for planning.

82. A: Deauthorization is the official process to remove a union's security clause and negotiating authority. Deauthorization removes the requirement that employees must join the union; the process is identical to decertification. Arbitration (Choice B) is a form of mediation that is a formal process to settle disputes prior to going to court. Mediation (Choice C) is generally the precursor to arbitration through a less formal process to resolve concerns and issues. Confrontation (Choice D) is also a form of mediation that is used when a stalemate occurs and neither side is willing to consider resolving the matter.

83. B: The Fair Labor Standards Act (FLSA) is also known as the Wage and Hour Law. The FLSA established employee classification and regulated issues related to wages and child labor. The Family Medical Leave Act (Choice A) allows eligible employees in an organization unpaid leave time to care for themselves and family while protecting their jobs. The Davis Bacon Act (Choice C) applies to contractors working on federally funded contracts over $2,000. The Walsh-Healy Act (Choice D) applies to contractors working on federally funded contracts over $10,000.

84. B: Systems thinking uses cognitive mapping, Choice B, to represent physical locations. Reviewing areas where each department connects to others can help identify more points of interaction that

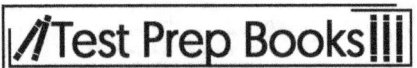

contribute to incidents. A centrist approach, scorecards, and technology to drive ideas, Choices A, C, and D, are not central to systems thinking.

85. A: Six Sigma is a method used by organizations to reduce inefficiencies and other cumbersome techniques that diminish profitability. It is a rationally organized process that is enlisted to constantly increase productive capacities by eliminating antiquated or outdated machinery and technology, making Choice A correct. Furthermore, Six Sigma may scrutinize opaque bureaucratic structures or wasteful practices that obstruct maximum profitability. Grounded in statistical analysis, this methodology exhibits a scientific and technical approach to solving critical problems facing an organization. Employee councils, feedback, and recruitment, Choices B, C, and D, are therefore not central to the purpose of Six Sigma.

86. C: Choice C, training, is the correct educational concept being used by the team leader. Training involves hands-on experiences, whether simulated or actual, to ensure competency with a new process. Choice A is not correct because competency is the term used to describe the efficacy of performing an action. Providing guidance does not guarantee competency. Choice B is not correct because knowledge is a broad concept that can be obtained through theory or experiences. Providing hands-on guidance goes beyond a knowledge base. Choice D is not correct because evaluation is a tool used to determine whether the implementation is successful.

87. C: The rate of employee satisfaction and morale (Choice C) is not an outcome of the performance management process. This rate is determined by an employee survey to establish what the organization does well and what needs to be improved. Standard outcomes of the performance management process are salary increases and promotions, growth and development opportunities, and disciplinary actions and training needs (Choices A, B, and D).

88. D: Diversity and inclusion (D&I) should be part of an organization-wide policy that involves all employees in each level of the organization, making Choice D correct. Choice A is not the best answer because key training messages may get lost in translation as they travel from leadership-level employees to their subordinates. Choice B is also not the best answer because it reacts to past problems rather than working to proactively create a workplace culture that avoids such conflict. Choice C is incorrect because long-standing employees also need training to adapt to changing workplace conditions.

89. B: The Patient Protection and Affordable Care Act is also known as Obamacare, making Choice B correct. This act made access to healthcare available to more Americans by providing healthcare purchase options and subsidies to ensure affordability.

90. C: HR staff members should help non-cooperating employees find common ground to work together toward an end goal, Choice C, rather than separating or punishing employees (Choices A and B). If there are too many failed attempts at resolution, it may be necessary to escalate tactics. Additionally, allowing the employees to solve the issue autonomously, Choice D, is not an effective leadership strategy.

91. B: The empirical-rational strategy assumes that individuals are, in general, rational and will follow a path that benefits them. This strategy to affect change works well when individuals are presented with the benefits that will be experienced by embracing a specific change.

92. A: Medicare Part A (Choice A) is mandatory hospital insurance coverage that most individuals do not have to pay for once qualified.

Answer Explanations #1

93. C: The statement provided in the question is the ANA definition of nursing practice: "The protection, promotion, and optimization of health and abilities, prevention of illness and injury, alleviation of suffering through the diagnosis and treatment of human response, and advocacy in the care of individuals, families, communities, and populations."

94. A: Medical libraries are great sources to find information that was validated and published in the past, especially when looking for older information such as the question suggests. Choice *B*, Web browsing, and Choice *D*, recent medical journals may only contain recently acquired data without describing past procedures in detail. Choice *C*, television dramas, can be left out entirely because they most likely contain fictional information that should not be used to further an investigation of disease.

95. A: Value-based payment models and value-based insurance design models are both forms of VBP, an innovative model of health insurance popularized by CMS and expanded under the ACA. Both value-based payment and value-based insurance design models seek to lower the overall cost of health care for customers and providers. Whereas value-based payment seeks to directly tie reimbursement to patient health outcomes, value-based insurance design seeks to incentivize its customers to utilize treatments previously determined to be effective, in hopes of reducing costs and improving health outcomes. Therefore, the correct answer is Choice *A*. Both types of models make use of both achievement and improvement scores, so Choice *B* is incorrect. Both models have also been shown to reduce costs across the board, so Choice *C* is incorrect. Finally, as previously mentioned, both models are examples of the VBP program, which has been largely promoted and popularized by CMS. Therefore, Choice *D* is incorrect.

96. D: It is appropriate for the nurse to delegate the task of recording output to a certified nursing assistant (CNA). Certified nursing assistants can also be delegated other routine care such as recording intake/output, vital signs, and activities of daily living as appropriate. The nurse should be able to assess if each task is necessary, appropriate, and within the CNA's scope of practice. Choice *A* is incorrect because passing medication is outside of the regular scope of a CNA's practice. The nurse should pass this medication if it was scanned and charted under their name and license. Choice *B* is incorrect because inserting a new IV is outside of the regular scope of practice for a CNA. Some facilities may allow training for CNAs for additional skills, so the nurse should be familiar with the policies at their facility. Choice *C* is incorrect because, although it is within the scope of practice for a CNA to reposition a patient, it is not appropriate to ask a CNA to independently reposition an obese patient. This task can cause injury to the CNA and patient; instead, the nurse should either assist the CNA or ensure the CNA has additional help.

97. B: On-call time during which the employee cannot do any other activities is called "engaged to wait" and is compensable. Choice *A* is incorrect since the employee can use their time for their own purposes. This type of on-call status is called "waiting to be engaged" and is not compensable. Choice *C*, an employee traveling from their home to their normal worksite, is not required to be compensable.

98. B: The new venous catheter in the intact sterile package is the best chance of preventing HAIs in this patient. Choice *A* is incorrect; assuming any break in a sterile environment is recent enough to be inconsequential is always dangerous, especially when this may very well reflect a situation of increased infection risk due to contamination. Choice *C* is incorrect because use of the sterile swab will only render the outside of the venous catheter mostly free of pathogens; it does nothing to remove pathogens from the interior of the tube through which blood or other fluids will flow. Choice *D* is incorrect because although returning the venous catheter in the torn package to the supply department for documentation and replacement is an appropriate method of tracking defects, it is not the next step.

Answer Explanations #1

99. A: Non-exempt positions fall directly under the regulations of the FLSA. Non-exempt positions do not involve the supervision of other employees, require specialized education or training, or use independent judgment for decision-making. Positions that are exempt, which include professional and administrative positions, do not fall under the regulations of the FLSA, so Choices *B, C,* and *D* are incorrect.

100. C: The abbreviation POS stands for point-of-service and refers to a specific type of private health insurance plan. Under a POS plan, an individual is assigned a primary care physician who accepts their insurance, and that physician is then able to refer the patient to specialists who also accept the insurance. POS plans are designed to strike a balance between the affordability of HMOs and the freedom of choice afforded by PPOs. The correct answer is Choice *C* because the other choices do not stand for POS.

101. B: An emergency response specifically refers to a planned and practiced protocol to be used in the event of an emergency. A strategic plan (Choice *A*) is an overall organizational plan specific to goals and objectives. An evacuation plan (Choice *C*) is a part of the emergency response and is a coordinated and planned exit from a specific location. A hazard communication (Choice *D*), also part of the emergency response, notifies employees when there is a physical danger regarding a hazardous chemical in the workplace.

102. A: With an HMO, a patient receives coverage only when they visit doctors and healthcare facilities that have negotiated with the insurance company. A PPO, on the other hand, allows patients to see out-of-network doctors, usually without any sort of referral. Therefore, the correct answer is Choice *A*. HMOs and PPOs are both examples of commercial insurance plans; therefore, Choice *B* is incorrect. The key distinctions between them are their price point and the degree of choice they offer, rather than following different reimbursement models, so Choice *C* is also incorrect. Choice *D* is incorrect because HMOs and PPOs are not the same type of plan, and there are key differences between the two.

103. C: FFS was once the industry standard when it came to health reimbursement. Under FFS models, healthcare providers billed only according to the number of medical services that were afforded to a client, not according to the effectiveness of the medical interventions prescribed. FFS models have largely been associated with practices such as overprovision, in which a healthcare provider overprescribes a patient in order to increase the billable fee. Such models are becoming increasingly unpopular because CMS has introduced and subsidized VBP programs. Therefore, the correct answer is Choice *C*. The other answer choices do not accurately reflect the current state of FFS payment models in the healthcare insurance marketplace.

104. D: When discussing healthcare reimbursement methods, overprovision refers to a phenomenon in which patients are overprescribed and overcharged by healthcare providers. Due to FFS models of healthcare reimbursement, it has historically been the case that healthcare providers received reimbursement based on the number of services they prescribed their patients and not according to the effectiveness or efficiency of those services. Therefore, the correct answer is Choice *D*. All the other answer choices refer to other phenomena, not to the practice of overprovision.

105. A: The database includes dates and details of who is restricted and who is excluded as well as a complete and up-to-date health history and immunization record for each employee. Choice *B* is incorrect because although the nursing supervisor may keep a complete list of all restricted or excluded personnel in the department, some restricted/excluded staff may work in other capacities, such as housekeeping or food care. Choice *C* is incorrect because restricted personnel still play some role in the

Answer Explanations #1

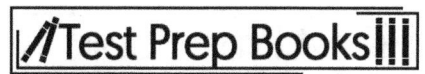

facility and should therefore not lose access. Choice D is incorrect; although distribution of a daily report is possible and likely helpful, if the information was not entered into the database in the first place, this report would not be possible or accurate.

106. C: Strategic plans are an ongoing and continuous process; therefore, Choice C is correct. Plans should be evaluated to determine effectiveness and whether new strategies or resources should be considered to accomplish the identified goals. Strategic plans should be regularly reviewed and updated as necessary to ensure the mission and vision of the organization are met.

107. C: Facilitating a patient's transition from one point on the health continuum to another requires caring practices in addition to advocacy and moral agency. Moral agency may be employed to ensure that the patient's wishes are considered, especially those wishes associated with end-of-life concerns. Developing cultural awareness is an example of a response to diversity, and the remaining two choices refer to the facilitation of learning.

108. A: At least 30% of eligible employees are required to sign authorization cards by the National Labor Relations Board before it will order an election where employees can vote on whether to be represented by a union.

109. B: Someone who allows their group to present ideas and solutions, but does not use the group's ideas, is said to be a consultative leader. In this leadership style, staff may feel that their input is being heard, even if it is not taken seriously into consideration. Choice A is incorrect because a democratic leader collaborates with their staff to hear ideas and solutions and will take those ideas into account when making their decision. Choice C is incorrect because participatory leadership is another name for democratic leadership and has the same meaning. Choice D is incorrect because in delegative leadership, similar to laissez-faire leadership, the leader is hands-off and assigns tasks and problems to their group to complete without the leader's instruction or input.

110. D: According to the updated Bloom's Taxonomy, the most complex level of cognitive learning listed is the step of evaluating. Bloom's Taxonomy outlines three different domains that are needed for effective learning: cognitive, affective, and psychomotor. The correct order of the steps from least to most complex in cognitive learning are as follows: remembering, understanding, applying, analyzing, evaluating, and creating. Choices A, B, and C are incorrect because they are not the most complex level of cognitive learning in Bloom's Taxonomy listed in the answer options.

111. D: Exempt employees are not required to be paid overtime. To be exempt, an employee needs to meet criteria set by the Fair Labor Standards Act (FLSA). Choice A is incorrect because FLSA does not distinguish between different jobs; instead, it defines the rule to be working for an employer more than forty hours a week. If an employee is working two different jobs, an employer still needs to track and pay overtime for their hours past forty. Overtime is calculated on a workweek; the employer can set what days that workweek starts and ends but is responsible for all hours past forty in a week regardless of the next week's hours, making Choice B incorrect. Lastly, there is no form to waive overtime, making Choice C incorrect.

112. A: When working with adult learners, it is important for the nurse to relate the teachings to real-world experiences. This acknowledges patients' prior knowledge and experience and helps provide a more robust teaching and understanding that adult learners can utilize. Choice B is incorrect because the nurse should not assume the patient has no prior knowledge, as this can come off as belittling and limit the extent to which the nurse can teach. Instead, the nurse should assess the prior knowledge the

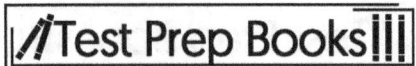

Answer Explanations #1

patient has and tailor the teaching level and material accordingly. Choice C is incorrect because by maintaining authority and control, the nurse does not allow the patient to be involved in learning and may invalidate concerns they have. This approach may also come off as disrespectful when trying to educate adult learners. Instead, the nurse should have a professional and collaborative approach. Choice D is incorrect because keeping objectives fluid and subjective may make it more difficult for patients to understand the goals they are trying to reach and more difficult for the nurse to assess their learning. Objectives should be clear, measurable, and goal focused.

113. C: The technology-innovation strategy is not a strategy for managing change, making Choice C incorrect. The text *The Planning of Change* outlines three strategies for managing change: normative-reductive, power-coercive, and empirical-rational, Choices A, B, and D respectively.

114. C: The Fishbone Diagram is a tool that seeks to analyze the primary causes of a problem. Ultimately, the diagram engages problems and investigates remedial efforts for improvement. In a group formation, a consensus is gathered to identify possible causes, such as employee performance, outdated technology, inefficient methods of production, or environmental implications. By isolating each factor, the diagram details organizational procedure to scientifically diagnose potential inefficiencies.

115. C: Any new orders should be read back to the provider to verify they are correct, and any additional questions or concerns should be addressed at this time. Choice A is incorrect because verbal orders should be avoided when possible, as there is a higher possibility of error. Instead, electronic orders or clearly legible handwritten orders should be used first. Choice B is incorrect because medical abbreviations should be avoided to help reduce the likelihood of medication errors. Choice D is incorrect because the nurse should utilize the electronic medical record to double-check orders and reduce incidences of medication error. Using electronic methods allows for medication barcodes and scanning, which is an additional check to decrease error.

116. A: It is not a requirement for the informed consent to list all members of the team involved in the treatment or procedure. However, the patient should still have a general understanding of the care they will be receiving from team members. Choices B, C, and D are incorrect because these are required components in informed consent. Other required components include risks and benefits of not having the procedure.

117. A: If a healthcare provider was to forgo completing an annual budget, they would be most likely to encounter difficulties when negotiating with financial lenders because many financial lenders still require the completion of some form of annual budget. Therefore, the correct answer is Choice A. A rolling forecast budget would actually help in all of the other circumstances because rolling forecasts use past and present trends to provide healthcare providers with up-to-date financial assessments and budget predictions.

118. C: Using "you" statements may place needless blame and pressure on the patient or learner. In the case of disagreement and communication, it is better for the nurse to use "I" statements to help them take responsibility for both ideas and feelings to help move a conversation forward. Choices A, B, and D are incorrect because these are encouraged communication tactics in successful assertive communication.

119. C: Most leadership theories have as a central concept the idea that good leadership can be taught and understood by non-leaders. However, the Great Man Theory of Leadership rejects this notion

Answer Explanations #1

outright, instead positing that good leadership traits and skills are innate and not transmittable. Therefore, the correct answer is Choice C. The other answer choices are all styles of leadership that demonstrate that good leadership is a teachable, transferable skill; therefore, they are all incorrect.

120. B: An organization's culture of civility must be rooted in its leadership. If employees sense that rules about workplace conduct do not apply to an organization's executives, or are applied inconsistently, standards of civil behavior are less likely to take hold throughout the organization. It is important to engage leaders from the C-suite (e.g., CEO, CFO, or COO) to lead by example, making Choice B correct. Choice A is not the best choice because some employees may prefer to keep their complaints confidential; experience with harassment may be personal and hurtful to share with a large audience. Choice C is not the best choice because, while guidance from the Department of Justice could be helpful, it is better to begin with leadership from inside the organization. Finally, while HR should be involved with all levels of this training, it is important to reach outside HR to leaders in other areas of the organization.

121. A: Six Sigma is a specific technique that works to improve business processes by implementing various tools and concepts to reduce errors and eliminate waste. Gap analysis, root cause analysis, and cause-and-effect diagrams (Choices B, C, and D) are incorrect because they are all tools that would be used to determine why goals were not achieved or if there was a discrepancy between the expected results and actual results.

122. D: Risk managers are trained in comprehensive evaluation of the potential for harm, outcomes of events, and patient safety, making Choice D correct.

123. B: An employer is required to offer COBRA to all qualifying former employees, including their dependents and spouses, that were covered under the employer's medical, dental, vision, and specialty medical plans. Choice A and Choice C are incorrect, since an employee must have medical insurance through the employer before leaving to be eligible for COBRA. Choice D is incorrect since COBRA is for the continuation of benefits after employment and would not impact current employees.

124. C: In order to effectively manage change with the empirical-rational strategy, it is important to incentivize the change. If employees undergo a change but understand how it can positively impact them, they are more likely to accept it and agree with it. While providing lunch, communication, and education are important (Choices A, B, and D), incentives increase the success rate of change.

125. C: Meeting dysfunctions have significant negative impacts on the progress of the project. Dysfunctional meetings impact the cost, schedule, and quality of the project and reduce the project manager's credibility within the team, making only Choice C correct.

126. B. The Family and Medical Leave Act does not provide for continued pay while on leave. Choices A, C, and D are all included in the legislation. FMLA is gender neutral and is available to both new mothers and new fathers. The employee will continue to have medical coverage during their absence. A position (either the same position or an equal position) will be maintained for the employee.

127. B: An operational budget allocates funds for staffing and the needs of the facility to carry out normal operating functions. Choice A is incorrect, as a functional budget focuses on a specific functional area of a business, such as sales, marketing, or staffing. An organizational budget, Choice C, is used in relation to a specific timeframe or event. Choice D is used to determine funds required for large expenses, such as equipment, and does not include staffing or operating expenses.

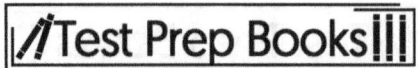

Answer Explanations #1

128. A: Public health is educating and connecting resources to the general public. Topics on healthy foods and chronic disease prevention are applicable to all members of a community. Choice B is incorrect, as healthcare law may refer to topics such as health insurance issues, filing grievances, or representation for navigating healthcare matters. Choice C is incorrect since home health refers to care needed inside the home for individuals with chronic and debilitating health problems, disabilities, or mental health issues. Patient rights, Choice D, is not correct since this type of advocacy assists patients with ensuring that their rights are protected.

129. C. The FLSA does not require that breaks or mealtimes are given to workers. This is left up to state regulations or an agreement between the employer and employee. Choices A, B, and D are incorrect since overtime pay, minimum wage, and time recording are provided for by the FLSA.

130. A: The rate of patient falls is considered a nurse-sensitive indicator. Of the options presented, patient falls are most directly affected by nursing practice. Choice B is incorrect because, while nurses should check for patient consent before procedures, the full responsibility of ensuring informed consent is obtained prior to medical procedures is not within the nursing scope of practice. Choice C is incorrect because preparation of blood products is primarily completed by blood bank staff. Choice D is incorrect because the responsibility for handwashing falls equally on all participants in direct patient care.

131. C. A nurse executive should not create broad job descriptions, as this could be used to demonstrate that an employer did not hire a person with disabilities based on a job function that is not required. Options A, B, and D are ways that the nurse executive should maintain compliance with the ADA.

132. C: Referral of the case to the ethics committee, Choice C, will provide unbiased guidance on how to uphold the patient and family's wishes from the perspective of the law in that state. Choice A is incorrect, as it is best for the ethics committee to review the case and ensure the correct steps are followed. Choices B and D are unprofessional and will break trust with the family.

133. C: A root cause analysis is a process used to examine all of the factors that contributed to an error, to analyze where changes are most appropriate, and to create a plan for change. Choice A is incorrect because it assumes the root cause is human error and takes a punitive approach. Choice B is incorrect since this is a risk-management approach to the problem, not a root-cause approach. Choice D is incorrect because, while a literature search on ways to prevent the problem in the future may be a final step in a root cause analysis, it does not best describe the overall goal.

134. A. The primary purpose of the NLRA is to protect workers from unfair labor practices. Choices B, C, and D are incorrect. While the NLRA encourages the formation of unions, it does not create them. The NLRA does not prevent strikes or picketing, since these activities are allowed under the act for reasonable purposes. Finally, the NLRA does not provide coverage for independent contractors.

135. D: This type of financial budget is called a rolling forecast, Choice D. Choice A is incorrect, as a fiscal year analysis looks at a specific time period. A performance-based budget, Choice B, is a method used to balance between funding and resources versus anticipated costs and outcomes. Choice C is a goal-oriented process that determines the resources that are available to be committed to a project.

136. C: The first step to supporting a just culture is to assess and understand the process that failed and allowed the safety event to happen. Choice A is incorrect, as this raises suspicion that the employee is at fault prior to learning about the whole situation. Choice B is incorrect since this option would degrade the patient's trust of staff prior to understanding the series of events that led to safety concerns. Choice

Answer Explanations #1

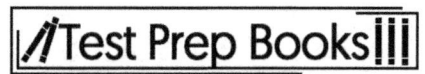

D is incorrect since applying a solution prior to a thorough investigation will not necessarily lead to improved outcomes.

137. A. Active listening is a key principle in communication for nurse executives. Choices *B, C,* and *D* are incorrect. Ambiguity should be avoided in communication, and speaking quickly can cause information to be lost in conversation. Finally, multitasking is not possible when actively listening.

138. D: Choice *D* measures the number of hours that clinical staff spend per patient. Increased hours per patient day is directly linked to predicting improved patient satisfaction scores, safer care delivery, and a decrease in quality concerns. Choices *A, B,* and *C* are tied to financial gain for an organization, not patient satisfaction.

139. D. Reflective communication is described as actively listening and restating the message in one's own words. Choices *A, B,* and *C* are incorrect. Engaging communication can be described as actively involving the audience through enthusiasm, imagery, or humor. Two-way communication occurs when one person communicates a message, and the recipient confirms with a response. Interviewing is described as questioning, listening, and speaking.

140. A: The "S" of a SMART goal is *specific*, not *standard*. Choices *B, C,* and *D* are all terms used to describe a SMART goal.

141. D: According to the Joint Commission, "An organization can have an unannounced survey between 18 and 36 months after its previous full survey."

142. A: Review of existing policies is completed during the assessment phase. Choice *B* is incorrect, as this is the implementation stage. Choice *C* is incorrect, since conducting a root cause analysis occurs during the identifying issues, problems, or trends stage of the process. Choice *D* is incorrect, as this describes the evaluation phase.

143. B. Backward communication is not a type of managerial communication. Choices *A, C,* and *D* represent different types of managerial communication.

144. A: Regulatory compliance standards required to maintain accreditation include infection control, staff qualifications, and emergency preparedness. Patient satisfaction scores, Choice *A*, are not part of the regulatory compliance review process. However, maintaining accreditation status will greatly increase the trust of patients and provide a positive impact on patient satisfaction.

145. D: Value-based purchasing bases the reimbursement for a service on the ability of an organization to meet benchmarks related to patient satisfaction and health-oriented outcomes. Because this model provides reimbursement based on meeting performance-based goals, use of evidence-based practice is encouraged and, therefore, the rate of adverse patient events is reduced. Oversight and funding of value-based purchasing comes from the Centers for Medicare & Medicaid Services (CMS), not the Joint Commission (Choice *D*).

146. D. The PICOT acronym in research refers to population, intervention, control, outcome, and time.

147. D. Perceiving is the missing key process in communication. The six key processes are thinking, encoding, transmitting the signal, perceiving, decoding, and understanding.

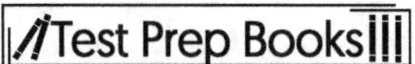

Answer Explanations #1

148. B: Quality standards and guidance can be found at NCQA for nurse executives to drive quality improvement initiatives. Choice *A* is incorrect, as the CDC provides information on disease prevention, maintenance, and public health matters. Choice *C* is incorrect, as CMS provides information and regulations regarding the joint federal and state insurance programs. Choice *D* is incorrect, as the WHO is an intergovernmental organization focused on improving health on a global scale.

149. D: In Rogers' Five-Stage Change Theory, communicating the reasons, content, and impact of the change to staff is the first step. Choice *A* is incorrect because it describes the last step in this approach. Choice *B* is incorrect because it best describes the third, or middle, step in this approach. Choice *C* is incorrect because it describes a top-down approach to the initiation of change, which is not reflected in Rogers' Five-Stage Change Theory.

150. D: Choice *D* describes informed consent best; it aims to ensure that a patient's autonomy is upheld by disclosing the information required to understand relevant details about a medical procedure or treatment. Choice *A* is incorrect; a patient must be competent in order for informed consent to be obtained, but competence alone is not enough. Choice *B* is incorrect; although there is a form to document a patient's signature, this form is not the consent process. It requires education and understanding of the medical intervention. Choice *C* is not correct since the informed consent process is voluntary for the patient and must not be used as a coercion tool.

Practice Test #2

1. The nurse is completing discharge teaching for a 35-year-old patient who is a lawyer at a local law firm. This patient was admitted following a new breast cancer diagnosis and initiation of chemotherapy. This patient's readiness to learn is most likely to be impacted by which barrier?
    a. Physical restriction
    b. Literacy barrier
    c. Emotional lability
    d. The patient will not be impacted by any barriers.

2. Which of the following employees would not be eligible to vote in an upcoming union election?
    a. An employee who is temporarily laid off
    b. An employee who is out sick with the flu
    c. An employee who is out on military leave right before the election
    d. A staff member who is out of the office on a medical leave of absence and who will not be returning to work

3. An operational budget is used to estimate:
    a. Costs associated with durable goods, such as patient beds and equipment
    b. Costs that apply directly to patients and other payors
    c. Costs associated with facility operation, personnel, and staffing
    d. Costs that are absorbed by government agencies like TRICARE and Medicare

4. The nursing unit recently discovered a high rate of UTIs amongst post-op patients. As a result, nurses have begun removing indwelling foley catheters within 24 hours after surgery, instead of 48 hours, to try to reduce the rate of UTIs. This nursing unit is at which stage of a problem-solving strategy?
    a. Evaluation of solution
    b. Development of solutions
    c. Identification of the problem
    d. Implementation of solution

5. When the nurse is communicating with patients and family members to give education and instruction, which communication approach should they use?
    a. Assertive
    b. Aggressive
    c. Passive
    d. Submissive

6. A nurse is developing a plan of care for a patient population that is culturally diverse. Which statement correctly identifies the appropriate nursing actions?
    a. The nurse follows the standard protocol for the predominant culture of the community.
    b. The nurse focuses on the cultural needs of the largest group in the population.
    c. The nurse identifies and acknowledges self-biases and addresses the needs of the patient.
    d. The nurse meets the needs of the group according to personal values and beliefs.

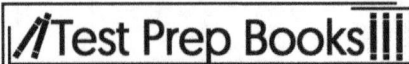

7. The nurse is caring for a terminally ill patient who is expected to pass within the week. A family member is insistent that the medical team tries a new treatment they saw online to help give the patient a longer life. This family member is exhibiting which stage of grief in the Kubler-Ross model of grief?
   a. Bargaining
   b. Anger
   c. Denial
   d. Depression

8. What function does the CMS serve?
   a. Directly oversees all activities of a healthcare facility, ensuring that care is up to an acceptable standard.
   b. Directly oversees all commercial insurance companies, regulating how they set rates and engage with clients.
   c. Provides select groups of Americans with health insurance through government programs.
   d. Provides healthcare organizations with low-cost advice and assistance with their annual budgets.

9. Albert is in charge of a committee that is tasked with coming up with better ways to address patients' dietary concerns. His team meets twice weekly, and Albert is responsible for scheduling those meetings and reporting the team's findings to his boss by the end of the month. What type of authority does Albert have?
   a. Line authority
   b. Team authority
   c. Management authority
   d. Staff authority

10. David is caring for a large number of patients, which ordinarily is not a problem. However, he was just assigned three new patients who are very sick and will require a great deal of time and attention. David's coworker was also assigned three new patients, but her patients do not require as much care. David is feeling a bit overworked with his new assignment. Which model of staffing is his unit likely using?
    a. Patient acuity model
    b. Nurse-patient model
    c. Functional planning model
    d. Budget-based model

11. What are the five rights of delegation the nurse must consider when delegating tasks?
    a. Right task, right person, right direction, right supervision, right dose
    b. Right supervision, right person, right dose, right assessment, right facility
    c. Right circumstance, right assessment, right direction, right task, right facility
    d. Right task, right circumstance, right person, right direction, right supervision

12. A nurse is reading a research article on new treatments for patients with COPD. In order to critically read, the nurse should actively try to determine all of the following aspects of the article EXCEPT:
    a. Thesis
    b. Process
    c. Outcomes
    d. Funding

13. A nurse consults with a busy emergency room doctor about the exact dosage of medication to give a patient after noticing that it is more than double the recommended dose. Is she practicing proper resource utilization, and why or why not?
    a. No. By interrupting the emergency room doctor, the nurse is preventing the doctor from effectively and efficiently carrying out their duties.
    b. No. By restricting the dosage of medication given to a patient, the nurse is attempting to limit the hospital's billable amount.
    c. Yes. By attempting to restrict the dosage of medication given to a patient, the nurse is ensuring that minimal resources are expended by each patient.
    d. Yes. By consulting with the doctor on the exact dosage, the nurse is ensuring that services provided to a patient are delivered as effectively and efficiently as possible.

14. Under the Taft-Hartley Act, which of the following is illegal?
    a. Creating a company-sponsored labor union
    b. An employee deciding to contribute to a charity instead of paying union dues
    c. An employer filing an unfair labor practice charge against a union
    d. A union representing nonunion employees in the bargaining unit

15. What type of bargaining occurs when groups negotiate terms for a contract while being mindful of the key issues to each side in the process?
    a. Distributive bargaining
    b. Principled bargaining
    c. Positional bargaining
    d. Coordinated bargaining

16. What is the goal of the improve phase of the DMAIC model?
    a. To enable the management team to visually analyze the KPIs (key performance indicators) of each individual on the healthcare team
    b. To assimilate all the ideas into a strategic plan that prioritizes opportunities for improvement and amends all processes associated with changes, including any process flows and job aids
    c. To implement strategies to determine the sustainability and benefits of the newly defined processes
    d. To enable team members to implement processes themselves

17. Delilah works in a unit where she is responsible for taking the vital signs of each patient in the unit. Her coworker, Anne, handles the medications for each patient. What type of nursing delivery model is being used here?
    a. Primary nursing
    b. Functional nursing
    c. Team nursing
    d. Modular nursing

18. Which nursing delivery model involves having a collaborative group of different nurses that work on the group's assigned patients?
    a. Primary nursing
    b. Modular nursing
    c. Team nursing
    d. Functional nursing

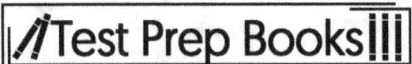

19. An employee files a grievance. After the employee discusses the grievance with the union steward and the supervisor (who are both in agreement), what is typically the next step in the formal grievance process?
    a. A committee of union officers will discuss the grievance with the appropriate managers in the company.
    b. The national union representative will discuss the grievance with designated company executives.
    c. The grievance will go to arbitration.
    d. The union steward will discuss the grievance with the supervisor's manager and/or the HR manager.

20. How might an institution best support diversity?
    a. By requiring all employees to speak a second language
    b. By providing mandatory cultural sensitivity training for all managers
    c. By offering alternative food services
    d. By providing alternative solutions to all patient requests

21. A nurse executive believes her team works best when goals and incentives are clearly communicated and quickly rewarded. What style of leadership could she best be described as having?
    a. Situational leadership style
    b. Autocratic leadership style
    c. Transactional leadership style
    d. Transformational leadership style

22. UnitedHealth Group, Cigna, and Aetna are all examples of what kind of organization?
    a. Commercial health insurance companies
    b. Healthcare providers
    c. Nongovernmental organizations (NGOs)
    d. Healthcare workers' unions

23. Which of the following statements best reflects the similar thinking that underlies both transformational leadership style and transactional leadership style?
    a. Leaders are most effective when there is the least oversight.
    b. Leaders are most effective when their team members are most satisfied in their work.
    c. Leaders are most effective when they listen to feedback.
    d. Leaders are most effective when they can adjust how they lead situation to situation.

24. A nurse is managing the care for three patients on a fully staffed unit with a CNA. During the morning care, the nurse has to pass medications for all their patients, complete two dressing changes, and give a bed bath to two incontinent patients. The nurse attempts to independently complete all of these tasks and is unable to do so. As a result, two of their patients do not receive their morning medications on schedule. What is this consequence most likely a result of?
    a. Poor staffing ratios
    b. Disorganization
    c. Failure to delegate
    d. Inappropriate patient assignment

25. Which staffing model specifically works to ensure that each nurse has a manageable mix of high-needs and lower-needs patients?
   a. Budget-based
   b. Nurse-patient
   c. Patient acuity
   d. Nurse-patient and patient acuity

26. The nurse involved in a research study wants to ensure that data was properly analyzed and collected. This nurse is ensuring what aspect of study design?
   a. External validity
   b. Generalizability
   c. Internal validity
   d. Replicability

27. Which of the following communication strategies is used to establish a relationship where employees feel comfortable speaking directly with management about problems and suggestions?
   a. Town hall meetings
   b. Management by Walking Around (MBWA)
   c. Open-door policy
   d. Department meetings

28. A patient who is alert, oriented, and exhibits no signs of cognitive deficits is completing an informed consent document for an upcoming surgery. Which parties must be present and sign this informed consent?
   a. Patient and performing provider
   b. Patient, performing provider, witness
   c. Patient, family member, performing provider, witness
   d. Patient, family member, witness

29. An emergency room calculates that it has an HPPD value for its nursing staff of 0.4. Which of the following statements provides the correct interpretation of that value?
   a. A patient at that emergency room saw an average of 0.4 nurses on a particular day.
   b. A physician at that emergency room saw each patient for 0.4 hours on average for a particular day.
   c. A patient at that emergency room saw nurses for an average of 0.4 hours on a particular day.
   d. A nurse at that emergency room saw an average of 0.4 patients an hour on a particular day.

30. Susan finds that she usually works best when she can go directly to whichever supervisor is responsible for handling the area in which she has a problem. Which type of authoritative structure would best suit Susan's work style?
   a. Line authority
   b. Team authority
   c. Management authority
   d. Staff authority

31. Which of the following hospital wards/centers would most likely have the lowest HPPD value?
    a. Neonatal intensive care unit (NICU)
    b. Burn unit
    c. Psychiatric ward
    d. Hospice care ward

32. Which of the following is an expected finding in a patient who is undergoing the imminent dying process?
    a. Increased coughing and clearing of secretions
    b. Decreased respiratory rate
    c. Increased urine output
    d. Periods of rapid breathing followed by apnea

33. How can HR leadership best communicate appropriate and acceptable behaviors within the workplace?
    a. Specifically communicate this information to employees during orientation
    b. Hang posters with federal and state regulations in break rooms and lunchrooms
    c. Consistently display ethical, reliable, and acceptable behaviors
    d. Communicate the required behaviors via email and newsletters on a regular basis

34. Which action is a proven method of reducing risk of healthcare-associated hepatitis B among caregivers in medical facilities?
    a. Regular, annual employee screening
    b. Declining to offer a job to unimmunized individuals
    c. Documenting immunizations for all employees
    d. Barring exposed employees from the building for seven days

35. What can HR specifically do to alleviate employees' fears and concerns about reporting unethical behavior and possible retaliation?
    a. Provide annual training regarding the policies and expectations
    b. Provide confidential and/or anonymous reporting methods
    c. Provide all employees with the handbook to ensure knowledge of the policy
    d. Provide frequent updates to the policies and procedures

36. Which action ensures the successful integration of remote monitoring?
    a. Training nursing staff on the proper use of remote monitoring equipment and software
    b. Establishing partnerships with remote monitoring device manufacturers
    c. Expanding telehealth services to new patient populations
    d. Conducting market research on the latest remote monitoring technologies

37. What is the correct order of the steps for a nurse to create and implement new evidence-based practice guidelines?
    a. Evaluate, appraise, ask, gather, act
    b. Ask, gather, appraise, act, evaluate
    c. Gather, ask, act, appraise, evaluate
    d. Ask, act, evaluate, gather, appraise

38. In which of the following elements of alternative dispute resolution are the parties required by law to follow the decision reached as a result of the arbitration process?
    a. Compulsory arbitration
    b. Binding decision
    c. Voluntary arbitration
    d. Constructive confrontation

39. Which of the following is a vital component of communication that builds trust?
    a. Empowerment
    b. Courage
    c. Collaboration
    d. Transparency

40. Using the Synergy Model, a nurse who is at a level 1 of clinical inquiry would have which of the following characteristics?
    a. Seeks new knowledge
    b. Questions industry standards
    c. Is aware of the problem and asks others for advice
    d. Deviates from industry standards using evidence-based practice

41. Which of the following is the most important consideration in remote monitoring?
    a. Patient safety and confidentiality
    b. Patient education on the remote monitoring system
    c. Access of data by the patient's PCP
    d. Provider training on remote monitoring

42. Stethoscopes should be disinfected with what level of liquid chemicals?
    a. High-level disinfectants
    b. Intermediate-level disinfectants
    c. Low-level disinfectants
    d. No disinfectant chemicals

43. Which of the following is representative of a common issue handled by a labor union?
    a. Advocating for fair wages
    b. Advocating for safe working conditions
    c. Advocating for the nurse's rights
    d. All of the above

44. An employee must file a complaint charge of discrimination with the Equal Employment Opportunity Commission (EEOC) within how many days of the alleged incident?
    a. 180 days
    b. 90 days
    c. 120 days
    d. There is no time limit associated with filing a complaint charge of discrimination with the EEOC.

45. Which of the following is NOT a right that patients and families have regarding their medical care?
   a. Accessing staffing schedules for their care team
   b. Obtaining medical records
   c. Receiving non-discriminatory care
   d. Participating in healthcare decisions

46. A novice nurse is caring for a patient who requires a blood transfusion. The patient, however, has refused the transfusion due to a religious objection. The nurse says, "I don't understand why the patient's sister can't donate the blood. No one should object to receiving blood from a family member when you need it." Which of the following statements correctly identifies the critical issue in this situation?
   a. The nurse is displaying an ethnocentric attitude.
   b. The nurse thinks that the patient is concerned about contracting an infectious disease.
   c. The nurse thinks that the patient doesn't understand the necessity of the blood transfusion.
   d. The nurse believes that blood donation from family members is safe.

47. Which of the following types of picketing is done by employees for the purpose of letting the public know that they are not represented by any one authority and thus plan to organize?
   a. Recognitional picketing
   b. Organizational picketing
   c. Consumer picketing
   d. Informational picketing

48. An 80-year-old patient with hearing aids is scheduled to start a new antibiotic regimen with their morning medications. As the nurse is hanging the new medications, they verbally explain what the new medications do and their possible side effects. This nurse is at which level of facilitation of nursing according to the Synergy Model?
   a. Level 1
   b. Level 2
   c. Level 3
   d. Level 5

49. The nurse is caring for a patient who comes from a different cultural background than themselves. The nurse respectfully asks the patient about different foods they prefer to eat in their culture so those foods can be discussed with the dietician. This nurse is at which level of responding to diversity in the Synergy Model?
   a. Level 1
   b. Level 2
   c. Level 3
   d. Level 5

Practice Test #2

50. What are an employer's responsibilities when an employee leaves for military duty under the Uniformed Services Employment and Reemployment Rights Act (USERRA)?
    a. If the employee gets called to active duty, the employer is required to re-employ them upon their return.
    b. When an employee is re-employed, they receive the full amount of employment benefits they would have received if they didn't leave for active duty.
    c. The employee has indefinite job protection as long as the employee is actively serving in the military the whole time.
    d. Both A and B

51. Which of the following correctly identifies a critical distinction between advocacy and moral agency?
    a. Advocacy is legally binding.
    b. Moral agency requires accountability for right and wrong decisions.
    c. Advocacy is implied in the paternalistic view of patient care.
    d. Moral agency only refers to support for at-risk populations.

52. The core portions of the SIPOC method include which of the following?
    a. Suppliers, inputs, processes, outputs, customers
    b. Scorecards, inputs, processes, outputs, customers
    c. Sponsors, investors, products, outputs, customers
    d. Suppliers, inputs, processes, opportunities, consumers

53. When creating a lesson plan to teach a new topic to a patient and their family, which of the following components would NOT help create and foster a comprehensive lesson plan?
    a. Set goals
    b. Create open-ended objectives
    c. Focus on one or two topics
    d. Assess the patient's understanding

54. A patient experiences a urinary tract infection (UTI) as a result of an improperly inserted catheter. Which of the following performance measures is the provider most likely to notice a change in as a result?
    a. Clinical outcomes
    b. Person and community engagement
    c. Safety
    d. Efficiency and cost reduction

55. Which of the following word pairs identifies the C's of caring practices that are most closely associated with the critical care certification in nursing?
    a. Compassion and curiosity
    b. Confidence and collaboration
    c. Conscience and creativity
    d. Commitment and competence

56. A nurse is involved in a research study with 500 participants for a new vaccine that would be recommended for all people 18 years of age and older. 450 of the participants were 50 years old and older. This study would likely suffer from which kind of bias?
    a. Reporting bias
    b. Recall bias
    c. Healthy participant bias
    d. Selection bias

57. A 75-year-old female patient who follows Orthodox Jewish traditions is admitted to the unit for pneumonia. She needs assistance cleaning up and receiving a partial bed bath. It would be appropriate for which of the following team members to participate in this care?
    a. A female nurse and female nursing student
    b. A female nurse and male nursing assistant
    c. A male nurse and female nurse
    d. A male nurse and male nursing assistant

58. Why are single-dose medication vials recommended when providing intravenous, intramuscular, intradermal, or subcutaneous medication?
    a. They reduce medication expenditures.
    b. They don't require any measurement.
    c. They're more convenient and are recyclable.
    d. The vials reduce risk of contaminating the medication.

59. Tina is scheduled to undergo carpal tunnel release surgery in one week. What effect, if any, will her value-based insurance have on the cost of her surgery as opposed to traditional insurance?
    a. No coverage; since carpal tunnel release surgery is elective, it is not covered by any insurance
    b. No effect; carpal tunnel release surgery generally costs the same with value-based or traditional insurance
    b. Less expensive; value-based insurance assigns fixed, low costs for any surgeries
    d. More expensive; value-based insurance assigns higher costs to elective surgeries

60. Under the Uniform Services Employment and Reemployment Rights Act (USERRA), which of the following actions are employers NOT allowed to carry out?
    a. Halting an employee's vacation accrual while they are out on military leave
    b. Continuing health care coverage at their expense for an employee who is out on military leave for six months
    c. Continuing to pay an exempt employee who is out on military their full salary, minus their earnings for serving in the military
    d. Making reasonable efforts to accommodate a disabled veteran returning from military leave

61. What are an employer's responsibilities to an applicant that has past, present, or planned future military service under the Uniformed Services Employment and Reemployment Rights Act (USERRA)?
    a. The employer is not allowed to discriminate against any military service and must work with applicants to understand comparable skills from previous service.
    b. The employer can choose to not hire someone based on future military service if they know that person will be deployed soon.
    c. The employer does have to consider any previous military experience towards job experience, since it is difficult to compare.
    d. USERRA is focused only on current employees and does not have rules for job applicants.

62. Which of the following is NOT one of the benefits of line authority?
    a. It is a temporary structure that lasts only as long as necessary.
    b. Each employee has only one "boss" to whom they report.
    c. Dealing with problems is a more straightforward process.
    d. There is a clear chain of command, eliminating confusion about who is responsible for what.

63. Which of the following is one of the key problems with relying on budget-based staffing?
    a. It does not account for variable patient needs.
    b. It does not include a determination of the nursing hours per patient per day.
    c. It uses an average number of patients per week.
    d. It is mathematically-based rather than patient-oriented.

64. An individual is unable to get referrals for doctors outside of their insurance network. What kind of insurance plan does this individual most likely have?
    a. POS
    b. HMO
    c. PPO
    d. EPO

65. The nurse is delegating the task of getting a set of vital signs to the certified nursing assistant (CNA). The nurse tells the CNA the task to complete, the CNA repeats the task instructions back to the nurse, and the nurse verifies that the message is correct. This is an example of what kind of communication?
    a. Closed-loop communication
    b. Call-out communication
    c. Feedback communication
    d. Open-loop communication

66. Which of the following communication types, while making it easy to distribute information to a large group of individuals very quickly, may also lead to "information overload"?
    a. Intranet
    b. Email
    c. Newsletter
    d. Word-of-mouth

67. The head doctor of a particular ward refrains from checking in frequently with the other doctors of the ward, believing that the best quality of care is provided when each doctor is allowed to work in their own way. What style of leadership might they best be described as having?
    a. Transactional leadership style
    b. Democratic leadership style
    c. Laissez-Faire leadership style
    d. Autocratic leadership style

68. The nurse is caring for a patient who is malnourished after weeks of severe nausea related to chemotherapy. The patient is interested in trying medical marijuana to help their appetite, but state laws do not allow for use of medical marijuana. This is an example of a barrier from what kind of external force?
    a. Political forces
    b. Regulatory forces
    c. Economic forces
    d. Social forces

69. A medical facility recommended that individuals in their waiting room use proper cough etiquette to contain coughs while waiting for medical attention; however, no reduction in infection transmission was seen despite compliance with this tried-and-true advice. What should they do?
    a. Go online to check the latest guidelines issued by the CDC.
    b. Stop recommending proper cough etiquette because it is a waste of time.
    c. Provide a public supply of hand sanitizer for use after a cough.
    d. Go online to research if any other health facility is facing this problem.

70. A manager likes to sit down with each of her employees toward the end of every week, checking in with them about their goals for the work week and their personal ambitions. Which of the following components of transformational leadership could this manager be described as exhibiting?
    a. Intellectual stimulation
    b. Individual consideration
    c. Inspirational motivation
    d. Idealized influence

71. What can ambiguity, or being vague, cause when communicating with employees?
    a. Opportunities for employees to go above and beyond
    b. Innovation, productivity, and motivation
    c. Confusion, conflict, and distress
    d. Lower turnover and increased job satisfaction

72. What steps are taken when an employee involved in patient care contracts a contagious illness?
    a. The employee calls out sick and goes to a doctor.
    b. The employee is sent home for a few days.
    c. The employee is transferred to a different department.
    d. The employee is excluded from all patient care.

73. What is the purpose of the cost-benefit analysis in process improvement?
    a. To determine the true costs of a potential solution compared to the actual benefits
    b. To ensure that the outcome actually solves the problem
    c. To confirm the passive and unplanned spread of new practices
    d. To find solutions before they become necessary

74. According to the Synergy Model, which of the following choices is associated with the patient's vulnerability?
    a. The patient is financially stable.
    b. The patient smoked cigarettes for thirty years prior to quitting five years ago.
    c. The patient is married.
    d. The patient actively participates in decisions related to the plan of care.

75. Which definition most accurately explains a whistle-blower?
    a. A person who reports any unethical information about an organization
    b. Someone hired by an organization to cover up illicit or unethical activity
    c. A person who reports or publicizes any illegal or unethical information about a private institution
    d. Someone who reports or publicizes any illegal or unethical information about a public institution

76. A nurse is caring for a patient who had a colectomy two days ago. While assisting the patient back to bed, the nurse notes that the patient's heart rate and respiratory rate are slightly elevated, and the patient states, "I can feel my pulse." The nurse assesses the patient for additional signs of heart failure. This intervention is an example of which of the following caring practices according to the Synergy Model?
    a. Engagement by a novice nurse
    b. Vigilance by an experienced nurse
    c. An expected response to predictable changes by the novice nurse
    d. Collaboration by an experienced nurse

77. The nurse is caring for a patient who is terminally ill. Which of the following actions can help mitigate ethical dilemmas in this patient population?
    a. Provide thorough explanations of care for decision making.
    b. Promote active treatments to help extend life.
    c. Use nursing expertise to help make decisions for the patient and the family.
    d. Give the patient the highest prescribed dose of analgesic for comfort.

78. A primary care physician notices that many of her employees are showing up late to work. Rather than scold or incentivize her employees directly, she instead endeavors to show up early herself every day, modeling to her employees the kind of behavior she would like to see. Which of the following components of transformational leadership is this manager exhibiting?
    a. Intellectual stimulation
    b. Individual consideration
    c. Inspirational motivation
    d. Idealized influence

79. Brian works in a unit where he reports directly to his immediate supervisor, Lucy. If need be, Lucy will take issues to other managers or departments for resolution. What type of authority is this?
    a. Team authority
    b. Staff authority
    c. Line authority
    d. Management authority

80. Which of the following ethical principles is MOST closely related to advocacy?
    a. Distributive justice
    b. Beneficence
    c. Nonmaleficence
    d. Fidelity

81. The nurse is planning to teach a newly diagnosed diabetic patient, their mother, and their spouse how to draw up and inject insulin before the patient is discharged from the hospital. Which teaching style would be most effective for this group and learning objective?
    a. Lecture
    b. Discussion group
    c. Online module
    d. Hands-on workshop

82. While discussing treatment plans for a patient with a stage IV pressure ulcer, the nurse works with a doctor, a nurse practitioner, a wound care nurse, and a registered dietitian. On which type of team is this nurse working?
    a. Primary medical team
    b. Secondary medical team
    c. Intradisciplinary team
    d. Interdisciplinary team

83. Which method of communication can spread information quickly but often becomes misinterpreted, misunderstood, and incorrect?
    a. Emails
    b. Newsletters
    c. Town hall meetings
    d. Word of mouth

84. What is the best way to determine who is responsible for identifying the tasks that must be done, who is available to do those tasks, and delegating authority to those people?
    a. Organizational chart
    b. Management list
    c. Supervisory status listing
    d. Shift-specific whiteboard

85. A nurse manager allows their staff to create and implement their own solutions for problems that they identify while working. This manager has which type of leadership style?
    a. Democratic
    b. Transactional
    c. Laissez-faire
    d. Autocratic

86. Resiliency and stability are examples of traits in which aspect of the Synergy Model?
    a. Nursing competencies
    b. Quality outcomes
    c. Client characteristics
    d. Healthcare environment

87. If a manager is questioning a union employee and it may ultimately lead to a disciplinary action via the Weingarten rights, the employee is entitled to have which of the following present?
    a. A relative or close friend
    b. An attorney
    c. A representative from the union
    d. Another manager

88. A nurse who is at a level 3 of team collaboration according to the Synergy Model has which of the following characteristics?
   a. Participates in collaborative efforts
   b. Initiates collaborative efforts
   c. Mentors others in collaborative efforts
   d. Teaches collaboration techniques to others

89. Which staffing method involves staffing the unit below the maximum and then adjusting the staffing as needed?
   a. Fixed staffing
   b. Semiflexible staffing
   c. Workload staffing
   d. Variable staffing

90. While creating an evidence-based practice guideline, a nurse is conducting research and wants to use research that has the highest level of evidence, level A. From which of the following studies should the nurse draw information?
   a. Meta-analysis
   b. Randomized-control trial
   c. Integrative interviews
   d. Cohort study

91. An influx of patients with a known or suspected communicable disease may indicate an act of bioterrorism or an outbreak of a particular disease that is unrelated to bioterror. How do medical personnel and public health officials monitor data in order to identify a situation that may require response protocols?
   a. Reference the CDC database for reported cases
   b. Use a syndromic surveillance system
   c. Receive Federal Emergency Management Agency (FEMA) notification
   d. Review electronic medical records

92. Having which of the following characteristics promotes a systems thinking approach?
   a. Independent work dynamic
   b. Organization-wide perspective
   c. Self-focused views
   d. Reliance only on past experiences

93. Despite intending his theory to be applied to the business world, Kurt Lewin first noticed three different styles of leadership while watching which of the following?
   a. Schoolchildren completing a project
   b. Professional athletes practicing and training
   c. Beavers building a dam
   d. Firefighters battling a blaze

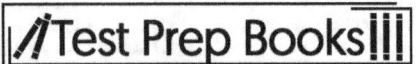

94. The nurse is caring for a 40-year-old female who comes from a Hispanic culture. The nurse knows that which family member is likely to be an integral part in medical decision-making?
    a. Paternal grandmother
    b. Father
    c. Mother
    d. Oldest son

95. If employees win the vote to decertify their union on August 31 in a given calendar year, what is the next earliest date that a new election can be held?
    a. After January 1 of the following year
    b. After one year
    c. After thirty days
    d. After ninety days

96. Which of the following statements best reflects the mindset of a healthcare provider engaging in overprovision?
    a. "I should double-check with the physician in charge of this patient's care to ensure that I understand the procedure I am tasked with performing."
    b. "I should send the patient for a neurological evaluation because I'm unsure if some neurological condition could be the cause of their distress."
    c. "I should send the patient for a neurological evaluation, although I'm certain they are just dealing with symptoms of shock."
    d. "I should ensure that this patient understands his options for care now that he's being sent home from the hospital."

97. A patient who has private insurance and Medicare is treated at a medical facility that is covered under their Medicare plan, however, the patient elects to pay out of pocket instead. In this case, who is considered the 'payor'?
    a. The patient
    b. The private insurance plan
    c. Medicare
    d. The medical facility

98. One difference between a health maintenance organization (HMO) and preferred provider organization (PPO) is:
    a. An HMO is generally more expensive than a PPO
    b. An HMO allows customers to see out-of-network doctors without a referral
    c. A PPO requires a higher premium than an HMO
    d. A PPO is more likely to have fixed-rate copays for in-service providers than an HMO

99. A patient passed away while their family members were in the room. Which of the following is NOT an appropriate action for the nurse to take immediately after death?
    a. Continue to refer to the patient by their name after death
    b. Assist with arrangements for funeral or burial facilities
    c. Escort the family out of the room to begin post-mortem care
    d. Encourage grieving and communication for the family

100. Which of the following styles of leadership is particularly beneficial when securing proper public health accreditation?
   a. Autocratic leadership style
   b. Transformational leadership style
   c. Transactional leadership style
   d. Situational leadership style

101. A blood transfusion is ordered for a patient with a hemoglobin of 5.8 g/dL. The nurse knows this patient is a practicing Jehovah's Witness. What is the most appropriate action for the nurse to take?
   a. Let the provider know you cannot give the blood since the patient is a Jehovah's Witness.
   b. Discuss alternative therapies with the patient and medical team.
   c. Explain to the patient that their religious belief should not be more important their health.
   d. Begin the transfusion and notify the charge nurse about the patient's religious beliefs.

102. Under the Pregnancy Discrimination Act of 1978, which of the following statements is TRUE?
   a. An employer can refuse to provide a pregnant woman with reasonable accommodation if she is unable to do her job and approaches her manager to that effect.
   b. An employer can ask a pregnant interview candidate when they are due and how much time they will plan to be off of work after the baby arrives.
   c. An employer must give a woman a comparable position to the one that she held prior to her maternity leave (if the company does so with employees on short-term disability).
   d. An employer can discriminate against an employee who has undergone an abortion if this act is against their personal convictions.

103. Nurses are responsible for which of the following elements of informed consent?
   a. Identification of alternatives to the planned procedure
   b. Description of associated risks and benefits
   c. Explanation of the planned procedure or diagnostic test
   d. Assessment of the patient's understanding of the information that is provided

104. Which of the following statements accurately explains how situational and transformational leadership styles are distinct from other leadership styles?
   a. They can be practiced in a variety of ways, with the philosophy reinforcing those actions being more important.
   b. They are used only in healthcare settings.
   c. They are proven to increase productivity in team members.
   d. They can be practiced by both leaders and subordinates.

105. A clerk observes a healthcare provider in a community clinic using a pair of gloves to change dressings on one individual with an infected wound and then using the same gloves to immunize an individual without symptoms of disease. What should the clerk's next step be?
   a. Recognize their own lack of medical expertise and ignore the situation.
   b. Be sure to watch this healthcare provider intentionally for the remainder of day.
   c. Call attention to the action by describing it out loud to warn other patients.
   d. Promptly and confidentially report the action to a member of senior medical staff on duty.

106. A patient who is Middle Eastern is admitted to the unit, and the nurse is informed that this patient follows typical Middle Eastern dietary restrictions. Which of the following food trays would be appropriate to give this patient?
   a. Grilled salmon with steamed vegetables and rice
   b. Cheeseburger with fries and broccoli
   c. Grilled chicken sandwich with Swiss cheese and side salad
   d. Eggs and bacon with whole wheat toast

107. A patient who is recovering from a stroke requests the incorporation of acupuncture in their care and recovery. What is the most appropriate response from the nurse?
   a. Tell the patient it is not recommended to start acupuncture because it is dangerous.
   b. Explain that acupuncture does not work and should not be added to their care.
   c. Suggest that the patient starts acupuncture care twice weekly in place of PT.
   d. Discuss the safety of incorporating acupuncture into the patient's current care regimen with the medical team.

108. Under the principles of resource utilization, what should be the most important factor in a patient's treatment plan?
   a. The efficacy of the selected treatments
   b. The overall cost of the selected treatments
   c. The total number of selected treatments
   d. The timing of the selected treatments

109. Which of the following communication techniques represents good therapeutic communication for the nurse to use with a patient?
   a. Asking simple yes or no questions
   b. Using silence when appropriate
   c. Using clichés to establish rapport
   d. Asking patients to explain their behavior

110. Which of the following is considered to be an illegal subject that cannot be discussed during a collective bargaining negotiation?
   a. Voluntary subjects
   b. Worker safety conditions
   c. Working conditions and terms
   d. Security clauses

111. Nursing practice is based on the principles of ethical behavior. Which of the following correctly identifies the moral principle that may require knowledge of the legislative process?
   a. Fidelity
   b. Autonomy
   c. Advocacy
   d. Beneficence

112. When the nurse is documenting a task that is delegated, which piece of information are they NOT required to include?
   a. What task was completed
   b. Location where the task was completed
   c. When the task was completed
   d. Duration in which the task was completed

113. Which staffing model involves calculating staffing needs based on HPPD?
   a. Nurse-patient ratio
   b. Patient acuity
   c. Functional planning
   d. Budget-based staffing

114. A patient is being discharged following a drug overdose. Before they leave, the nurse prints out information that has resources for support meetings, local mental health clinics, and crisis hotline numbers. This nurse is at which level of systems thinking in the Synergy Model?
   a. Level 1
   b. Level 3
   c. Level 4
   d. Level 5

115. When used to implement evidenced-based practice, clinical inquiry can result in which of the following?
   a. Replacing an outdated nursing intervention
   b. The nurse becoming an innovator
   c. Matching patient needs with nursing competencies
   d. All the above

116. The Synergy Model views the practice of expert nurses as which of the following?
   a. Being able to anticipate patient needs
   b. Being able to address change
   c. The point where clinical reasoning and clinical inquiry are inseparable
   d. Being able to incorporate research findings

117. When is the critical period for cleaning medical instruments?
   a. Within one day of use
   b. Right before use
   c. Immediately after use
   d. According to manufacturer recommendations

118. Which of the following is NOT one of the four key elements of an effective staffing plan?
   a. A statement of philosophy
   b. Clear, specific objectives
   c. Employee shift preferences
   d. Defined job descriptions

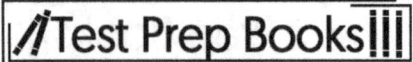

119. Which term refers to the people within an organization who are hired to do a specific job?
    a. Scheduling
    b. Authority
    c. Nurse executive
    d. Staff

120. The nurse is caring for a patient from China who speaks Mandarin as their first language. They have just received news that their cancer has returned and will need to restart chemotherapy. When the nurse comes in the room to try to speak with the patient, they are looking away and are closed off to discussing their feelings with the nurse. What is the most appropriate response by the nurse?
    a. Encourage the patient to maintain eye contact for better communication.
    b. Suggest therapeutic techniques so they can work on expressing their feelings.
    c. Contact the patient's family so they can offer their support and help to the patient.
    d. Use an interpreter to let the patient know the nurse is there to answer any questions.

121. A patient is being discharged with a chest tube following a pneumothorax. They request to have a printed diagram showing steps on how to empty the chest tube. This patient is most likely which type of learner?
    a. Auditory learner
    b. Reader learner
    c. Visual learner
    d. Kinesthetic learner

122. A patient is able to follow the steps in written instructions from a nurse to get their blood glucose level using a new glucometer. According to Bloom's Taxonomy, this patient is at which step of psychomotor learning?
    a. Complex overt response
    b. Guided response
    c. Mechanism
    d. Perception

123. A patient with preexisting conditions is wary of transitioning to an insurance plan with value-based insurance design, fearing they may have to pay more to see certain specialists related to their conditions. Is this fear reasonable, and why or why not?
    a. Yes. Insurance plans with value-based insurance design usually do not allow patients with preexisting conditions to have coverage provided for specialty doctors related to their condition.
    b. Yes. Insurance plans with value-based insurance design usually have decreased rates for low-cost, widely effective treatments but, consequently, their rates for specialty doctors are increased.
    c. No. Insurance plans with value-based insurance design usually allow patients to see any specialty doctors of their choice and will cover the cost for those patients.
    d. No. Insurance plans with value-based insurance design will typically vary which services are offered at a reduced rate depending on the individual needs of the consumer.

124. On January 1, 2015, an employer had 1,000 employees, and on December 31, 2015, the same employer had 1,200 employees. During the year, the employer had 125 employees exit from the organization. What is the employer's turnover rate for 2015?
   a. 10.42%
   b. 11.36%
   c. 12.5%
   d. 62.5%

125. The nurse is caring for a terminally ill patient with congestive heart failure. A patient's family member expresses concern to the nurse that the patient should have their IV fluids increased because the patient's mouth is dry, and they may be thirsty. What is the most appropriate action for the nurse to take?
   a. Tell the family member the doctor's orders need to be followed
   b. Increase the rate of IV fluids to 50 mL/hr
   c. Dampen the patient's lips with a moist towel
   d. Encourage the family member to use swabs to keep the patient's mouth moist

126. Which of the following staffing models involves evaluating the needs of the patients on the unit, and then staffing based on those needs?
   a. Acuity-based staffing model
   b. Primary nursing model
   c. Team nursing model
   d. Nurse-patient ratio model

127. An adverse event leads to the identification of a gap in a patient safety process. The executive nurse leader engages the assistance of a multidisciplinary team to develop an action plan. What type of leadership is this?
   a. Democratic
   b. Laissez-faire
   c. Autocratic
   d. Transactional

128. What is the purpose of the ANA Code of Ethics?
   a. Defines nursing practice and ethical duties
   b. Promotes pay grades for nurses
   c. Defines nurse-to-patient ratios for safe care
   d. Differentiates between the moral compass for nurses versus primary care providers

129. Which of the following describes the skill mix staffing model?
   a. Ratio of different types of nurses: intensive care, progressive care, and medical-surgical
   b. Ratio of staff to planned admissions according to patient acuity status
   c. Ratio of different types of personnel: RN, LPN, and CNA
   d. Matching clinical skills of nurses to the unit matrix

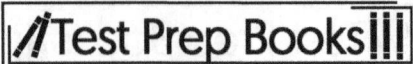

130. According to the American Association of Critical-Care Nurses (AACN), the six standards of a healthy work environment are skilled communication, true collaboration, effective decision-making, meaningful recognition, appropriate staffing, and which of the following?
    a. Authentic leadership
    b. Competitive compensation
    c. Appropriate resources
    d. Fair accountability

131. Which of the following describes a staffing model that involves assignment of a defined number of patients to each nurse or CNA on the unit?
    a. Nurse-patient ratio model
    b. Team nursing model
    c. Total patient care model
    d. Functional nursing model

132. The initial data collected for analysis of a problem is called what?
    a. Aggregate data
    b. Baseline data
    c. Correlative data
    d. Qualitative data

133. The National Patient Safety Goals are determined and measured by which organization?
    a. The Institute of Medicine (IOM)
    b. The National Institutes of Health (NIH)
    c. The Joint Commission (TJC)
    d. The American Hospital Association (AHA)

134. What type of scheduling can best help with hiring and retaining nurses?
    a. Block scheduling
    b. Flexible scheduling
    c. Centralized scheduling
    d. Decentralized scheduling

135. What is an advantage of a health maintenance organization (HMO) over a preferred provider organization (PPO) from the consumer's perspective?
    a. Provider choices are limited.
    b. Third-party care is covered, but coverage may be reduced.
    c. Cost of care is capped, with set prices for services.
    d. Patient care is delivered at a higher quality.

136. The nurse executive must ensure that the healthcare staff is proficient in responding to a choking incident. Which of the following is the first step in demonstrating this competency?
    a. Ask for the full name and date of birth.
    b. Verify choking and call for help.
    c. Swipe the person's mouth with a bare finger.
    d. Encircle the person's torso with arms and thrust the fist deep into the epigastric area.

137. Which aspect of employee performance management is defined as identifying when an employee has demonstrated knowledge and ability to do certain work?
    a. Mentoring
    b. Coaching
    c. Teaching
    d. Competency validation

138. What is a risk with the fee-for-service model of healthcare payor system?
    a. Care is managed to meet quality metrics.
    b. Increased diagnostic services are ordered.
    c. Quality measures are incentivized for facility and provider reimbursement.
    d. Readmission rates are reduced.

139. What is NOT a purpose of employee performance appraisals?
    a. Assessment of employee performance
    b. Development of an action plan for advancement
    c. Editing job description and job duties
    d. Encouraging continued development

140. The nurse executive is preparing a proposal to advocate for the hiring of a neurointerventional team that will better serve the facility's response to traumatic brain injury (TBI). The nurse executive knows that which of the following is the most common cause of TBI?
    a. Falls
    b. Assaults
    c. Motor vehicle accidents
    d. Unknown etiology

141. The nurse executive is looking into a medication error and learns that a nurse who witnessed the error did not file a quality report through the hospital's quality reporting system. The nurse says, "I didn't want to get anyone in trouble." What is the best response by the executive?
    a. "I promise I won't punish anyone. We just need all of the information."
    b. "Quality reports are important so that we can correct individual behavior."
    c. "Patient safety is the most important thing. Disciplining lapses in behavior will make everyone safer."
    d. "Quality reports aren't meant to get people in trouble. They are meant to help us find and fix failures in the system."

142. The executive leadership team has created a committee to develop measures that will improve response to chest pain-related 911 calls in order to prevent a delay in care. What discipline would be most effective in affecting the outcomes of these goals?
    a. ED healthcare provider
    b. Cardiac critical care nurse
    c. EMS personnel
    d. Primary care provider

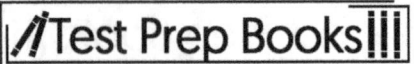

143. Employee competency validation does NOT provide which of the following?
    a. Risk mitigation
    b. Nursing knowledge and clinical skill
    c. Standardization of care
    d. Critical thinking

144. A patient developed shortness of breath and tachycardia while having a CT diagnostic exam. The time to call for help was delayed due to lack of a clear policy for staff to follow. What intervention would be most effective in improving this staff's knowledge of calling for help during an emergency?
    a. Develop an algorithm to define emergencies and appropriate clinical responses.
    b. Reassign staff to other non-patient areas of the hospital.
    c. Provide additional BLS training to staff in the emergency department.
    d. Quiz staff on the policy to assess their knowledge.

145. How does the nurse executive drive the mission of providing safe and affordable care through budgetary and fiscal knowledge?
    a. Aims for best outcomes through capitalizing on resource management
    b. Ensures supplies are ordered from companies owned by employee friends and family
    c. Mitigates risk management by providing monetary compensation for adverse patient events
    d. Advocates for higher-than-average staffing ratios to prevent patient harm

146. When changing practice on a nursing unit, which is the most appropriate first step?
    a. Implement a pilot test of the practice change.
    b. Announce the change to the affected staff and give a timeline.
    c. Plan the steps to accomplish the change.
    d. Solicit the support of senior executives.

147. Performance appraisals and the regular evaluation of performance issues have all of the following in common EXCEPT what?
    a. Employee development
    b. Recognizing accomplishments
    c. Determining training needs
    d. A set time frame

148. The nurse executive is developing an initiative for telephone triage of poisonings to increase the speed in connecting callers with the poison control hotline. Which of the following would be most effective in meeting this goal?
    a. Give the caller the phone number and direct them to hang up and call the hotline.
    b. Direct the caller to the website for further information.
    c. Place a sticker with the poison control hotline number in a noticeable place at each telephone station and transfer the call.
    d. Notify the charge nurse of the initiative.

149. Which research provides the strongest evidence to support a proposed change in practice?
    a. A single randomized controlled trial (RCT)
    b. A meta-analysis of multiple RCTs
    c. A prospective cohort study
    d. A meta-analysis of multiple retrospective case-control studies

150. A review of benchmark scores indicates that a facility is lower than average for infection prevention in their surgical department. What strategy would aim to better this metric?
    a. Provide education on infection prevention.
    b. Schedule fewer surgeries until the metric improves.
    c. Administer antibiotics with each surgery.
    d. Insist that the metrics are incorrect and blame patients for noncompliance.

Answer Explanations #2

1. C: This patient has recently received the difficult news that she has cancer and has just started chemotherapy, all of which can be very emotionally taxing. Being in a heightened or overly emotional state may make it more difficult for a patient to comprehend new knowledge and decrease their readiness to learn. There is not an indication that this patient has any physical restrictions that may affect learning; therefore, Choice A is incorrect. Choice B is incorrect because the question stated that the patient is educated and can work in a high-functioning position, so the patient would likely not suffer from a literacy barrier. Choice D is incorrect because this patient would most likely suffer from emotional lability. Even if a patient is educated, they can still have barriers to learning. It is important to assess every patient fully for barriers that may not be apparent and adapt one's teaching style accordingly.

2. D: An employee who is out of the office on a medical leave of absence and who will not be returning to work would not be eligible to vote in an upcoming union election. An employee who is temporarily laid off, out sick with the flu, or out on military leave right before the election would all be eligible to vote in an upcoming union election.

3. C: There are two categories of budgets that are typically within a healthcare budget: a capital budget, which is used to estimate the costs of durable goods like beds and equipment, and an operational budget, which is used to estimate costs associated with facility operation and staffing.

4. D: This team is now at the implementation stage of problem-solving because their team is actively using their possible solution by removing catheters within 24 hours of surgery. Choice A is incorrect because evaluation would be the next step in this process and would include the team seeing if this is an effective strategy in reducing UTIs. In this scenario, the nursing team has already identified a problem, in this case high UTI rates, and developed a possible solution of removing catheters earlier in the post-op period; therefore, Choices B and C are also incorrect.

5. A: When teaching and communicating with patients and families, nurses should strive for an assertive communication style. In this style, nurses communicate and convey their thoughts and beliefs without coming off as antagonistic or unsure of their ideas. Choice B is incorrect because aggressive styles of communication do not encourage collaborative communication and may come off as offensive to patients. Choices C and D are incorrect because passive and submissive communication styles may make it seem as though the nurse lacks confidence and knowledge. Additionally, nurses may not complete their intended educational goals and objectives with this style if they cannot competently present their knowledge or ideas.

6. C: Nurses must acknowledge their own biases and recognize that those biases will affect their ability to provide culturally sensitive care. Standard protocols related to cultural beliefs and practices are an imperfect solution to the problem of culturally sensitive care because they are not individualized to the specific patient. Meeting the needs of the largest group in a population generally means that the cultural needs of the minority groups within the population are not met. As previously stated, culturally competent care results when caregivers first consider their own biases and the possible effect of those beliefs on patient care. If nurses base their care only on their own beliefs, the patient's beliefs and practices will be ignored.

Answer Explanations #2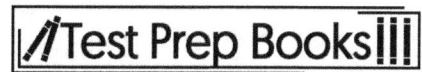

7. A: This patient's family member is exhibiting the bargaining stage of grief where they attempt to offer trades to help improve the outcome for their family member. Bargaining may be directed towards treatment and providers or spiritual powers. The Kubler-Ross stages of grief include denial, anger, bargaining, depression, and acceptance. These are the common stages and orders in which grief occurs; however, it is possible that a person grieving may not experience all stages or may experience them in a different order. Choice *B* is incorrect because in the anger stage a person may become irritated, aggressive, or even violent. Choice *C* is incorrect because the denial stage may have a person refusing to accept a prognosis and could impact their decision making. Choice *D* is incorrect because in the depression stage, a person may begin to accept their grief but become withdrawn, upset, and sad.

8. C: CMS is a governmental organization that provides government-sponsored health insurance to specific groups of Americans. Under the Medicare program, CMS provides coverage for older Americans and Americans with select conditions. The Medicaid program provides coverage for many lower-income Americans. The correct answer is therefore Choice *C*. Choices *A* and *B* are incorrect because CMS does not oversee healthcare facilities or commercial insurance companies. Choice *D* is incorrect because CMS does not provide healthcare organizations with budgetary advisement.

9. B: Team authority is a structure used to manage particular tasks or committees. While Albert does report the team's findings to his immediate supervisor, suggesting line authority (Choice *A*), Albert is in charge of his committee. Choice *D* refers to an organizational structure in which employees report to the supervisors of whichever department is having the issue.

10. B: The nurse-patient model assigns a number of patients to each nurse. This model does not, however, account for the level of care required by the patients. If David's unit was using the patient acuity model, Choice *A*, the patients would be assigned to nurses based on the level of care required by each patient rather than just by numbers. A budget-based staffing model, Choice *D*, relies on mathematical calculations to determine staffing needs. Choice *C* is not a real staffing model.

11. D: The five rights of delegation are right task, right circumstance, right person, right direction, and right supervision. If the nurse is unsure if a task falls within these guidelines, they should not delegate that task and should check their facility policy for future delegation. When the nurse is delegating a task to unlicensed assistive personnel, they must make sure they include the five rights of delegation for the safety of the patient as well as coverage for their own license. Choices *A*, *B*, and *C* are incorrect because they do not correctly outline the five rights of delegation.

12. D: When critically reading a new research article, it is not imperative that the nurse sees where funding comes from for the research. While funding can have some influence over research and should be examined when appraising research, it is not necessary when trying to critically read and understand new research information. Choices *A*, *B*, and *C* are incorrect because the nurse should determine the thesis, process, and outcomes when critically reading research.

13. D: One of the key principles of proper resource utilization is that each member of a care team, from the doctor in charge to the orderlies responsible for transporting a patient, should understand the treatments prescribed and their roles in that process as thoroughly as possible. For the nurse in this situation, proper resource utilization involves confirming with the doctor when a dosage seems inaccurate. It may be that the doctor incorrectly wrote the dosage or is prescribing that larger dose for a particular reason. By consulting with the doctor, the nurse is ensuring that resources are used properly and that the patient's treatment is as effective and efficient as possible. Therefore, the correct answer is Choice *D*. Although Choice *C* is correct in identifying that the nurse used proper resource utilization

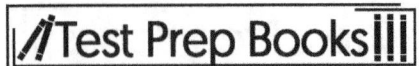

Answer Explanations #2

techniques, the reasoning is faulty—following proper resource utilization does not entail ensuring that minimal resources are expended on each patient. Instead, proper resource utilization is about ensuring that whatever resources are expended on a patient are effectively and efficiently contributing to the patient's treatment plan. Therefore, Choice C is incorrect. Choices A and B are incorrect because the nurse was practicing proper resource utilization.

14. A: Under the Taft-Hartley Act, creating a company-sponsored labor union is illegal, making Choice A correct. The actions listed in Choices B, C, and D are not addressed by the Taft-Hartley Act.

15. B: Principled bargaining occurs when groups negotiate a contract while being aware and mindful of the key issues to each side. Principled bargaining is a process of finding solutions so that both sides gain from the agreement. Choices A and C, distributive and positional bargaining, both refer to bargaining that takes place to achieve a specific objective. Choice D, coordinated bargaining, refers to bargaining that occurs when multiple unions within one organization meet to negotiate as one group to benefit all employees.

16. B: The goal is to assimilate all the ideas into a strategic plan that prioritizes opportunities for improvement and amends all processes associated with changes, including any process flows and job aids. Choice A, visually analyzing team members' performance, may come before this, while Choice C, implementing strategies, would come after.

17. B: Functional nursing means that each nurse is responsible for an aspect of patient care, such as taking vitals or dispensing medications. Primary nursing, Choice A, is where one nurse handles the patient's care throughout that patient's hospitalization. Team nursing, Choice C, is where a team of nurses collaborates on the patient's care, and Choice D, modular nursing, is where nurses are assigned based on the location and proximity of the patients.

18. C: Team nursing involves having a collaborative team that cares for its assigned patients. Primary nursing, Choice A, involves having the same nurse care for the patient throughout the patient's hospital stay. Modular nursing, Choice B, assigns nurses based on a group of patients within a given proximity, such as in a particular hallway or room cluster. Functional nursing, Choice D, assigns one nurse to handle a specific task for a group of patients.

19. D: The next step in the grievance process would involve the union steward discussing the grievance with the supervisor's manager and/or the HR manager. Then, a committee of union officers should discuss the grievance with the appropriate managers in the company, Choice A. The national union representative would then discuss the grievance with designated company executives, Choice B. If, after this process, the grievance is still not settled, it would then go to arbitration, Choice C.

20. C: The institution can support diversity by providing resources that satisfy cultural practices, such as dietary rules. Institutions also may provide interpreters, information sessions for employees, and accommodations for religious observances. Under normal circumstances, requiring employees to speak a second language would severely limit the pool of eligible employees and would not be an effective strategy; therefore, Choice A is incorrect. Educational programs should be provided for all employees and should not be limited to supervisory staff, so Choice B is wrong. Choice D is incorrect as offering alternative solutions to all requests for accommodation could be viewed as paternalistic and culturally insensitive. The institution is required to consider ways to satisfy all reasonable patient requests.

Answer Explanations #2

21. C: A leader who believes her team members work best with clear-cut incentives and rewards can best be described as having a transactional leadership style. In a transactional leadership style, the main focus is the transactional aspect of the relationship between leader and team member. The belief is that team members are most likely to find satisfaction with their own work when the leader is clear about expectations and incentives. Therefore, the correct answer is Choice C. All of the other answer choices describe distinct styles of leadership that are not in line with the scenario described.

22. A: UnitedHealth Group, Cigna, and Aetna are all examples of commercial health insurance companies. The three companies are among the largest commercial insurance companies in the United States, and commercial insurance companies in general continue to account for a significant portion of health insurance policies. The correct answer is therefore Choice A. All of the other answer choices describe different types of organizations, which are not examples of commercial health insurance companies.

23. B: Transformational leadership style and transactional leadership style are two distinct theories of leadership that share the same central premise: a leader's effectiveness is directly related to their team members' ability to feel satisfied and fulfilled in their work. The distinction between the two leadership styles lies in how they believe team members are most satisfied. With transactional leadership style, the belief is that team members are most satisfied when they can best sense the potential rewards associated with their good performance. On the other hand, transformational leadership style is more concerned with transforming team members' relationship to their work and the leader, with the hope of aligning their personal goals and development with that of the organization. Therefore, the correct answer is Choice B. Choice A is incorrect because there is nothing about either leadership style that is concerned with oversight for leaders and their decisions. Choice C is incorrect because it is an example of democratic leadership style thinking. Choice D is incorrect because it is an example of situational leadership style thinking.

24. C: This nurse exhibited a failure to delegate appropriate tasks and therefore fell behind schedule. They had multiple time-heavy tasks to complete in the morning that were difficult to carry out independently. Since the nurse is on a fully staffed floor that includes nursing assistants, the nurse should delegate the bed baths because this task is within the scope of practice for the nursing assistant to complete. This would allow the nurse to complete the other tasks that require nursing-level competency. Choice A is incorrect because the nurse is working on a fully staffed unit, so it is unlikely that staffing ratios would be the cause of this delayed care. Choice B is incorrect because regardless of organization and planning, the nurse may not be able to complete all of these tasks independently in a certain amount of time. Instead, tasks should be delegated appropriately. Choice D is incorrect because a nurse may have patients that have very involved care, and delegating tasks helps the nurse complete all of their care in the appropriate time.

25. C: Patient acuity staffing takes into consideration the level of care required by each patient when assigning nurses. Budget-based staffing, Choice A, uses mathematical calculations to determine staffing needs. Nurse-patient staffing, Choice B, assigns patients based on the number of patients to the number of nurses. A combination of nurse-patient and patient-acuity, Choice D, would likely result in a good combination of the number of patients and the care level required by those patients assigned to each nurse; however, the question asked for which method specifically targets need levels.

26. C: Checking that data is properly collected, analyzed, and from an unbiased source ensures that data for a study is internally valid. Choice A is incorrect because external validity is ensuring that results in the study participants can be applied to other outside populations. Choice B is incorrect because

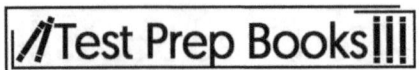

generalizability is a type of external validity where the study results can be useful to larger groups of the population. Choice D is incorrect because replicability is the ability for a study to be reproduced and generate outcomes similar to the original study.

27. C: An open-door policy is used to establish a relationship where employees feel comfortable speaking directly with management about problems and suggestions. Town hall meetings, Choice A, are formal gatherings for the entire company that are commonly referred to as "all-hands meetings" and tend to focus on sharing information "from the top down" concerning the overall organization. These meetings are not usually designed to allow feedback from employees about smaller detail issues. Management by Walking Around (MBWA), Choice B, as the name suggests, involves having managers and supervisors physically get out of their offices and interact with employees in person. MBWA allows management to check on employee progress, inquire about potential issues, and gain other feedback without relying on employees to "make the first move." Finally, department meetings, Choice D, are formal gatherings of employees and management in a given department that typically take place on a set day and time, allow everyone involved to share ideas, and offer solutions to company challenges.

28. B: Informed consent is a legal document that is required when a patient is undergoing an invasive medical procedure to ensure they have complete understanding of the procedure. Since this patient has no cognitive deficits and is alert and oriented, they must sign their own consent, along with the performing provider and a witness. A family member does have to be present if the patient is incapacitated, incapable of understanding the education regarding the procedure, and unable to sign the consent themselves. Choices A and D are incorrect because they do not include all necessary members needed for this scenario's informed consent. Choice C is incorrect because a family member does not have to be present for the informed consent described in this scenario.

29. C: HPPD is a common metric used to assess effectiveness and efficiency of care provided. By dividing the total number of hours worked by a particular kind of medical professionals (e.g., nurses, physician's assistants, medical technicians) by the total number of patients seen at a particular healthcare center over the same 24-hour period, HPPD provides a healthcare provider with an average of how many hours were spent attending to each patient for that particular day. In other words, HPPD estimates how much time the average patient received medical attention by that group of workers over that 24-hour period. Therefore, the correct answer is Choice C. All of the other answer choices do not provide the correct interpretation of an HPPD value of 0.4.

30. D: Staff authority is a management system wherein supervisors are responsible for their areas of expertise. Employees would go to whichever supervisor is in charge of the area in which there is a problem. Line authority, Choice A, refers to a structure in which employees report to their direct supervisor only, and that supervisor will seek out other supervisors if the need arises. Team authority, Choice B, is usually task- or committee-based.

31. C: A good rule of thumb when considering HPPD as a metric is that the more intensive and continuous care a patient or patient type requires, the higher the HPPD value for that ward will be. A psychiatric ward may have many patients living and existing more or less independently of healthcare professionals' direct intervention. Therefore, the correct answer is Choice C. The NICU, burn unit, and hospice care ward are all wards that care for high-risk patients who often require intensive, around-the-clock care.

32. D: While a patient is in the process of imminently dying, they may have a respiratory pattern that has periods of rapid breathing followed by apneic periods. This pattern of breathing is also called

Cheyne-Stokes respirations and is common in individuals who are dying. Choice A is incorrect because patients who are dying may have decreased cough and an inability to clear their own secretions. These secretions may need to be suctioned if appropriate for the patient and their comfort. Choice B is incorrect because patients may experience an increased respiratory rate during the dying process. Choice C is incorrect because dying patients are more likely to have decreased and darkened urinary output.

33. C: The best way for HR leadership to communicate appropriate and acceptable behaviors within the workplace is to consistently behave in an ethical, reliable, and acceptable manner. Choices A, B, and D are all acceptable best practices to ensure that the message of what is appropriate behavior is communicated frequently; however, the best way to communicate this is to model the behavior daily.

34. C: Since the hepatitis B vaccine became available in 1982, risk of healthcare-associated hepatitis B among caregivers in medical facilities has been significantly reduced. Use of PPE and environmental controls also help reduce risk. Choice A is incorrect because screenings are done for TB, not hepatitis B. Choice B is incorrect because not every previous work experience requires hepatitis B immunization. A "catch-up" period is advisable to ensure adequate staffing rather than refusing to hire unimmunized individuals. Choice D is incorrect. Although seven days is the minimum duration of time that hepatitis B pathogens can survive outside of a host, once exposed, there is no guarantee that this action will prevent the care provider from contracting the disease.

35. B: HR can specifically alleviate employees' fears and concerns about reporting unethical behavior and possible retaliation by providing them with a confidential and/or anonymous reporting method. This will protect their identity while still allowing for a proper and thorough investigation to occur. Although Choices A, C, and D are all appropriate actions to ensure a robust policy that is compliant with the law and understood by employees, these actions may not specifically address employees' concerns about making a report.

36. A: When implementing remote monitoring in a telehealth program, a priority for the nurse administrator is to ensure that nursing staff are trained on the proper use of remote monitoring equipment and software. Adequate training is vital to ensure accurate data collection, interpretation, and appropriate response to patient data received through remote monitoring. Choice B may be a consideration, but training nursing staff is more essential to the successful integration of remote monitoring. Choice C is a broader goal that may be pursued after ensuring the successful implementation of remote monitoring. Choice D is not the top priority in ensuring the successful integration of remote monitoring, although this option can be valuable for staying informed.

37. B: When creating and implementing new evidence-based practice guidelines, the nurse should ask a question of clinical inquiry, gather evidence, appraise this evidence, act and implement new guidelines, and then evaluate the effectiveness of their guidelines. Choices A, C, and D are incorrect because they do not have the steps of evidence-based practice inquiry in the correct order.

38. B: In a binding decision, the disputing parties are required by law to follow the decision reached as a result of the arbitration process. In compulsory arbitration, Choice A, the disputing parties are required by law to go through the arbitration process. In voluntary arbitration, Choice C, the disputing parties choose to undergo the arbitration process. Finally, constructive confrontation, Choice D, is a type of mediation used in some extremely complicated or contentious disputes, particularly ones where neither party is able to agree to a compromise.

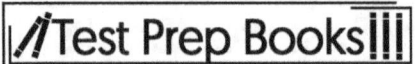

39. D: Transparency is a vital component of communication that builds trust within an organization and between employees. Empowerment and courage, Choices A and B, are not related to components of communication. Collaboration, Choice C is a form of communication, not a component of it.

40. C: A nurse at level 1 of clinical inquiry in the Synergy Model, the most basic level, has awareness that a problem exists and may ask others for assistance and guidance. Choices A and B are incorrect because these are characteristics that reflect level 3 clinical inquiry. Choice D is incorrect because using evidence-based practice to change delivery of care, even if it goes against industry standards, is the highest level of clinical inquiry, level 5.

41. A: Patient safety and confidentiality is the most important consideration when it comes to remote monitoring. Data should be transferred to the patient's overseeing provider through secure networks to protect their private health information. Choices B and D are both important considerations but not the most important, making them incorrect. Choice C is also an important consideration, but the data recorded via remote monitoring doesn't necessarily go to the patient's PCP; instead, it goes to the provider that ordered the remote monitoring. However, the PCP can review data to provide continuity of care if needed.

42. C: Because stethoscopes only come into contact with patient skin, they only need low-level disinfection. Tools that penetrate the skin require the higher levels of disinfection and stronger solutions.

43. D: Common issues handled by labor unions include advocating for fair nursing contracts, wages, working conditions, and rights, making Choice D correct.

44. A: An employee must file a complaint charge of discrimination with the EEOC within a period of 180 days of the alleged incident.

45. A: Patients and families do not have the right to access staffing schedules; however, they should be kept informed regarding who is actively participating in their care. Choices B, C, and D are incorrect because these are all rights that patients and families have in the healthcare setting. They have the right to obtain and review their medical records, receive capable and non-discriminatory care, and actively join in medical care decisions.

46. A: The novice nurse is comparing her own beliefs to the patient's beliefs and lacks the knowledge to understand the patient's point of view. This is the definition of ethnocentrism, which can adversely affect the nurse-patient relationship. The remaining observations could potentially affect the patient's refusal of the therapy; however, the patient's refusal in this example is clearly related to the religious objection.

47. D: Informational picketing is done by employees for the purpose of letting the public know that they are not represented by any one authority and thus plan to organize. Recognitional picketing, Choice A, is done by employees for the purpose of encouraging their employer to recognize their union as their representative. Organizational picketing, Choice B, is done by employees for the purpose of convincing other employees to join their union. Finally, consumer picketing, Choice C, takes place when employees picket to discourage the public from doing business with the employer in question.

48. A: In the AACN Synergy Model, there are three levels: levels 1, 3, and 5. A nurse at a level 1 in facilitation of learning can deliver their planned education to a patient; however, this may be done without fully assessing learning readiness and ability. The ability to competently and expertly facilitate learning requires the nurse to not only create their educational content, but also assess any barriers and adapt these lessons to the individual patient or group. Choice B is incorrect because level 2 is not one of the levels in the ability to facilitate learning. Choice C is incorrect because level 3 facilitation would exhibit the nurse tailoring some of their teachings to the basic needs or obstacles in a patient's learning. Choice D is incorrect because level 5 facilitation of learning would have the nurse able to completely understand the patient's preferred learning styles, teaching methodology, and ability to learn. The nurse would then also be able to fully adapt their teaching and lesson plan to these preferences.

49. C: There are three levels of responding to diversity in the Synergy Model: levels 1, 3, and 5. According to the Synergy Model of responding to diversity, a nurse who is seeking information about the cultural background of a patient and beginning to incorporate some of this diversity into the patient's care is said to be at a level 3 of diversity response. Choice A is incorrect because at level 1, the nurse is just beginning to assess different cultural backgrounds with basic questions and may not be incorporating these findings into diverse care. Choice B is incorrect because level 2 is not one of the levels of responding to diversity in the Synergy Model. Choice D is incorrect because level 5 is when the nurse is actively incorporating diverse cultural knowledge into the patient's care and can help think of alternative or preferred models for delivery of care that are aligned with the patient's diverse cultural beliefs.

50. D: An employer is required to bring the veteran back to their position or equivalent position if they leave for active military service. Additionally, they must provide all length of service benefits they would have received if they were actively working for the employer at the time they left to serve. Choice C is incorrect, as the employer is responsible to maintain the position for up to five years.

51. B: Moral agency refers to decision-making that includes accountability for right and wrong decisions by the moral agent. Advocacy is an ethical principle that is not legally enforced, making Choice A incorrect. Many argue that paternalism is contrary to advocacy because of the assumption that the "system" knows what is best for the patient without concern for the patient's wishes. Choice D is incorrect because moral agency is not restricted to a specific population; however, the nurse will assess the ability of all patients to make informed decisions.

52. A: SIPOC stands for suppliers, inputs, processes, outputs, and customers. It is a process improvement tool used to define each step of a process before it is implemented.

53. B: When creating a lesson plan, the nurse should create definite and measurable goals and objectives. Creating open-ended objectives makes it more difficult to create a structured lesson and assess if the learner gained the desired knowledge. Choices A, C, and D are incorrect because these are all accurate and important components to include in a lesson plan when educating a patient. Additionally, the material in the lesson should encompass both the goals and objectives of the teaching.

54. C: Situations such as the one described in the question, in which a patient experiences an infection following medical treatment, can be measured using the metric HAI. Such a metric is used to determine a healthcare provider's performance in the safety performance domain. Therefore, the correct answer is Choice C. All of the other answer choices describe the other performance domains, none of which HAI is used to calculate.

55. D: The nurse demonstrates professional competence as a result of a commitment to lifelong learning that is required for all areas of nursing. The other choices each contain only a single element of the five elements of caring: commitment, conscience, competence, compassion, and confidence.

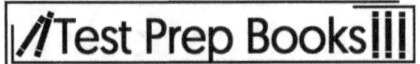

Answer Explanations #2

56. D: Since most of the participants are over 50 years old and the treatment is for all adults over 18 years old, these participants do not accurately reflect the population for which the vaccine is intended. This can lead to skewed results due to a selection bias, a bias that comes from study participants not being reflective of the true population. Choice A is incorrect because reporting bias comes from under-reporting or over-reporting certain characteristics or variables to skew results. Choice B is incorrect because recall bias is when participants are not able to accurately or completely remember information that is asked in a study. Choice C is incorrect because healthy participant bias is when someone is more likely to participate in a medical study if they are already careful and considerate about their health.

57. A: Patients who practice Orthodox Judaism often follow practices where unnecessary touching from non-family members and any physical contact from members of the opposite sex is not allowed. A female nurse and female nursing student would be an appropriate care team to handle this patient's care. Choices B, C, and D are incorrect because each of these care teams includes at least one male team member, which would not be appropriate for this patient's care based on their religious beliefs. In medical emergencies, these practices may have exceptions, but it is important that cultural and religious preferences be respectfully discussed and honored with patients throughout their care.

58. D: Single-dose vials are key to reducing risk of transmitting bloodborne pathogens, such as hepatitis B, hepatitis C, and HIV, as is consistent use of aseptic techniques. Choices A, B, and C are incorrect since single-dose vials are unlikely to reduce medication expenditures. Medication must still be measured because the prescribed dose may not represent the entire contents of the vial, and not all single-dose vials are recyclable.

59. D: In general, value-based insurance assigns higher costs to treatments that have not been proven effective, as well as elective surgeries. Since carpal tunnel release surgery is an elective surgery, having value-based insurance will likely cause it to be more expensive for the patient.

60. A: Under USERRA, employees who are out on military leave are expected to receive the same seniority-based benefits that they would have received had they not been out of work on leave, such as vacation time and 401(k) contributions. After the first month of military leave, employers are not required to continue group healthcare coverage at their expense, so Choice B is incorrect. An employer is expected to continue to pay exempt employees who are out on military leave their full salary, less any compensation that they receive for serving in the military, Choice C. Additionally, employers are encouraged to make reasonable efforts to accommodate disabled veterans returning from military leave, Choice D.

61. A: An employer cannot discriminate against employees that have or plan to serve in the military. There also is an obligation to review candidates and use comparable skills from their military experience to the job that they are applying for. USERRA rules are for applicants and current employees. Choice B is incorrect because not hiring based on future service would be discrimination. Choice C is incorrect since previous military experience should be considered. Choice D is incorrect since USERRA has rules for applicants as well as current employees.

62. A: Team authority is a temporary structure lasting only as long as the task or committee is needed. Choices B, C, and D are all benefits of line authority, in which each employee has one immediate supervisor to whom they report.

63. A: Budget-based staffing does not account for the ebb and flow of patient needs during any given shift or day. Budget-based staffing does calculate the number of nursing hours per patient per day

(HPPD), Choice *B*, and it factors in the average number of patients per day, not week, as in Choice *C*. While budget-based staffing is mathematically-based, it is still oriented towards the end goal of helping the patients, Choice *D*.

64. B: If a patient is entirely unable to get out-of-network referrals, they most likely have an HMO plan. Under such a plan, treatment is only covered if it is with a healthcare provider that has negotiated with the payor (usually a commercial health insurance company). Therefore, the correct answer is Choice *A*. All the other answer choices are different kinds of insurance plans that all offer coverage for out-of-network referrals to some extent.

65. A: The communication style in which someone sends a message or instruction, someone receives the message, the receiver repeats the message back, and then the initial sender verifies the message is called closed-loop communication. Closed-loop communication is important in the healthcare setting and when delegating tasks to ensure that the instructions are clear and received accurately. Choices *B* and *C* are incorrect because they are each only one step of the closed-loop communication style. Choice *D* is incorrect because in open-loop communication there is no feedback step and the person receiving the instruction does not repeat it back for verification. This communication style is faster but allows more room for error.

66. B: Email makes it easy to get information to a lot of people very quickly. However, this communication method can result in employees suffering from "information overload" from too many emails. The intranet, Choice *A*, has the benefit of no risk of important information being accessed by someone outside the organization. Intranets can be effective at communicating important ongoing information about the company, such as policies and procedures. Newsletters, Choice *C*, can provide a variety of information and have the potential to do so in an engaging and welcoming manner. However, newsletters can be labor-intensive. Finally, word-of-mouth, Choice *D*, can quickly spread information throughout a group of people. However, information can become muddled, misinterpreted, and unrecognizable as it is passed from person to person.

67. C: A leader who is not particularly involved in the decision-making process of their teammates may be described as having a laissez-faire leadership style. Under the philosophy of laissez-faire leadership style, team members work best when supervised least because each member knows their own strengths and weaknesses and does not feel hampered by the expectations of the leader. Therefore, the correct answer is Choice *C*. All of the other answer choices describe separate and distinct styles of leadership and do not align with the scenario described.

68. A: Federal and local laws that affect the type of care that patients are given are called political forces. The nurse should be aware of different external forces that may affect the care they can provide for patients at their healthcare facility. Choice *B* is incorrect because local, state, and community regulations that affect the kind of care that can be delivered is considered a regulatory force. Choice *C* is incorrect because economic forces affect the funding or allocation of resources that may impact testing, treatment, and other aspects of care that can be given. Choice *D* is incorrect because social forces refer to the pressure to provide certain care as influenced by societal expectations.

69. A: The CDC and the World Health Organization constantly review and update recommendations of risk reduction measures based on the latest scientific data; therefore, conducting research for a better answer is the best approach. Choice *B* is incorrect because entirely stopping any previous CDC recommendation is not the best answer. Choice *C* is incorrect because hand sanitizer will not remove the airborne infectious particles launched by the cough into the air that others are breathing. Choice *D* is

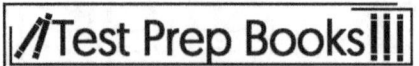

incorrect because although researching other facilities may reveal shared challenges, this type of research will not always provide a solution for improvement in risk reduction measures.

70. B: Individual consideration refers to a transformational leader's ability to serve as a direct mentor to their team members. Rather than merely engaging in a transactional relationship, individual consideration asks that leaders take a more involved role in their team members' work lives and goals. By doing so, the hope is that each team member feels listened to and prioritized and is consequently more likely to put their best effort in at work. Therefore, the correct answer is Choice B. All of the other answer choices are different components of transformational leadership style with distinct actions and mentalities.

71. C: Ambiguity when communicating with employees can cause confusion, conflict, and distress. When employees do not have a clear direction, they will not be motivated or engaged to do their best work, and therefore, Choices A, B, and D are incorrect. When an organization's leader is ambiguous in their communications, results will not include employees going above and beyond, innovative and productive work, or lower turnover and higher satisfaction.

72. D: The work exclusion lasts until a doctor confirms full recovery or that the proper course of medication has been completed. Choices A and B are incorrect because although the employee may call out sick, go to a doctor, and/or be sent home for a few days, neither of these choices reflects the regulated process that must be in place for patient safety or the required amount of recovery time to contain the contagion. Choice C is incorrect because transferring the employee to a different department only risks infection of different patients.

73. A: A cost-benefit analysis is used in the Lean Six Sigma methodology to determine the true costs of a potential solution, as compared to the actual benefits. Choices B, C, and D are not goals of a cost-benefit analysis.

74. B: According to the systems thinking model, vulnerability refers to the presence of any stressor, actual or potential, that could adversely affect the patient's health. A history of smoking increases the patient's vulnerability to additional health alterations. Socioeconomic status (Choice A) and being married (Choice C) are related to resource availability, which refers to the availability of financial and emotional resources that are necessary to support the patient's recovery. The patient's active participation in the plan of care (Choice D) is considered to have a positive effect on care outcomes.

75. A: A whistle-blower reports or publicizes any illegal or unethical information about an organization or industry. An example of a whistle-blower is former tobacco industry official Jeffrey Wigand, who confessed in a televised interview that the tobacco industry was intentionally packing cigarettes with addictive levels of nicotine. Whistle-blowers are generally perceived as villains to institutions, while others believe they risk their livelihood for a just cause. Whistleblowers can operate in public or private institutions, making Choices C and D incorrect.

76. B: Vigilance refers to the ability of the nurse to recognize and respond to changes in the patient's condition. According to the Synergy Model, vigilance as a caring practice is a learned behavior that evolves with clinical experience, which means that the novice nurse will identify predictable alterations in the patient's condition, while the experienced nurse will identify and respond to more subtle changes. The most experienced nurse is capable of intervening to prevent some adverse events. Choice A is incorrect; engagement refers to committing to the patient care relationship, rather than responding to changes in the patient's condition. The changes noted in the patient's condition are early, subtle

Answer Explanations #2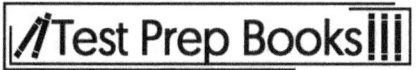

indications of heart failure. The novice nurse would initially associate the changes with the surgical procedure, while the experienced nurse would assess the patient for heart failure. Although collaboration with other providers may have been an outcome of the nurse's assessment, the initial care was an independent action.

77. A: Providing thorough explanations of continuing or changing care can help terminally ill patients and family members make the most informed decisions for themselves. Choice *B* is incorrect because although active treatments may help extend life, they may not be curative, and the patient could experience a worsened quality of life due to deteriorating health and side effects of treatment. Choice *C* is incorrect because the nurse and medical team should not make decisions for the patients or family members. The patient and family members should be encouraged to make their own decisions to help gain control and ensure their end-of-life care is within their preferences. Choice *D* is incorrect because giving a higher dose of an analgesic, even if prescribed, should be discussed with the patient and family first. Higher doses of analgesic may decrease a patient's awareness, feelings, and interactions with family, and may even speed up the dying process.

78. D: Idealized influence refers to a transformational leader's ability to serve as a role model to their team members. Rather than directly instruct team members on proper performance, a transformational leader can impact team members' performance simply by modeling such behavior correctly. Therefore, the correct answer is Choice *D*. All of the other answer choices are different components of transformational leadership style with distinct actions and mentalities.

79. C: Line authority refers to a chain of command structure where employees report directly to their immediate supervisor, and the supervisor is responsible for moving issues "up the chain" as needed. Staff authority, Choice *B*, divides responsibility based on areas of expertise, and team authority, Choice *A*, is usually a temporary organizational structure involving particular tasks or committees. Choice *D* is not an actual type of authority.

80. A: Distributive justice refers to the allocation of scarce resources, and advocacy is support for policies that protect at-risk populations. The nurse understands that scarce resource allocation may be sub-standard in certain populations. In nursing, nonmaleficence (Choice *C*) refers to the act of inflicting the least amount of harm possible in order to reach a favorable result. Fidelity (Choice *D*) refers to faithfulness but does not specifically address resources or the patient population. Beneficence (Choice *B*) refers to doing good to others in the care of patients.

81. D: Using a hands-on workshop would be a beneficial teaching style for drawing up and injecting insulin since this is a hands-on, tactile technique to learn. Additionally, hands-on workshops are also conducive for small group settings, such as this one with a patient, spouse, and parent. Choice *A* is incorrect because lecture-style learning would be more beneficial for a large group setting. It may also be more difficult to learn a practical procedure in a lecture setting. Choice *B* is incorrect because, although a discussion group is a good style for a smaller group, it does not have the benefit of being able to teach the practical and technical skills needed for insulin administration. Choice *C* is incorrect because online or computer-based learning would be more beneficial if the learners were remote; however, this group is still in the hospital before being discharged.

82. D: A team that is made of healthcare professionals from multiple disciplines, such as doctors, specialized nurses, nurse practitioners, and dietitians is an interdisciplinary team. Choices *A* and *B* are incorrect because they are not types of medical teams that a nurse works on. Choice *C* is incorrect because an intradisciplinary team is made up of members that are all from the same profession or

Answer Explanations #2

discipline. In the healthcare setting, nurses will work on both intradisciplinary and interdisciplinary teams and should be comfortable in both settings.

83. D: Word-of-mouth communication can spread information quickly; however, individuals may inaccurately represent the information, which can lead to misinformation and misunderstandings. The individual who initiated the information can quickly lose control over the message, its accuracy, and its effectiveness. All other choices are reliable in being able to represent and understand information.

84. A: An organizational chart is used to define who is responsible for managing each aspect of the organization. It helps staff know who their direct supervisor is and who they should contact them with any issues that come up during their shift. Choices B, C, and D are not real types of tools.

85. C: A leader who is hands-off and allows their staff to control the process of finding problems and creating solutions is said to have a laissez-faire style of leadership. Although this style gives people independence, little may be accomplished because the manager is not truly leading and guiding their staff. Choice A is incorrect because in the democratic leadership style, the leader works with their staff to hear problems and potential solutions but will ultimately choose the appropriate solution to implement. Choice B is incorrect because in transactional leadership, the leader is task-oriented and will offer rewards or punishments as they see appropriate. Choice D is incorrect because autocratic leaders rely on their own knowledge and skills to make decisions without receiving input from those around them.

86. C: The Synergy Model shows how client characteristics and nursing competencies work together in a healthcare environment to affect quality outcomes. Resiliency and stability are aspects of client characteristics in the Synergy Model. Other client characteristics include vulnerability, resource availability, participation in care, decision-making ability, predictability, and complexity. Choices A, B, and D are incorrect because these characteristics are not part of those sections of the Synergy Model.

87. C: Via the Weingarten rights, a union employee is entitled to have a union representative present if they are being questioned by a manager in a discussion that may ultimately lead to a disciplinary action.

88. B: According to the AACN Synergy Model, a nurse who is at a level 3 of team collaboration helps initiate collaborative efforts with interdisciplinary team members and actively tries to find activities that continue collaboration. Choice A is incorrect because only participating in collaboration with team members is level 1. Choices C and D are incorrect because teaching and mentoring others to continue to spread and grow collaboration is level 5, the highest collaborative level in the Synergy Model.

89. D: The variable staffing method involves staffing the unit below the maximum and then making adjustments as needed. Fixed staffing, Choice A, involves staffing the unit based on the maximum workload. Semiflexible staffing, Choice B, maintains a small, fixed staff and fills in with need-based staff. Choice C is not a staffing method.

90. A: Evidence is usually graded on a letter scale, with A being the highest level of evidence. The type of research with the highest level of evidence is a meta-analysis. Choice B is incorrect because a randomized-control trial is the second highest level of evidence, level B. Choices C and D are incorrect because integrative interviews and cohort studies have a moderate level of evidence and are both level C.

91. B: Electronic syndromic surveillance systems may be used locally, state-wide, or nationwide. The national version receives data from local and state facilities as well as the Center for Disease Control and

Prevention (CDC). This type of system can predict an outbreak or threat based on symptoms even before a diagnosis is confirmed. Choice A is incorrect; although the CDC does maintain a database of health issues to monitor outbreaks, the CDC database relies on reports from other health professionals and facilities. Choice C is incorrect because FEMA directs efforts to prepare for and recover from natural disasters. FEMA does not collect health data. Choice D is incorrect because although electronic medical records are great tools to track individual patients, these software programs do not offer an option to track diagnostic data among populations.

92. B: Having an organization-wide perspective can help promote systems thinking because it allows nurses to collaborate with more team members, define problems they see in healthcare, and implement solution strategies. Choices A, C, and D are incorrect because these characteristics are barriers to systems thinking. Instead, strong group dynamics, prospective thinking, and an organization-wide perspective should be used to encourage systems thinking.

93. A: Psychologist Kurt Lewin, although certainly not the first man in history to speculate on and identify common traits of great leaders, is often credited with popularizing the idea that there are distinct styles of leadership. In the mid-20th century, Lewin conducted research in which he observed schoolchildren completing an art project together. From his observations, Lewin delineated three distinct styles of leadership—autocratic, democratic, and laissez-faire. Therefore, the correct answer is Choice A. All of the other answer choices incorrectly identify the conditions under which Lewin first formulated his theories on leadership.

94. B: Hispanic cultures are typically patriarchal, and fathers or other prominent older male figures in a patient's family are often the decision makers, regardless of the patient's age. Choices A and C are incorrect because it is unlikely that other females in the family will oversee medical decisions if the patient's father is present. Choice D is incorrect because it is more likely that an older male, such as a patient's father, will be involved in medical decisions rather than their child.

95. B: If employees win the vote to decertify their union on August 31 in a given calendar year, a new election cannot be held until after one year has passed.

96. C: Overprovision is a phenomenon associated with FFS reimbursement models in which healthcare providers overprescribe patients, subjecting them to more tests and scans than are absolutely necessary. Because FFS models reimburse healthcare providers solely for the number of services they render to a patient and not how effective those services were, healthcare providers have a direct incentive to expend as many resources and services as possible on each patient. By having their patient undergo another evaluation while not believing it to be necessary for their treatment, the healthcare provider in Choice C is embodying the practice of overprovision. All other answer choices describe practices that are in line with proper resource utilization and therefore are representative of a mindset that is very much counter to the practice of overprovision.

97. A: Since the payor is defined as the individual or entity who is responsible for paying the cost of a patient's care, the payor in this circumstance is the patient themselves, Choice A, since the patient chose not to use either private or government insurance (Medicare).

98. C: A PPO generally requires a higher premium than an HMO. That is because a PPO allows customers to see out-of-network doctors without a referral, which an HMO does not, making PPOs more expensive. Also, HMOs are more likely to have fixed-rate copays for in-service providers than PPOs because they are generally less flexible plans.

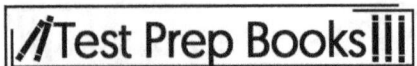

Answer Explanations #2

99. C: Following a patient's death, the family members should not be immediately asked to leave the room. The family should be allowed to stay in the room with the patient to grieve, process their emotions, and participate in care if safe and appropriate. Choices *A, B,* and *D* are incorrect because these are appropriate actions for the nurse to take to help provide support to the family and remain respectful to the patient.

100. D: Situational leadership style emphasizes the specific situation or scenario a leader finds themselves in as the most important factor as to how they should govern themselves and their team. When a healthcare provider is attempting to secure proper public health accreditation, situational leadership style can be especially effective because the provider will need to be prepared to be tested in a variety of ways. Therefore, the correct answer is Choice *D*. All other answer choices represent other leadership styles that, although potentially effective in accreditation situations, are not considered to be particularly effective in the way situational leadership style is.

101. B: Jehovah's Witnesses often avoid or refuse blood products as part of their religious beliefs and practices. If a patient who is a practicing Jehovah's Witness does need a blood product, information should be explained factually to the patient. Additionally, alternatives that are not against their religious practices, including hemoglobin-based blood substitutes, should be discussed with the patient and care team. Choice *A* is incorrect because the nurse should never automatically assume that this patient will refuse the blood product. These medical decisions should always be explained and discussed with the patient first. Choice *C* is incorrect because this response is judgmental and shames the patient for their beliefs. Choice *D* is incorrect because the transfusion should not be given before discussing the care and possible alternative measures for this patient.

102. C: Under the Pregnancy Discrimination Act of 1978, an employer must give a woman a comparable position to the one that she held prior to her maternity leave (if the company does so with employees on short-term disability). An employer may not refuse accommodations, ask about pregnancy status, or in any way discriminate against an employee for reasons related to pregnancy, making Choices *A, B,* and *D* incorrect.

103. D: While the physician is legally responsible for satisfying all elements of informed consent, nurses are ethically responsible for assessing the patient's ability to process and understand the implications of informed consent. Nurses protect the patient's autonomy by raising these questions and concerns. The remaining elements of informed consent are required of the physician, rather than the nurses.

104. A: Situational and transformational leadership styles are both styles of leadership that are more focused on the philosophy a leader brings to their position. In situational leadership style, the focus is on the leader's ability to adapt and, specifically, their ability to know how best to use their team members in different scenarios. In transformational leadership style, the focus is on the leader's ability to inspire change in their team members. Consequently, both styles can be taught and practiced in a variety of ways. This wouldn't be true of, for example, autocratic leadership style, which has a much more singular mentality and disposition. Therefore, the correct answer is Choice *A*. Choice *B* is incorrect because all styles of leadership discussed can be applied to a variety of contexts, not just medical ones. Choice *C* is incorrect because no such link has been proven, and most leadership styles will be effective at increasing productivity in different contexts. Choice *D* is incorrect because no such distinction is made about who can and cannot practice different leadership styles.

105. D: An important aspect of an infection prevention program is that all employees can recognize noncompliance and should be encouraged to report the incident confidentially using recommended

Answer Explanations #2

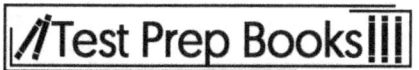

protocols. Choice A is incorrect; every employee in a medical facility should take responsibility for compliance by reporting noncompliance in a confidential manner; therefore, ignoring the situation is not an option. Choice B is incorrect; intentional observation will serve no purpose and may interfere with overall patient care and safety, particularly if this action becomes a distraction. Choice C is incorrect because calling attention to the action and describing it in a loud voice has great potential to violate HIPAA privacy regulations.

106. A: A patient who follows traditional Middle Eastern practices may follow certain dietary restrictions, such as not eating pork or mixing meat and dairy products. Grilled fish with vegetables and a grain would be in line with this culture's dietary restrictions. Culture and traditions should never be automatically assumed; the nurse should always respectfully discuss with the patient what their dietary preferences and restrictions are. Choices B and C are incorrect because they mix meat and dairy on the same plate. Choice D is incorrect because bacon is pork, which is often not allowed in Middle Eastern diets.

107. D: When a patient requests complementary therapies, the nurse should not discourage or immediately deny their request. Instead, this request should be discussed with the medical team to ensure it is safe and will not interfere with their current prescribed therapy and recovery. Choice A is incorrect because the nurse should not deny the request and state it is dangerous without further review. Choice B is incorrect because, in addition to denying their request without further review, many complementary therapies are tied to cultural and religious practices and denying their benefit may be offensive and insensitive. Choice C is incorrect because, before starting new complementary therapy such as acupuncture, benefits and risks should be reviewed. Additionally, complementary therapy should not take the place of prescribed therapies; rather, they should be used in conjunction with traditional therapies and medications.

108. A: Resource utilization, in the most general sense, can be used to refer to any scenario or action in which a healthcare provider is ensuring that medical resources (whether physical resources or team resources) are being used to their maximum effectiveness and efficiency in the course of a patient's treatment. The cornerstone of proper resource utilization is how effective the selected treatments are, with cost-efficiency concerns only factoring in after that primary concern. Therefore, the correct answer is Choice A. All of the other answer choices reflect variables in a patient's treatment plan that, although valid to discuss and plan for, should not take primacy over the efficacy of the selected treatments, according to the principles of resource utilization.

109. B: When indicated and appropriate, using silence allows time for the patient to reflect on how they are feeling, process their thoughts, and come up with their own solutions. Choice A is incorrect because yes or no questions can be limiting; instead, open-ended questions should be used to garner more information from the patient and allow for better communication. Choice C is incorrect because clichés can come across as insincere and may add little meaning to the conversation. Choice D is incorrect because asking patients to explain their behavior may come across as accusatory and cause a patient to close off their communication.

110. D: Security clauses are considered an illegal subject that cannot be discussed during a collective bargaining negotiation. Voluntary subjects, worker safety conditions, and working conditions and terms are all legal subjects that can be discussed during a collective bargaining negotiation.

111. C: Advocacy involves supporting appropriate programs and actions for marginalized or at-risk populations. At the community level, a nurse in the role of advocate may need knowledge of the

Answer Explanations #2

legislative process to bring about change. In direct patient care, the nurse will be the advocate for the patient by providing the information necessary for informed choices and supporting those choices in the development of the plan of care. Fidelity refers to trust. Autonomy refers to the right of self-determination. Beneficence refers to acting in the best interest of other individuals in society.

112. B: The location where the task was completed is not a required piece of documentation when delegating a task. In charting this would often be redundant to include, as the patient's room or location would automatically be linked in their health record. Choices A, C, and D are incorrect because these are the three essential components to include in charting when a task is delegated.

113. D: HPPD refers to the number of nursing hours per patient per day. Budget-based staffing, Choice D, uses calculations such as HPPD to determine staffing needs. Choice A, nurse-patient ratio, calculates staffing needs based on the number of patients assigned to each nurse. Choice B, patient acuity, determines the level of care required by each patient when staffing nurses. Choice C is irrelevant.

114. D: For systems thinking according to the AACN Synergy Model, a nurse who has a deep understanding of community resources outside of themselves and can actively promote these to assist in a patient's care and recovery is at the highest level of systems thinking, level 5. Choice A is incorrect because a nurse at level 1 systems thinking is only able to offer themself as a resource and does not know or offer outside resources. Choice B is incorrect because a nurse at level 3 systems thinking can look for external resources and help for a patient, but may not have an expert understanding. Choice C is incorrect because level 4 is not one of the levels of systems thinking.

115. D: When used to implement evidenced based practice, clinical inquiry can result in replacing an outdated, even counter-productive nursing intervention with an intervention that effectively addresses the needs of the patient. Matching patient needs with nursing competencies means that professional nurses are responsible for challenging all nursing interventions to be sure that they represent current best practice standards. As innovators, nurses are in the best position to research, implement, and evaluate alternative care practices.

116. C: Expert nurses are those who reach the point in their clinical practice where clinical reasoning and inquiry are intertwined, allowing the nurse to make clinical judgements quickly and appropriately, according to best practice standards. Nurses may be able to anticipate a patient's needs and address change at all levels, making Choices A and B incorrect.

117. C: Medical tools need to undergo cleaning as soon as they have been used. This ensures that bacteria do not have time to continue to grow or spread. Then, the tools can be prepared for disinfection or sterilization. Choice A, waiting one day, would be too long. Choice B, cleaning before use, would not be needed if the tool has already been through the cleaning, disinfection, and sterilization process, and Choice D, using a manufacturer recommendation, would be unnecessary.

118. C: While employee preferences should be addressed whenever possible, that is not one of the primary concerns of a staffing plan. Choices A, B, and D, along with an understanding of the care requirements for the patients, are the four key elements of an effective staffing plan.

119. D: Staff refers to the people within an organization. Scheduling, Choice A, refers to the task of determining who will be working when and what they will be responsible for during their work shift. Choice B, authority, refers to the individual who is responsible for oversight of the organization and handling any issues that arise. The nurse executive, Choice C, is often a manager who has the authority to handle scheduling and staffing.

120. D: Using a hospital interpreter helps bridge language barriers and increases a patient's understanding of their medical care. Patients who come from certain Asian cultures may not outwardly express their emotions and grief and may appear stoic. It is important that the nurse still offers a line of respectful communication so the patient can ask questions and process this news as they feel appropriate. Choice A is incorrect because patients from Asian cultures may not maintain eye contact as a sign of respect, and this cultural preference should be understood and respected by the nurse. Choice B is incorrect because patients from Asian cultures may see it as a sign of weakness to express their feelings or grief. The nurse should be respectful of how the patient wishes to process and show their emotions in relation to their cultural beliefs and traditions. Choice C is incorrect because patients who are sick may feel a sense of shame and want to hide their illness from their families; the nurse should respect the patient's wishes and only contact the patient's family if the patient directly asks them to.

121. C: Patients who prefer to use diagrams, visual aids, charts, and videos are likely visual learners. The four types of learning styles are visual, auditory, reader/writer, and kinesthetic. Choice A is incorrect because auditory learners prefer to learn through listening and may benefit from lectures, discussion groups, and audiotapes. Choice B is incorrect because reader learners, also called reader/writer learners, prefer to learn through handouts, written instruction, and taking their own notes. Choice D is incorrect because kinesthetic learners prefer hands-on learning where they can physically hold the equipment or explore the teachings in a tactile manner. Patients may prefer one or a combination of multiple styles of learning. The nurse should be able to assess the styles and tailor the teaching approaches to meet these preferences.

122. B: In the psychomotor domain of Bloom's Taxonomy, a person who can follow detailed instructions to complete a practical task is at the guided response level. The complete steps of the psychomotor domain from least to most complex are perception, set, guided response, mechanism, complex overt response, adaptation, and origination. Choice A is incorrect because complex overt response is an expert level of proficiency where the learner can perform certain tasks proficiently without hesitation or separate guidance and instruction. Choice C is incorrect because mechanism is basic proficiency where the learner has some confidence, and psychomotor response has become habitual. Choice D is incorrect because perception is the most basic level where the learner is only aware of certain sensory clues and can guide their motor activity for completion of basic tasks.

123. D: Value-based insurance design seeks to redefine how insurance policies operate. Under such a design, coverage will typically be extended to treatments that have been shown to be broadly effective and efficient. However, most insurance plans with value-based insurance design will also vary their rates and which services they provide coverage for, depending on the health needs of the consumer. Therefore, the correct answer is Choice D. All other answer choices do not accurately reflect how insurance plans with value-based insurance design operate.

124. B: The turnover rate is calculated by taking the number of employees that exited the company during the year, dividing it by the average number of employees during the year, and then multiplying that amount by 100. In this example, this equates to $\frac{125}{1100} \times 100$, which is 11.36%.

125. D: A patient with congestive heart failure is at an increased risk of complications from fluid overload and should have their fluid intake closely monitored. If the patient is experiencing discomfort due to dry mouth, the nurse should encourage using mouth swabs to help keep their mouth moist

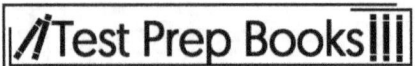

Answer Explanations #2

without increasing their fluid intake. Additionally, patients who are terminally ill, regardless of medical condition, should have their fluid intake closely monitored as increased fluids can cause edema, skin breakdown, and incontinence. The reasoning for these medical decisions should always be explained to the patient and family member so they can understand the choices being made.

Choice A is incorrect because this dismisses the family member's concern without providing an explanation for the patient's care. Choice B is incorrect because IV fluids should not be increased without approval from the provider. It may also not be recommended to increase the fluids for this patient because they are terminally ill and have congestive heart failure. Choice C is incorrect because dampening the patient's lips can draw moisture out and make their lips drier. Instead, a mouth swab should be used inside of the patient's mouth and a lip balm can be applied to the lips if appropriate.

126. A: An acuity-based staffing model involves assessing the needs of the unit to properly manage patient acuity and then staffing based on those needs.

127. A: Choice A, a democratic leadership style, defers to the expertise of a team to gain insight and guidance for decision-making. Choice B is a hands-off approach that allows other individuals to develop solutions and employ action. Choice C is an authoritarian style, where input from the outside is not required. Choice D is a style that encourages team input through a reward system.

128. A: The ANA Code of Ethics provides guidance for performing nursing duties in an ethical manner. Choice B is not correct because the code does not define pay scales or tables for nursing compensation. Choice C is not correct since this is defined in ANA's Principles for Nurse Staffing, not the Code of Ethics. Choice D is incorrect since only the ethical considerations of nurses, not primary care providers, are covered.

129. C: Skill mix is using a ratio of different types of staff by proportion—for example, 50 percent RN staff, 30 percent LPN staff, and 20 percent CNA staff. Choices A and B are not recognized staffing models. Choice D is budget-based and allows for a certain number of staff for a certain number of patients, regardless of acuity.

130. A: Authentic leadership is one of the six standards of the AACN's healthy work environment. Choices B, C, and D are not included in the six standards of a healthy work environment.

131. A: The nurse-patient ratio model consists of holding a certain number of RNs or LPNs to a certain number of patients, as well as holding a certain number of assistants to a certain number of patients. Choice B is incorrect, as team nursing is a collaboration between the RN and the LPN. The RN delegates to the LPN as they care for a certain number of patients, with appropriate tasks assigned to each role. Choice C is incorrect. The total patient care model is described as an RN who gives total care to a certain number of patients, such as in private duty nursing. Choice D is also incorrect, as the functional nursing model gives tasks to each type of staff (e.g., RN, LPN, and assistant) instead of assigning patients.

132. B: When data is initially collected for analysis, the first set of data points is considered the baseline. Choice A is incorrect since this is a compilation of similar data. Choice C is incorrect since this is data that is compared with other data to seek a mutual relationship. Choice D is incorrect since qualitative data refers to a characteristic, a quality, or an individual's experience.

133. C: The National Patient Safety Goals are an initiative of the Joint Commission.

Answer Explanations #2

134. B: Flexible scheduling can help to hire and retain nurses by providing opportunities to work on specific days, at specific times, and for an amount of time that works for them. This allows for a better chance of filling openings with available staff.

135. C: Choice C is correct, as this type of health insurance allows the consumer to know set prices up front. Choice A is incorrect, as the consumer may have to pay more to see certain providers. Choice B is incorrect since cost of service varies between facilities and providers based on network coverage. Choice D is incorrect since the care delivered would not differ; however, the cost may be different.

136. B: The first responder should verify that the person is choking and immediately call for help. Choice A is incorrect, as this could waste valuable time if the person's airway is compromised. Choice C is incorrect since this action may push a food bolus further into the airway. Choice D is not correct, as this would be completed after verifying choking, calling for help, and assisting the person into a standing position.

137. D: Competency validation is when the knowledge and skills of a nurse are verified for a particular task.

138. B: Choice B is the correct answer, since overprovision—a phenomenon where more services are ordered than necessary—has been linked to the fee-for-service model. Choices A and C are incorrect, as they describe value-based insurance that approves services based on a return on investment. Choice D is incorrect, as this metric is applied to value-based reimbursement.

139. C: Editing job descriptions and job duties is not part of the purpose of a performance appraisal. Choices A, B, and D are incorrect. Assessing employee performance, developing an action plan for advancement, and encouraging continued development are all components that should be addressed during a performance appraisal.

140. A: Falls are the most common cause of traumatic brain injury. Choice B is incorrect since assaults are the fifth most likely cause. Motor vehicle accidents, Choice C, are the fourth leading cause. Choice D, unknown etiology, is the second most likely cause.

141. D: Quality reporting systems are intended to be used in a non-punitive way to help reveal systemic weaknesses, so Choice D is the best response. Choice A is incorrect because the frontline nurse should be encouraged to trust the reporting process, not just the direct manager's word. Choice B is incorrect because quality reports are not primarily a means of targeting individual behavior, but rather of addressing systemic flaws that can affect anyone. Choice C is incorrect because treating errors in a punitive manner discourages transparency and reporting, which hides systemic flaws.

142. C: EMS personnel are the first responders to 911 calls and therefore can facilitate expeditious transport and reporting to the scene. Choices A, B, and D are incorrect, as they are not the first contact with the patient in relation to 911 calls.

143. D: Critical thinking skills are not provided through competency validation. Instead, this often comes from experience and thinking through processes. Choices A, B, and C are all provided by validating the competency of employees.

144. A: An algorithm provides guidance for staff to autonomously respond to an emergent situation. Choice B is incorrect since this would not solve the issue. Choice C is incorrect; beyond Basic Life Support (BLS) training, development of an algorithm is also needed. Choice D is incorrect; although quizzing staff

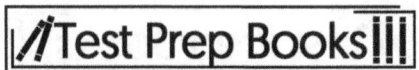

may reveal their base level of knowledge, education on the policy and appropriate response would improve staff knowledge of emergent response.

145. A: Choice A is correct, as this provides a balance between resource allocation and sustainability. Choice B is incorrect since nepotism is unethical and may be an illegal practice. Anticipating risks and employing strategies to mitigate harm supports ongoing safety and should be prioritized over Choice C, paying reparations for adverse patient events. Choice D is incorrect, as it is not fiscally responsible and has not been shown to improve patient outcomes. Using appropriate staffing ratios, based on patient acuity and census, balances budget and safety.

146. C: "Plan" is the first step in the Plan-Do-Study-Act cycle for accomplishing successful change. Choice A is incorrect because this step should be taken after careful planning and communication with staff. Choice B is incorrect because this action takes a top-down approach and does not involve careful planning. Choice D is incorrect because, while senior executive support may be important, it should be solicited with a clear plan for the change.

147. D: Performance appraisals are completed on a set time frame (typically on an annual basis), but evaluation of performance issues can occur on an ongoing basis. Employee development, recognition of accomplishments, and determining training needs—Choices A, B, and C—are shared components of performance appraisals and regular evaluations.

148. C: Choice C allows staff to easily locate the number and provide a warm transfer between the person calling with a poison emergency and the experts for assisting with this medical emergency. Choice A is incorrect, as there should always be a warm transfer in urgent calls to ensure the caller and the recipient are connected. Choice B is incorrect, as this is not the best way to ensure the caller is connected with an expert to assist. Choice D does not disseminate information to all staff that are affected and are responsible for knowing the process.

149. B: A meta-analysis of randomized controlled trials is the highest level of evidence to support a practice change. Choice A is incorrect because a single trial is weaker evidence than multiple trials of the same subject. Choices C and D are incorrect because neither a prospective cohort study nor a meta-analysis of retrospective case-control studies is stronger evidence than a meta-analysis of RCTs.

150. A: Increased education is the most effective method to improve the metric of preventing infections within the surgical department. Choice B is fiscally irresponsible, would cause delays in care, and would not improve infection control practices. Choice C does not demonstrate effective stewardship of antimicrobial strategies and may increase antimicrobial resistance. Blaming patients, Choice D, is conducive to a lack of trust and negates promoting patient-centered care. Metrics should be thoroughly reviewed for accuracy but acted upon in good faith to reduce potential risks.

Nurse Executive Practice Test #3 & #4

To keep the size of this book manageable, save paper, and provide a digital test-taking experience, the 3rd and 4th practice tests can be found online. Scan the QR code or go to this link to access it:

testprepbooks.com/online387/nurseexecutive

The first time you access the tests, you will need to register as a "new user" and verify your email address.

If you have any issues, please email support@testprepbooks.com.

Dear Nurse Executive Test Taker,

Thank you for purchasing this study guide for your Nurse Executive exam. We hope that we exceeded your expectations.

Our goal in creating this study guide was to cover all of the topics that you will see on the test. We also strove to make our practice questions as similar as possible to what you will encounter on test day. With that being said, if you found something that you feel was not up to your standards, please send us an email and let us know.

We have study guides in a wide variety of fields. If the one you are looking for isn't listed above, then try searching for it on Amazon or send us an email.

Thanks Again and Happy Testing!
Product Development Team
info@studyguideteam.com

Online Resources & Audiobook

Included with your purchase are multiple online resources. This includes the practice tests in an interactive format and this book in audiobook format. There is also a convenient study timer to help you manage your time.

Scan the QR code or go to this link to access this content:

testprepbooks.com/online387/nurseexecutive

The first time you access the page, you will need to register as a "new user" and verify your email address.

If you have any issues, please email support@testprepbooks.com.

Thank you for letting us be a part of your studying journey!